AF352124

Punishment and Ethics

Punishment and Ethics

New Perspectives

Edited by

Jesper Ryberg
University of Roskilde, Denmark

and

J. Angelo Corlett
San Diego State University, USA

First published 2010 by
PALGRAVE MACMILLAN

Palgrave Macmillan in the UK is an imprint of Macmillan Publishers Limited,
registered in England, company number 785998, of Houndmills, Basingstoke,
Hampshire RG21 6XS.

Palgrave Macmillan in the US is a division of St Martin's Press LLC,
175 Fifth Avenue, New York, NY 10010.

Palgrave Macmillan is the global academic imprint of the above companies
and has companies and representatives throughout the world.

Palgrave® and Macmillan® are registered trademarks in the United States,
the United Kingdom, Europe and other countries.

ISBN 978–0–230–24097–1   hardback

This book is printed on paper suitable for recycling and made from fully
managed and sustained forest sources. Logging, pulping and manufacturing
processes are expected to conform to the environmental regulations of the
country of origin.

A catalogue record for this book is available from the British Library.

Library of Congress Cataloging-in-Publication Data

Punishment and ethics : new perspectives / edited by Jesper Ryberg,
    J. Angelo Corlett.
      p. cm.
    ISBN 978–0–230–24097–1   (hardback)
  1. Punishment—Moral and ethical aspects.   I. Ryberg, Jesper.
    II. Corlett, J. Angelo, 1958–
    K5101.P86 2010
    172'.2—dc22

                                                        2010023950

10   9   8   7   6   5   4   3   2   1
19 18 17 16 15 14 13 12 11 10

Printed and bound in Great Britain by
CPI Antony Rowe, Chippenham and Eastbourne

Contents

Foreword

State punishment constitutes one of the cardinal issues in legal and social philosophy. That this is the case is not hard to understand. Punishment, after all, involves the infliction of death, suffering, or deprivation on citizens and thereby enacts the very type of treatment of people that would, under normal circumstances, be regarded as abhorrent and as a conspicuous case of morally forbidden behaviour. Such a practice certainly calls for some ethically persuasive justification. Moreover, once one starts analyzing current punishment practices or engages in more detailed reflections on penal questions – such as in what manner and how severely different crimes should be punished – a plethora of challenging ethical problems arise, all calling for thorough consideration. Thus, both the obvious moral significance of the issue and the variety of the problems which a punishment practice gives rise to have contributed to placing punishment as a subject at the heart of legal and social theorizing.

The essays in this book concern aspects of the basic question of the justification of a penal practice, as well as a number of more detailed challenges which such a practice gives rise to. The aim has not been to provide the reader with a systematic overview of rival positions or problems. Nor do the essays provide introductions to the field. Rather, the authors have been asked to present argued papers on what they regard as interesting problems. Thus, the chapters can be read in any order. The reader may choose to pick out one chapter which is of particular interest, or read the entire collection – thereby, hopefully, getting some sort of snapshot of recent research within the field. We hope that the reader will find the book valuable and that it will constitute one small step forward in the ongoing discussion of the ethics of punishment.

We would like to thank the authors for their contributions and enthusiasm. Moreover, we wish to thank the publisher and all other persons who have kindly helped to bring this work about.

Jesper Ryberg and J. Angelo Corlett

Notes on Contributors

Christopher Bennett is Senior Lecturer in the Department of Philosophy, University of Sheffield, UK. Among other things, he is the author of *The Apology Ritual: A Philosophical Theory of Punishment* (CUP, 2008). His main interests lie in ethics, political philosophy and moral psychology.

Thom Brooks is Reader in Political and Legal Philosophy at the University of Newcastle, UK. His recent books include *Hegel's Political Philosophy: A Systematic Reading of the Philosophy of Right* (2007) and *The Global Justice Reader* (2008). He is currently completing a monograph on punishment and a collection on Rawls's Political Liberalism co-edited with Martha Nussbaum. His interests include British and German Idealism, democratic theory, global justice, human rights, jurisprudence and the philosophy of punishment. He is founder and editor of the *Journal of Moral Philosophy*.

J. Angelo Corlett is Professor of Philosophy & Ethics at San Diego State University, and the author of more than 100 books and articles, including *Heirs of Oppression* (Rowman & Littlefield, forthcoming), *The Errors of Atheism* (Continuum, 2010), *Responsibility and Punishment* (Springer, 2006, 2004, 2001), *Race, Rights, and Justice* (Springer, 2009), *Interpreting Plato's Dialogues* (Parmenides, 2005), *Race, Racism, and Reparations* (Cornell, 2003), *Terrorism: A Philosophical Analysis* (Kluwer, 2003), *Analyzing Social Knowledge* (Rowman & Littlefield, 1996). He is also the editor-in-chief of *The Journal of Ethics: An International Philosophical Review* and editor of *Equality and Liberty: Analyzing Rawls and Nozick* (MacMillan, 1991). His articles have appeared in such journals as the *American Philosophical Quarterly*; *Analysis*; *The Classical Quarterly*; *Journal of Social Philosophy*; and *Philosophy*.

David B. Hershenov is a Professor of Philosophy at the University at Buffalo. His primary research interest is in the practical implications of the metaphysics of personal identity. He is currently working on a book titled 'The Metaphysical Foundations of Bioethics'.

Stephen Kershnar is a Professor of Philosophy at the State University of New York at Fredonia and is also an attorney. He focuses on applied ethics and political philosophy. Kershnar has authored over fifty articles on such diverse topics as torture, affirmative action, pornography, hell, adult-child sex, the most valuable player, equal opportunity, slavery and the nature of pleasure. He is the author of four books: *Desert and Virtue: A Theory of Intrinsic Value* (Lexington Books, 2010), *Sex, Discrimination, and Violence* (University Press, 2009), *Justice for the Past* (SUNY Press, 2004) and *Desert, Retribution, and Torture* (University Press, 2001).

Kasper Lippert-Rasmussen is Professor of Political Theory at the University of Århus, Denmark. He is associate editor of *Ethics* and member of the editorial boards of *Utilitas* and *Economics and Philosophy*. Recent publications include 'Scanlon on the Doctrine of Double Effect', *Social Theory and Practice*, 36(4) (2010); *Nationalism and Multiculturalism in A World of Immigration* (Palgrave Macmillan, 2009), co-edited with N. Holtug and S. Lægaard; and 'Against Self-Ownership', *Philosophy and Public Affairs*, 36(1) (2008). Presently, he is working on a book-length project on the (im)morality of discrimination.

Jesper Ryberg is Professor of Ethics and Philosophy of Law at the University of Roskilde, Denmark. His recent books include *The Ethics of Proportionate Punishment* (Kluwer Academic Publishers, 2004), *The Repugnant Conclusion* (Kluwer Academic Publishers, 2004), *Normative Ethics: Five Questions* (Automatic Press, 2007 co-edited with T. S. Petersen), *New Waves in Applied Ethics* (Palgrave Macmillan, 2007, co-edited with T. S. Petersen). He is the author of numerous articles and book contributions. His current interests lie primarily in criminal justice ethics and other parts of applied ethics.

Thomas S. Petersen is Associate Professor of Ethics and Philosophy of Law at the University of Roskilde, Denmark. His recent books include *Normative Ethics: Five Questions* (Automatic Press, 2007 co-edited with J. Ryberg), *New Waves in Applied Ethics* (Palgrave Macmillan, 2007, co-edited with J. Ryberg). He is the author of numerous articles and papers, for example, *Bioethics, Criminal Law and Philosophy, Journal of Medical Ethics, Journal of Happiness Studies* and *Theoria*, and several book contributions. His current interests lie primarily in criminal justice ethics and the ethics of sport.

Leo Zaibert is the Chair of the Department of Philosophy at Union College, in New York, USA. He is the author of *Five Ways Patricia can Kill her Husband: A Theory of Intentionality and Blame* (Open Court, 2005), and of *Punishment and Retribution* (Ashgate, 2006). He is the author of numerous articles and book contributions. His current interests lie primarily on punishment, forgiveness and on the political implications of state responses to wrongdoing.

1
Punishment and the Socratic Roots of Retributivism

J. Angelo Corlett

Much ado has been made in punishment theory over the past several decades over the plausibility status of retributivism, especially in philosophical circles.[1] Indeed, there are about as many interpretations of retributivism as there are defenders and opponents of the view, or cluster of views, rightly called 'retributivism'. Whether pure or mixed versions of the theory, what all punishment theories worthy of the name 'retributivism' share with one another is that the justification of both the institution and particular forms of punishment[2] are primarily matters of deservedness, however 'desert' and its cognates (words pertaining to desert) are understood by the various retributivists themselves. According to the standard retributivist line of thinking, those who are responsible for a harmful wrongdoing deserve to be punished (positive retributivism). The innocent are never to be punished for any reason whatsoever (negative retributivism). And the guilty ought to be punished in proportion to the kind and degree of harm their wrongful actions caused to others. Strong versions of retributivism, such as Immanuel Kant's, hold that the state has a perfect moral duty to punish all offenders, while weak retributivists[3] hold that the state has an imperfect duty to punish them. While some retributivist theories also admit (in accordance with certain statements made by Kant) that considerations of social utility (deterrence, rehabilitation and so on) might serve as secondary justifications of the institution and particular forms of punishment,[4] all retributivisms[5] hold that the notion of desert is central to why, if ever, punishment and punishments are morally justified.

And while what Kant wrote of punishment (especially in the *Rechtslehre*) surely counts as retributivist if only impurely,[6] he is hardly the philosophical founder of retributivism. This article will reveal the Western philosophical roots of retributivism in Socrates as his arguments and analyses are expressed in Plato's works, though no argument is made herein that Socrates is the ultimate founder of the view. Focus in the expository section of this project will be given to what Socrates argues concerning desert and some related concepts in the context of punishment. And it may surprise many that Socrates' version of retributivism is not purist.[7] Instead, it, like Kant's, is impure in important ways.[8] Indeed, most contemporary philosophers of law will be surprised to find that the idea that Plato's works reveal a kind of moral education 'theory'[9] of 'punishment'[10] is at best only part of what we find in Plato's corpus of writings. And even those, such as A. D. Woozley, who recognize the varied nature of the concept of punishment in Plato's works, seem to miss the rather strong retributive element in them: 'For Plato, the purpose of punishment is twofold: making good to the victim the damage actually suffered, and encouragement to the offender to reform'.[11] Indeed, it will be revealed that such a view of 'punishment' as rehabilitation or reform of offenders – when attributed to Plato or Socrates – is quite misleading as it fails to understand the essentially retributivist leanings of Socrates, that is, according to many of the arguments placed in his 'mouth' by Plato. Thus not only is it unclear whether Socrates expresses in Plato's dialogues a theory of punishment, it is quite unclear whether what he says about punishment amounts to what some refer to as moral education. Whether or not Socrates expresses a theory of punishment, the content of what he does express is clearly retributivist.

Assumed in my approach to Plato's writings is that they are neither strictly unitarian nor strictly developmentalist, but rather a hybrid of these approaches.[12] While it is dubious that we can decipher Plato's own views from the content of the corpus of his writings,[13] the topic of this paper is what might be reasonably ascribed to Socrates as his arguments and analyses are depicted in Plato's written work. And since even the most responsible ways to date Plato's works are fraught with difficulties,[14] any claims to the unity or development of Socrates' arguments and analyses must be done with the understanding that this is at best rather general and contingent on an unproblematic dating of Plato's writings. Moreover, it faces the fact that it is not always clear whether what Plato places in the mouth of Socrates (especially in the 'Socratic dialogues') represents something Socrates actually said, historically speaking, or whether it is Plato having the character Socrates express something that is nonhistorical. In the latter case, Plato might well put in the mouth of Socrates ideas that only those closest to Socrates heard him express, perhaps in order to enhance the philosophical level of such dialogues. In light of these seemingly insurmountable challenges, my approach to the Socratic roots of retributivism is to look closely at what can be found in Plato's writings along these lines, while respecting the fact that perhaps the most that can be said with reasonable plausibility about such Socratic roots is that they are somewhat tenuous. Nonetheless, it is vital that such roots be explored both for the sake of accuracy in the history of philosophy and for the sake of correcting a common misunderstanding among philosophers of law concerning retributivism and its conceptual roots.

It is noteworthy that the philosophical work on Plato or on Socrates and punishment does not even mention that desert words such as *axios*, *kalos* and their cognates appear numerous times throughout Plato's works both in and aside from punishment contexts. Moreover, Plato's Socrates uses desert words in the context of punishment. When these facts are brought to light, it may appear that the entire framework of what most philosophers attribute to Socrates (or Plato) concerning punishment is in need of rethinking. Whatever Socrates expresses in terms of moral education must take into account that Socrates is indeed a retributivist. But as I will argue, a retributivist can without contradiction or conceptual confusion accommodate the concerns of moral education as a by-product of retributive punishment.

Since what characterizes retributivisms is predominantly their commitment to the idea of desert in contexts of punishment and compensation, Socratic expressions of desert words in these contexts will be the focus of this investigation. And we might begin with Plato's *Apology* 38b, where Socrates in addressing the court of Athens, states that he does not believe that he deserves to be punished. But his use of desert words does not simply apply to his perception of his own innocence. Rather, it applies, as it does with typical retributivists, to whether or not others might deserve blame: 'but they thought they were hurting me, and for this they deserve blame' (*Apology* 41e). So in Plato's *Apology*, where Socrates is defending his own life from Meletus' charges of corrupting the youth of Athens and of atheism, Socrates argues that he is not deserving of punishment, but that those who seek to do him harm deserve blame, presumably, for seeking to have him punished unjustly. Thus far, Socrates' use of desert words is quite consistent with any retributivism worthy of the name.

But retributivism is not simply about what the guilty and blameworthy deserve in terms of punishment or forced compensation. It is, as Socrates states in *Phaedo* 113e, also a matter of rewarding those who deserve praise: 'they are also suitably rewarded for their good deeds as each deserves'. In fact, it is in this context that Socrates employs a notion of proportional punishment, another primary principle of retributivisms:

> Those who have been deemed incurable because of the enormity of their crimes, having committed many great sacrileges or wicked and unlawful murders and other such wrongs – their fitting fate is to be hurled into Tartarus never to emerge from it. Those who are deemed to have committed great but curable crimes, such as doing violence to their father or mother in a fit of temper but who have felt remorse for the rest of their lives, or who have killed someone in a similar manner, these must of necessity be thrown into Tartarus, but a year later the current throws them out, those who are guilty of murder by way of Cocytus, and those who have done violence to their parents by way of the Pyriphlegethon.
>
> (*Phaedo* 113e–14a)

One thing to notice about what Socrates states here is the retributivist blending of the idea of proportionality with that of desert. In so doing, Socrates makes it rather difficult, if not embarrassing, for those who would seek to attribute to him some moral education 'theory' of 'punishment' as 'Plato's theory of punishment'. There is nothing of the sort in this passage, which is consistent with the ones from Plato's *Apology*.

In *Rival Lovers*, considered by many scholars to constitute one of the various apocryphal writings of Plato, Socrates asks the young polymath: 'And isn't it also the case that cities are well governed when the unjust are punished?' (138b). This is an indication that, even in the secondary[15] writings of Plato, there is confirmation of a retributive idea expressed by Socrates: in states that are reasonably just ones, the guilty deserve to be punished. It is noteworthy that here too, as in Plato's *Apology* and *Phaedo*, there is no mention of moral education.

So it is clear that Socrates argues for the punishment of the unjust because they deserve it, and in proportion to the gravity of the injustice. But it is not until Plato's *Protagoras* that the matter of the significance of such punishment is addressed. According to Protagoras, 'the true significance of punishment lies in the fact that human beings consider virtue to be something acquired through training' (324a–b). And it is Protagoras, not Socrates, who espouses what centuries later becomes known as a utilitarian view of the justification of punishment as found in the philosopher Jeremy Bentham:[16] 'Reasonable punishment is not vengeance for a past wrong – for one cannot undo what has been done – but is undertaken with a view to the future, to deter both the wrong-doer and whoever sees him being punished from repeating the crime. This attitude towards punishment as deterrence implies that virtue is learned' (324b–c). What is noticeable in Socrates' reply to Protagoras at 329f is that, while Socrates compliments Protagoras on the beauty of his speech, he never concurs with the words on punishment and addresses only Protagoras' notion that virtue can be taught. While this in itself hardly makes Socrates a retributivist, it likewise hardly makes him a proponent of punishment as moral education for harmful wrongdoing.

Perhaps more than any other Platonic dialogue, the *Gorgias* has Socrates address issues of punishment and desert (unless one assumes that the Athenian in the *Laws* is meant to be Socrates). There is Socrates' statement that the one who murders is to be pitied and is miserable because doing what is unjust 'is actually the worst thing there is' (469b), and the concurrence of thought between Socrates and Polus on the idea that it is sometimes better to put people to death or banish them or seize their assets as methods of punishment for certain kinds of wrongdoing (470b) so long as these punishments are meted out justly (470c), and the ultimately retributivist idea that those who are unjust are miserable, but those who do not get their just deserts are even more miserable – and the less so to the extent that those who deserve punishment pay their due 'at the hands of both gods and men' (472e). It is clear to Socrates that the one who is worst off, morally speaking, is the one who escapes punishment. This is consistent with Kant's point that the state has a perfect moral duty to punish criminals. Why might this be the case? Socrates provides the answer to this question at *Gorgias* 479d: 'doing what's unjust is the second worst thing. Not paying what's due when one has done what's unjust is by its nature the first worst thing, the very worst of all'. What is implied here is that harmful wrongdoers ought to have sufficient moral virtue to do the right thing and undergo punishment without having to be punished by the state:

> that he should accuse himself first and foremost, and then too his family and anyone else dear to him who happens to behave unjustly at any time; and that he should not keep his wrongdoing hidden but bring it out into the open, so that he may pay his due and get well; and compel himself and the others not to play the coward, but to grit his teeth and present himself with grace and courage as to a doctor for cauterization and surgery, pursuing what's good and admirable without taking any account of the pain. And if his unjust behavior merits flogging, he should present himself to be whipped; if it merits imprisonment, to be imprisoned; if a fine, to pay it; if exiled, to be

exiled; and if execution, to be executed. He should be his own chief accuser, and the accuser of other members of his family, and use his oratory for the purpose of getting rid of the worst thing there is, injustice, as the unjust acts are being exposed.

(Gorgias 480c–d)

Thus 'injustice is the worst thing there is for the person committing it' and 'that person's failure to pay what's due is something even worse' (509b). Those lacking such moral virtue are indeed miserable, as Socrates argues, as injustice is a very bad thing, but not wanting to be punished for it is even worse. This is a clear statement in support of punishing those who deserve to be punished. At the very least, it is consistent with a common general justifying aim of retributive punishment and compensation. As with the previous passages, there is no indication in the *Gorgias* passages that Socrates believes in moral education in terms of it being the main goal of punishment. Instead, Socrates seems to be arguing repeatedly that punishment is required to achieve or retain moral virtue. And moral virtue is important for the moment of death: 'For no one who isn't totally bereft of reason and courage is afraid to die; doing what's unjust is what he's afraid of. For to arrive in Hades with one's soul stuffed full of unjust actions is the ultimate of all bad things' (*Gorgias* 522d). And for third parties who seek to avoid getting involved with cases of harmful wrongdoing, Socrates urges them to demonstrate a genuine concern for the wrongdoer and attempt to pay the fine where fines are relevant to cover the cost of the injustice (480a–b).

Aside from the fact that those who wrongfully harm others deserve to be punished in proportion to their injustices, Socrates adds at *Gorgias* 525b–c that 'it is appropriate for everyone who is subject to punishment rightly inflicted by another either to become better and profit from it, or else to be made an example for others, so that when they see him suffering whatever it is he suffers, they may be afraid and become better'. This utilitarian justificatory aim of punishment is immediately tied to a retributive one wherein 'the ones whose errors are curable … their benefit comes to them … by way of pain and suffering, for there is no other possible way to get rid of injustice' (525b–c). This latter point seems to be a retributivist one in that it appeals to a notion of paying one's debt for injustice that one has caused. But the first quotation from Socrates above is our first putative indication that something akin to rehabilitation might serve an educational function in society where punishment is employed. But this is simply one possible implication of the passage, as one can be rehabilitated without moral education accruing to one, just as one can serve as a deterrent to others without moral education having anything to do with the deterrent punishment in question.

Perhaps *Republic* 591a–c sheds light on the idea that Socrates has in mind some kind of moral education in the rehabilitative process of punishment when he states of lawbreakers:

> Doesn't the one who remains undiscovered become even more vicious, while the bestial part of the one who is discovered is calmed and tamed and his gentle part freed, so that his entire soul settles into its best nature, acquires moderation, justice, and reason, and attains a more valuable state than that of having a fine, strong, healthy body, since the soul itself is more valuable than the body?

Yet there is a limit to the extent to which rehabilitation plays a role in dealing with the unjust, according to Socrates. Sure, the souls of the unjust 'indeed die of injustice' (*Republic* 610d). But there are those who meet with death due to their injustice (*Republic* 610d).

However, the bulk of Socrates' statements on desert are found in Plato's *Laws*. In the *Republic*, desert is linked to punishment at 337d. And at 349b–d, desert underlies what ought to happen to the just person, on the one hand, and to the unjust person, on the other. But in *Laws* 626d, naming one after a god or goddess, Clinias states, is a matter of merit. And considerations of philosophical discussion can deserve due attention at *Laws* 645c. And in *Laws* 657e–658c, prizes for competitions are said to be matters of merit, while whatever benefits people most deserves a most fitting honour or prize (*Laws* 698d–e). Respect and offices in life are said to be deserved when they are merited (*Laws* 738e). Politicians are said to deserve their positions of power when they are the right candidates for the positions (*Laws*751c–d; 917a). And those making their wills are to decide who deserves to be heirs (*Laws* 923c). Parents deserve good treatment (*Laws* 931e), so much so that those who kill their parents will suffer death.

But the Athenian declares at *Laws* 663a that some words deserve legal condemnation. A society striving for genuine happiness will find it 'necessary for it to distribute honors and marks of disgrace on a proper basis', argues the Athenian at *Laws* 697b. So long as one pays proper respect to the gods, one will receive the award one deserves from them (*Laws* 718a). Furthermore, those who prevent others from committing a wrongdoing deserve to be quite highly respected (*Laws* 730d). In fact, justice amounts to 'granting the "equality" that unequals deserve to get' (*Laws* 757d). *Laws* 762f lists a number of punishments, not modes of moral education, that are linked to the commission of certain harmful wrongdoings, amounting to a kind of sentencing guide for the legal system. Severe beatings are mentioned for those who abandon their posts, and the right to have authority over the young is stripped from those who know of harmful wrongdoing, but fail to do anything about it (*Laws* 762c–d). The harshest punishments are saved for foreigners and slaves, while some citizens will be fined for their offences (*Laws* 764b). Former husbands who violate court orders regarding their children can be beaten by '*anyone who wishes*', and not suffer punishment for it *Laws* 784d). Whippings (hardly construable in terms of moral education the way most philosophers of law understand these terms) are also said to be deserved at *Laws* 949c for refusing to participate in a public ceremony. But certain 'social evils' are deemed trivial and are indecent to punish by law (*Laws* 788b). For as the Athensian states: 'I maintain that serious matters deserve our attention, but trivialities do not' (*Laws* 803c). Dances of peace and war are examples of serious matters, as stated in *Laws* 815d. A person's lifestyle can make her deserving of her fate as being slothful and fat (*Laws* 807a–b). For boys and their tutors who misbehave, punishment is in order, according to *Laws* 808e. It is noteworthy that the picking of '"dessert" grapes or figs' from another's trees is to be met with punishment to amount to a lash with a whip for the number of fruits taken' (*Laws* 844e–45a).s

Perhaps the most interesting feature of Plato's *Laws* is at 846b, where judges who judge poorly (say, out of bias), are to be punished such that they receive twice the damages that the plaintiff deserves. Thus not even judges are above the law. And punishment and moral education are conjoined at *Laws* 844d–e, where temple thief is to be punished with whippings in order to, perhaps, 'teach him restraint and make him a better man: after all, no penalty imposed by law has an evil purpose, but generally achieves one of two effects: it makes the person who pays the penalty either more virtuous or less wicked'. There is no good reason to think that there is some anti-retributivism being propounded here. Rather, it is quite consistent to hold that temple thieves deserve to be punished (on the one hand) and that 'perhaps' the thief will learn a valuable moral lesson from his punishment (on the other). Capital punishment is again suggested for those who commit unspeakable offences against the gods, the state, or their own parents (*Laws* 854e). It is difficult to understand how this is not a statement in favour of retributivism, especially when it permits no moral education or curing of the perpetrator of such wrongdoings – even though it does allow for other citizens to learn from those who are banished from the state for their crimes (*Laws* 855a). However, it is vital to note that punishment, on this view, never nullifies some of the rights of the criminal as a citizen of the state (*Laws* 855c). This includes various procedural rights that such wrongdoers possess. All of these statements are consistent with any plausible version of retributivism.

The Athenian further argues that judges, when deciding who is to provide rectification to another, ought always to do so in a way that reconciles the parties as 'friends' provided that 'atonement' has been made by the wrongdoer (*Laws* 862c). For whenever there is lawbreaking, the law will combine 'instruction and constraint' both for reasons of deterrence and so that the wrongdoer will pay for the damage she has done (*Laws* 862d). In cases of theft, criminals deserve proportional punishment, but because of the probability of the thief's curability (*Laws* 941d). For those criminals who are curable, any means necessary can be used to make him hate injustice and embrace true justice. Yet for the incurable, death is the best thing for everyone (*Laws* 862e; 942a). But it is only the incurable who ought to receive death as a punishment for their crimes (*Laws* 863a). Murderers must receive death, and the murderer's assets must be given to the family of her victim (*Laws* 866d), that is, if the murder is committed intentionally. For there are different kinds of murder (*Laws* 866e–7c), and some do not justify capital punishment, but rehabilitation (*Laws* 867c–d). But there are even said to be cases where capital punishment is justified where the crime does not result in the death of a human being (*Laws* 946d–e). When the topic of criminal recidivism is discussed, there is a double standard pertaining to the punishment of those who murder slaves versus those who murder citizens (*Laws* 868).

Perhaps the most obvious retributivist passage in all of Plato's *Laws* is 869b–d, where it is stated that 'if one man could die many times, the murderer of his father or mother who has acted in anger would deserve to die the death over and over again. To this one killer no law will allow the plea of self-defense; no law will permit him to kill his father or mother, who brought him into the world'. The death penalty is further elaborated at *Laws* 871d–2c. In fact, there is even mention of vengeance in punishment for murder at *Laws* 871b and 872e, though of course no vengeance theory of punishment ought to be confused with any plausible version of retributivism, for reasons that Joel Feinberg and Robert Nozick (respectively) have pointed out.[17]

Plato's *Laws* 877a–b raises and answers the matter of failed criminal attempts, an issue that has gained the attention of the most respected twentieth-century philosophers of law.[18] And the answer that is given is quite nuanced: 'If a man deliberately intends to kill a fellow citizen ... and wounds him without being able to kill him, no pity should be wasted on the man who has inflicted a wound with that sort of intention: he should be treated with no more respect than a killer, and made to stand trial for murder. But we should have due respect for the luck that has saved him from total ruin ... *He who* has inflicted the wound shall be spared the death penalty.' Further minutiae are discussed concerning punishment and compensation at *Laws* 877c–9b.

Capital punishment, Plato's *Laws* 881a admits, is not always a (successful) deterrent. So appeal is made to 'the sufferings said to be in store for these people in the world to come' which are 'much more extreme than' capital punishment. Nonetheless, 'the punishments men suffer for these crimes here on earth while they are alive should as far as possible equal the penalties beyond the grave' (*Laws* 881b). If this is not a bold form of retributivism, then there is no such theory as retributivism. Yet it astounds the serious student of punishment theory, and of Plato's works, that these passages never seem to be brought into discussions of 'Plato's "theory" of "punishment"'. The state's not being able to adequately punish certain offenders proportionally is not used as an excuse for not fulfilling what Plato (and later Kant) argue is the state's moral duty. Rather, inadequate punishments are said to meet with true justice in the world to come. Also important in this context is the fact that 'deserves' is tied to the details of whippings, capital punishment, reprimands, and so on, for various and sundry crimes (*Laws* 881c–3c). And for those who still do not comprehend the fact that in Plato's works the notion of retribution is central in punishment contexts, there is the distinction between different kinds of 'prisons', including one 'to convey the notion of "punishment"' (*Laws* 908a). The key point here is that one of the other 'prisons' is dubbed a 'reform center'. But the first is clearly not for reform, but for punishment! Underlying this point in Plato's *Laws* is the retributivist notion of proportional punishment: the punishment must 'fit' the crime, however approximately.[19] That centuries later the famous utilitarian Bentham devotes several pages of a major work of his to devising 13 principles of proportional punishment is hardly sufficient reason not to understand that the problem of proportional punishment, though faced by both retributivist and utilitarian theories of punishment, is so important to retributivists that some notion of proportional punishment sits at the very core of retributivism. That proportional punishment is a recurrent notion expressed in various of Plato's works suggests that important retributivist themes are argued for here and there throughout them.

Plato's *Laws* 933d–4b details rules about capital punishment,[20] along with those of proportional punishment – and even 'an additional penalty appropriate to his crime, to encourage him to reform'. Each of these notions (except the reformatory one) is central to retributivism. And as noted earlier, reform is not in principle incompatible with retributivism. Other details about deserved capital punishment are found at *Laws* 952d–8c.

Now if the words of the Athenian in the *Laws* are really those of Socrates, then the argument for Socrates' retributivism is beyond reasonable dispute. However, even if the Athenian's desert words are not meant by Plato to reflect Socrates' convictions, the textual evidence for the Socratic roots of retributivism remains strong.

Deservedness is so important to Socrates that even aside from punishment contexts, he is unwilling to say anything about himself that would inflate or overstate his person (*Lesser Hippias* 372d). Even in death, people ought to get what they deserve in terms of caring for the dead (*Menexenus* 236d), and in praising them for courageous service (*Menexenus* 242d). Those who give in friendship deserve praise also, according to the author of *Letter XIII* 362b. In *Republic* 375d, Socrates believes that he deserves to be hit because of his inability to stay on track concerning an analogy that was used. And at *Republic* 382c, a question is asked about what is deserved concerning the use of false words. Sympathy and pity are said to be deserved (or not) at *Republic* 539a. And a question is asked at *Republic* 574a about a child deserving to do better than her parents. Finally, the title of being wise ought only to be bestowed on those who deserve it (*Epinomis* 974b).

What these final uses of desert words seem to indicate are statements of oughtness. When Socrates says that someone deserves this or that, what he means at the very least is that they ought to be treated in such and such a way: Those guilty of a harmful wrongdoing ought to be punished in proportion to it; those who have performed supererogatory acts ought to be praised, presumably, in proportion to how well their action served the interests of others, and so on.

Now all of this renders rather dubious much of M. M. Mackenzie's study on 'Plato's theory of punishment'.[21] After defining 'retributivism' such that it is distinct from 'benefit' or rehabilitation theories of punishment, Mackenzie reads into each passage from Plato's works (that is, the few of them that she cites) Plato's putative theory of punishment. Mackenzie even goes so far as to interpret Protagoras' words in Plato's *Protagoras* as suggestive of Plato's theory of punishment: 'This suggests that Plato, as a penologist, would not acknowledge the claims of retributivism – whether real or ideal.'[22] This is quite astounding given that, first, nowhere is there sufficient evidence, textual or otherwise, to indicate that what we find expressed in any work of Plato's amounts to Plato's own views, a point that has been argued extensively since Mackenzie's work.[23] Second, even if 'mouthpiece interpreters' like Mackenzie could demonstrate that what we find in Plato's works amounts to what Plato believed, it is incumbent on them to explain which characters in Plato's works represent Plato's views and which do not. But in the passage quoted from Mackenzie, it is Protagoras who represents Plato's supposed denial of retributivism, as Mackenzie herself construes retributivism. Third, even if it could be shown which characters in Plato's works express Plato's views and which do not, it is surely a stretch beyond credulity to think, as Mackenzie does, that what we find in Plato's works is anything even akin to a *theory* of punishment. Perhaps there is the foundation of such a theory, but to think that what we have studied thus far from Plato on punishment and desert amounts to a theory is to grossly misunderstand the nature of a theory, or to use 'theory' in such a fast and loose way that it loses its essential meaning. Finally, as we have seen, in nearly every work of Plato's in which the discourse of punishment is found in the mouth of Socrates, we find a desert-based idea of punishment, contrary to Mackenzie's above-cited assertion that Plato 'would not acknowledge claims of retributivism'.

It is important to study Plato's works such that we permit them to speak for themselves, without reading into them our own preconceived biases for or against this or that 'theory' of punishment. When we study Plato's works with our attention focused on notions of punishment and desert, we find inescapable expressions of retributivism. Whether or not this view belongs to Plato, it is difficult to know. But to assert as Mackenzie does that Plato's works express anything but a retributivist idea of punishment, or more specifically that they express a moral education theory of punishment is to not read the passages as they appear to us, or it is to misunderstand tremendously the nature of punishment, moral education, and retributivism. This also applies to Jean Hampton's work that attributes, however tentatively, a moral education theory of 'punishment' to Plato as she cites Mackenzie's work.

For all Mackenzie and others[24] point out regarding the reasons for Socrates' embracing of something like moral education for wrongdoers, that Socrates might have supported some kind of moral education for those who are not beyond the pale of reform is in no way inconsistent with any plausible version of retributivism. And in light of the textual evidence, it is clear that Socrates espouses both retributivism and reform. But he must hold to some meaningful version of a desert-based notion of punishment, lest he fall prey (which he does not) to the implausible view that deservedness does not matter in punishment, a crudely utilitarian view that John Rawls spent a great deal of time and energy attempting to revise and rescue from legitimate charges of injustice.[25]

The expository aim of this chapter has demonstrated that several passages in Plato's works contain explicit references to and uses of desert words in punishment contexts. If it is objected that Plato's *Laws* does not necessarily reflect either Plato's or Socrates' views, as the 'Athenian' might not be meant to speak for either or because some find it dubious that Plato authored the *Laws*, then there remains sufficient textual evidence from the dialogues of Plato to support the attribution to Socrates of various desert words of Socrates in punishment contexts to show that Socrates articulated a version of retribution worthy of the name. That Socrates also here and there expresses the idea of moral education in penal contexts in no way discounts his obvious and consistent retributivist leanings, as both views of how the state ought to address criminal wrongdoing are compatible with one another. It is time that philosophers recognize that Socrates was not the singularly minded moral education 'punishment' theorist that so many think he was.

Notes

All passages from Plato's works cited herein are taken from the translations in John M. Cooper and D. S. Hutchinson, eds (1997), *Plato: Complete Works* (Indianapolis: Hackett Publishing Company).

1. For a bibliography that contains such works, see J. Angelo Corlett (2006), *Responsibility and Punishment*, 3rd edn (Dordrecht: Springer), Library of Ethics and Applied Philosophy, Volume 9, 231–47.
2. The distinction between the justification of the institution of punishment versus the justification of particular forms of punishment is found in Stanley I. Benn, Anthony Quinton, and John Rawls, later 'borrowed' by H. L. A. Hart (Corlett, *Responsibility and Punishment*, 'Introduction' and Chapter 2).
3. See, for example, J. Angelo Corlett (2001), 'Making Sense of Retributivism', *Philosophy*, 76, 77–110; Corlett (2003), 'Making *More* of Retributivism', *Philosophy*, 78, 277–85.
4. Corlett, *Responsibility and Punishment*, chapters 3–4.
5. Except, of course, those of the legal positivist variety.
6. See Corlett, *Responsibility and Punishment*, chapter 3.
7. Compare M. M. Mackenzie (1981), *Plato on Punishment* (Berkeley: University of California Press).
8. The only philosophical work that has even hinted at this view of Socrates on punishment is Thomas C. Brickhouse and Nicholas D. Smith (2007), 'Socrates on How Wrongdoing Damages the Soul', *The Journal of Ethics*, 11, 337–56.
9. I say 'theory' here in that it is hardly obvious that what Socrates says in Plato's dialogues concerning punishment amounts to a theory at all in light

of the criteria for a theory of punishment found in Jeffrie G. Murphy, 'Does Kant Have a Theory of Punishment?' *Columbia Law Review*, 87, 509–32. Using Murphy's criteria as a propaedeutic, one might argue plausibly that a theory of punishment requires at least the following: (a) a definition of 'punishment'; (b) a statement of the moral and legal justifications of punishment; (c) a distinction between the justification of punishment as an institution and particular forms of punishment; and (d) an account of proportional punishment. While Socrates' words on punishment seem to satisfy (a) and perhaps to a lesser extent (d), it seems implausible to think that they satisfy (b) and (c). However, this is not to say that a Socratic basis for a theory of punishment so construed cannot be pieced together by what Socrates says of punishment and other Socratic statements made that might relate indirectly to punishment. Hence, it might be possible to piece together a Socratic theory of punishment, one that, it is cautioned, ought not to be confused with that of Socrates' view of punishment given what he says in Plato's dialogues. Thus while the texts of Plato on punishment do not amount to a theory of punishment, especially regarding the words placed therein in Socrates' mouth, rational reconstruction might possibly provide something of a Socratically-based theory of punishment.

10. Jean Hampton (1984), 'The Moral Education Theory of Punishment', *Philosophy and Public Affairs*, 13, 208–38; Thomas C. Brickhouse and Nicholas D. Smith (2002), 'The Problem of Punishment in Socratic Philosophy', *Aperion*, 95–107. I write, 'punishment', because it is not at all clear that such a view amounts to a belief about punishment at all if by 'punishment' is meant 'hard treatment' (Joel Feinberg) and treatment normally considered to be unpleasant (Rawls) (Corlett, *Responsibility and Punishment*, chapter 2). For if *Laws* 728c is correct, then punishment is 'suffering that follows a wrongdoing', just as capital punishment ensures the safety of others in society. It is quite unclear how moral education amounts to punishment in any sense of the term 'punishment'. This confusion of moral education or curing wrongdoers with punishment as hard and unpleasant treatment is replete among philosophers.

11. A. D. Woozley (1979), *Law and Obedience: The Arguments in Plato's* Crito (London: Duckworth), 130.

12. A globally unitarian approach to Plato sees the entire body of Plato's works as setting forth a consistent set of beliefs, doctrines, or theories about a select group of subjects throughout Plato's works, while a globally developmentalist approach construes the ideas in Plato's works as evolving from one dialogue to the next. There are, of course, moderate and local versions of these views.

13. J. Angelo Corlett (2005), *Interpreting Plato's Dialogues* (Las Vegas: Parmenides Publishing).

14. Cooper and Hutchinson, eds, *Plato: Complete Works*, pp. xii–xviii.

15. 'Secondary', because it is unclear on precisely what legitimate (non-ideologically driven) grounds such writings are to be denied canonical or primary textual status.

16. Jeremy Bentham (1948), *An Introduction to the Principles of Morals and Legislation* (New York: Hafner).

17. Joel Feinberg (1995), 'The Classic Debate', in Joel Feinberg and Hyman Gross, eds, *Philosophy of Law*, 5th edn (Belmont: Wadsworth Publishing Company),

613–18; Robert Nozick (1981), *Philosophical Explanations* (Cambridge: Harvard University Press), 366–8.

18. For example, see Joel Feinberg (2003), *Problems at the Roots of Law* (Oxford: Oxford University Press), chapter 4. For a discussion of Feinberg's views on failed criminal attempts, see J. Angelo Corlett (2006), 'The Philosophy of Joel Feinberg', *The Journal of Ethics*, 10, 146–51.
19. As opposed to Hammurabi's code, which includes the dictum: 'An eye for an eye, a tooth for a tooth.'
20. Including for the fourth crime of perjury (*Laws* 937c) and frivolous law suits (*Laws* 938c)!
21. Mackenzie, *Plato on Punishment*, chapter 11.
22. Mackenzie, *Plato on Punishment*, 181.
23. Corlett, *Interpreting Plato's Dialogues*, chapter 1.
24. Brickhouse and Smith, 'The Problem of Punishment in Socratic Philosophy'.
25. John Rawls (1999), *Collected Works* (Cambridge: Harvard University Press), chapter 2.

2
Punishment and British Idealism

Thom Brooks

Theorists of punishment have traditionally aligned themselves with various camps. For example, theorists have defended either retributivism (see Cottingham 1979), deterrence (see Beccaria 1986), rehabilitation (see Hampton 1987), expressivism or communicative theories (see Feinberg 1970 and Duff 2001), restorative justice (see Braithwaite 2002), and other positions.[1] Proponents of these camps have been at loggerheads with perhaps the best example being the longstanding disagreement between advocates of retributivism and those of deterrence. While there have been a few attempts to overcome these deep divisions, these have been largely unsuccessful.[2] The task of theorists today may appear then to be to side with one camp and continue to help fortify their respective positions.

In this essay, I shall not offer a philosophical history of the various debates between these different camps. Instead, my aim is to introduce the reader to one important attempt to contribute to moving the debate forward offered by the British Idealists. The British Idealists grew to prominence during the late nineteenth century and their influence began to wane after the outbreak of the First World War. The movement produced several important figures, such as Bernard Bosanquet, F. H. Bradley, and T. H. Green. While there are many significant differences between these and other Idealists, there is also significant overlap. One such overlap is an attempt to view theories of punishment from a new perspective, namely, as part of a single, coherent and unified theory of punishment rather than rival camps opposed to unification.

I shall begin by first discussing the legacy of Kant's and Hegel's writings on the British Idealist view of punishment. I will then briefly discuss the problems they encountered with justifying punishment before outlining their unified theory of punishment. While the work of British Idealists may be too often overlooked today, my hope is that fleshing out certain primary motivating features of their theory of punishment might solicit greater interest from a wider audience.

2.1   The legacy of Kant and Hegel

The British Idealists were notable at their time for introducing the work of Immanuel Kant and G. W. F. Hegel to an Anglophone audience and, in turn, Kant and Hegel were an important influence on British Idealist philosophy. Punishment is one such example.

Kant held retributivism to be a penal ideal, although he also recognized important limitations (Brooks 2003a). For instance, he argued that punishment must have at least two features. The first is that punishment must be deserved. In other words, we only punish those who deserve to be punished. An innocent person can never be subjected to punishment simply because she has done nothing to merit punishment. The second feature of punishment is that punishment should be proportionate to the crime for which punishment is deserved. The more serious the criminal wrongdoing, the more severe the corresponding punishment. For example, Kant argues for 'the law of retribution' where

> whatever undeserved evil you inflict upon another within the people ... you inflict upon yourself. If you insult him, you insult yourself; if you steal from him, you steal from yourself; if you strike him, you strike yourself; if you kill him, you kill yourself.
>
> (Kant 1996 [6:332])

There is then an equality between the severity of crime and punishment. Thus, punishment should correspond to the gravity of the offence. Capital punishment is then justified, for Kant, as the most grave punishment for an equally grave crime.

Kant recognized a genuine practical problem with such a theory of punishment. He says:

> The real morality of actions, their merit or guilt, even that of our own conduct, thus remains entirely hidden from us. Our imputations can refer only to the empirical character. How much of this character is ascribable to the pure effect of freedom, how much to mere nature, that is, to faults of temperament for which there is no responsibility, or to its happy constitution (*merito fortunae*), can *never* be determined, and upon it therefore no *perfectly* just judgements can be passed.
>
> (Kant 1958: 475n [A552/B580] and see Kant 1991: 19 [4:407])

We punish the guilty to the degree that they are guilty for their crimes. However, we face a serious epistemological problem: we cannot safely ascertain the guilt of others, not even of ourselves. Our judgements will always be no better than best guesses based upon limited information. We cannot be certain in any case that a criminal is punished to the degree he deserves because we may be mistaken on how deserving he is.

This problem with Kant's theory is recognized by the British Idealist T. H. Green. He says:

> If [the state] could only punish justly by making this pain proportionate in each case to the depravity implied in the crime, it could not punish justly at all. The amount of pain which any kind of punishment causes to the particular person depends on his temperament and circumstances, which neither the state nor its agent, the judge, can ascertain.
>
> (Green 1941: §192)

Thus, punishing criminals to the degree of their moral wrongdoing is seriously undermined by our inability to properly assess not simply *the degree* of their moral wrongdoing, but also *the fact* of their moral wrongdoing. The problem is then more than just a question of getting proportionality generally correct. Indeed, the problem for retributivists is that they cannot ascertain with safety whether a criminal is, in fact, guilty.

This epistemological problem is also well stated by the British Idealist F. H. Bradley:

> If you can acquire the right to punish only by proving moral crime, it seems hard to be sure that this right is really secured. Thus the principle is good, but its aplication is seriously embarrassed.
>
> (Bradley 1894: 274)

Instead, we require a theory of punishment that can avoid justifying punishment on less vicarious grounds. This is not to say that we should then abandon the view that persons can only be guilty if they have performed a crime or that punishment should be set in proportion to its corresponding crime. On the contrary, we merely abandon the view that criminal wrongdoing is linked with moral wrongdoing.

For the British Idealists, Hegel offered a way forward. Hegel argues that punishment should 'cancel' crime (Hegel 1991: §101). However, punishment should be seen in its 'proper context' where the form that punishment might take may be several (Hegel 1991: §99R). For Kant, the criminal is thought to effectively set his own punishment: we punish him to the degree he deserves punishment and this desert is grounded in the wickedness of his crime. The problem to be solved is our inability to determine his responsibility for any wickedness. For Hegel, the criminal does *not* effectively set his own punishment. Instead, the community plays an important role. Hegel says:

> The fact that an injury to *one* member of society is an injury to *all* the others does not alter the nature of crime in terms of its concept, but in terms of its outward existence ... its *danger to civil society* is a determination of its magnitude ... This quality or magnitude varies, however, according to the *condition* of civil society.
>
> (Hegel 1991: §218R)

There are several different positions we might discern from this statement. The first is that we should punish crimes as crimes. Our concern is with a crime's 'outward existence' – and not its inner moral, existence as such. By punishing crimes as crimes, we retain an understanding of desert, namely, an individual must have performed a crime to deserve punishment. However, we can then sidestep the problem of having to discern the moral desert a criminal possesses when determining the severity of his deserved punishment.

A second feature is that the community's view of the crime matters when setting the penal tariff. One reason is because crime is a public, not private, affair. A theft may appear to be a wrong against the victim alone. However, in view of theft's existence, the property rights of all come under threat. Therefore, crimes are public affairs that are a concern for all. The more the political community is concerned about the crime, the more severely the crime should be punished. Hegel notes that a crime's perceived 'danger to civil society' determines its penal severity. Legal punishment then aspires to satisfy societal maintenance: we punish crimes in relation to the threat they pose to the continuation of our community. Thus, treason (followed closely by murder) poses the greatest threat to civil society and, unsurprisingly, we find no society in the world that does not punish treason with the highest permissible tariff in that society. This reading of Hegel's theory of punishment can help us make better sense of this fact.

Furthermore, few commentators seem even aware of an important statement by Hegel on punishment found in his *Science of Logic*, a work that – at least in his eyes – provided the cornerstone for his larger philosophical system. Hegel says:

> Punishment, for example, has various determinations: it is retributive, a deterrent example as well, a threat used by the law as a deterrent, and also it brings the criminal to his senses and reforms him. Each of these different determinations has been considered the *ground* of punishment, because each is an essential determination, and therefore the others, as distinct from it, are determined as merely contingent relatively to it. *But the one which is taken as ground is still not the whole punishment itself.*
>
> (Hegel 1999: 465)

This passage is very revealing. It is perhaps the first time that we find the statement that retribution, deterrence, and rehabilitation are each 'an essential determination' of what is punishment: each is a legitimate side of punishment. However, the three fit together in a particular way, namely, with retribution serving as a ground within a larger, unified theory of punishment incorporating the other perspectives.[3]

Hegel is distinguishing between the various grounds of punishment and essential, the 'true', ground of punishment. Hegel nowhere denies that punishment may legitimately have a deterrent effect. His argument is merely that the ground of punishment is retribution and by this he means that punishment must always be 'deserved' by the criminal and in proportion to their crime. Punishments may satisfy this ground in any number of ways. What is deserved is not a criminal's culpability as such, but the degree to which their criminal act presented a 'danger to civil society' (see Hegel 1991: §218R). Hegel's theory of punishment accommodates more functions than retributivism alone. These functions are justified within a certain framework where deterrent and rehabilitative functions are secondary to the necessity of desert and proportionality. Punishment is, strictly speaking, neither retributivist, deterrent nor rehabilitative, but a *unification* of these three distinct functions within a single, coherent framework.

To complete this part of the discussion, Hegel does not offer further substantive argument as to how retribution, deterrence, and rehabilitation might become unified in one theory of punishment. Commentators on Hegel's theory of punishment universally pay little, if any, attention to the *Science of Logic*'s claim (see Cooper 1971 and Wood 1990). Hegel is not explicit about how his theory of punishment in the *Philosophy of Right* might have a unified character, although there is no inconsistency between his arguments in the *Science of Logic* and the *Philosophy of Right* on punishment (Brooks 2007). The challenge of developing a unified theory of punishment which brings together retribution, deterrence, and rehabilitation into one coherent theory will be taken up by the British Idealists.

2.2   The Idealist's unified theory of punishment

My aim has been to highlight a particular strand of interpretation beginning with Kant and leading to Hegel. The purpose of this section is to explain not simply what British Idealists thought of certain problems with the aforementioned accounts of punishment, but what their distinctive alternative theory of punishment is.[4]

The British Idealists held that laws are necessary for the continuation of society. Political stability is impossible without laws. Inevitable conflicts will arise as individuals come together to create a shared community. This is not because people are naturally antagonistic, but rather that people will disagree. A system of law is then necessary in order to resolve such differences. This is not to say that a community needs law alone in order to be politically stable, but it is to say that law is a necessary, albeit not sufficient, condition for political stability.

Our community then requires a system of law.[5] Together, these laws help us govern our affairs. Some of these laws will be more central than others, such as laws against murder or treason. Other laws will play a more minor role in this project, such as laws against leaving chewing gum on a sidewalk. Therefore, some laws may have greater importance than others at a given time. We may revise how we view this importance over time and revise what we believe should serve as law. Nevertheless, these laws fit together into a system, a legal system. Its existence as a system is clear whenever we discover apparent conflicts between existing laws and seek to return greater coherence to our system of law.

It is important to point out that the British Idealists did not hold the view that legal systems have a right to continuation. On the contrary, the community and its laws were not held to exist in isolation, but rather for the benefit of the individuals within the community. Law serves a special purpose in helping safeguard and develop the rights and liberties of individuals.[6] Individuals must find satisfaction in their community and the laws designed for their community's continuity (Ritchie 1905: 321). The law exists for the benefit of individuals and not *vice versa*. Furthermore, as Green rightly notes, 'The justice of the punishment depends on the justice of the general system of rights' and that 'the proper and direct object of state-punishment [is] ... the general protection of rights' (Green 1941: §189, 204). Therefore, we cannot mete out just punishments from an unjust legal system. Instead, our punishments may be no more just than the legal system that sanctions them.

The British Idealists held that punishment can only be directed against crime.[7] This may seem obvious: after all, no mainstream theorist argues for punishment of innocent people. However, there is a difference in the approach of the British Idealists. Many theorists might argue that we punish crime because crime is evil or wrong in some moral sense. The British Idealists disagreed. For example, Bernard Bosanquet argues that there must be some 'overt act' performed in the past that triggers the possibility of punishment (Bosanquet 1918: 193). Punishment is then '*prima facie* retrospective' at its core (Bosanquet 1918: 188). We do not punish a criminal for what might happen, but for what did happen. Our primary concern is whether a crime has taken place. Punishment is then a response to crime. However, it is a response to crime *as crime* and not as moral wrong. The British Idealists were broadly favourable to the legal positivist's separability thesis and they argued that it would be a mistake to legislate against all forms of immorality or to view crime as immorality.[8]

This approach to desert is different from other approaches, such as retributivism. Retributivists might argue that a crime is wrong and, as wrong, criminals should be punished on account of their performing wrongdoing. Punishment should be in proportion to the wrong of the criminal activity. For British Idealists, criminals are punished solely on account of their breaking the law. Thus, they argued that we should punish as a reaction to the existence of crime: punishment exists only because of crime.

How then should punishment react to crime? The British Idealists were opposed to 'adding a new evil to an old one' and causing pain for its own sake (Bosanquet 1918: 189). Instead, they held a revised Hegelian account. Recall that on their view laws form a system. Together, this system of laws is necessary for the continuation of our society: societal maintenance is impossible otherwise. Some laws will be more central than others. Laws serve the function of protection, namely, the protection of rights (see Green 1941: §15; Seth 1907: 304). Punishment should be understood in this context. For example, T. H. Green argues:

[Punishment] is a disapproval founded on a sense of what is necessary for the protection of rights ... It is founded essentially on the outward aspect of a man's conduct, on the view of it as related to the security and freedom in action and acquisition of other members of society.

(Green 1941: §197)

The proportionality of punishment then corresponds to the centrality of a right within a system of law and not the immorality of its violation.[9] Thus, we find Green argues that punishment should be seen in light of 'a sense of what is necessary for the protection of rights, not on a judgment of good and evil' and 'punishment of crime, then, neither is, nor can, nor should be adjusted to the degree of moral depravity, properly so called, which is implied in the crime' (Green 1941: §197).

This position has much to recommend it. Not all crimes are signs of immorality, or at least not in any straightforward sense. For example, consider drug offences and traffic offences. Consider a cannabis smoker. It is far from clear how such a person is performing a greater immorality than, say, a consumer of alcohol. Or consider traffic offences. It is far from clear how speeding is immoral. A critic might respond that speeding demonstrates a lack of concern for others. However, the speed limits are established for regular driving conditions for regular citizens. Suppose that you have the driving skills of F1 driving legend Michael Schumacher and the driving conditions are ideal. It is unclear how such a person in similar circumstances necessarily fails to demonstrate a sufficient lack of concern for others. After all, such a person is able to drive better than most people. We can see the convenience of adhering to set speed limits to all, but hopefully we can also recognize that speeding is not necessarily immoral. If it is not necessarily immoral, then it may well remain open that some individual speeders are engaged in wrongdoing when they speed, but that the criminality of speeding at its heart is merely the fact of its being prohibited and not its being immoral.

I raise the examples of drug offences and traffic offences because these are the offences that most people actually do commit and become imprisoned.[10] Perhaps we have all at some time committed a traffic offence whether it be for illegal parking, speeding or some similar offence. Strictly speaking, traffic offences are criminal offences (see Cunningham 2008). Likewise, perhaps we have all at some time committed a drug offence whether it be for using cannabis or some other controlled substance. Drug offences are also part of the criminal law and most prisoners have been convicted of their use. If it is the case that most of the crimes we commit and punish are not immoral in any straightforward sense, then this is an important reason to become attracted to theories of punishment – like that offered by the British Idealists – that understand punishment as a reaction to crime, not immorality.

If the British Idealists do not punish crimes to the degree they are 'wrong' or 'immoral', then how are punishments set in proportion to crimes? Perhaps the clearest statement is offered by James Seth. He says:

> This view of the object of punishment gives the true measure of its amount. This is found not in the amount of moral depravity which the crime reveals, but in the importance of the right violated, relatively to the system of rights of which it forms a part ... The measure of the punishment is, in short, the measure of social necessity; and this measure is a changing one.
>
> (Seth 1907: 305; Hetherington and Muirhead 1918: 129)

The amount of punishment is determined by its object. The object of punishment is its corresponding crime. Crimes are not equal in value. However, what differentiates crimes from each other is not how immoral one crime is over another (or its 'moral depravity'), but the importance of the legal right violated by a crime. We determine the importance of the legal right violated in relation to its place within the system of rights, or the legal system.[11] This is summarized well by Green:

> a violation of a right, requires a punishment, of which the kind and amount must depend on the relative importance of the right and of the extent to which its general exercise is threatened. Thus every theory of rights in detail must be followed by, or indeed implies, a corresponding theory of punishment in detail.
>
> (Green 1941: §177)

A theory of rights requires a theory of punishment. This is because punishment's aim is to protect our rights.

Let us consider why we punish murder more than theft. Some theories of punishment might hold that both are moral wrongs, but the taking of a life is a more grave moral wrong than the taking of another's property. Note that such a position on punishment can only be compelling where all crimes are moral wrongs. The British Idealists would also punish murder more than theft, but not because one is more immoral than the other. Instead, the reason is that the right violated by murder is more central than the right violated by theft. What does this mean? An example may help. Some crimes can be more easily tolerated than others. If many citizens stole from each other, then there would exist a real problem of mutual trust and property rights would be threatened. However, if many citizens were being murdered, then the right violated is far greater. We may not risk any genuine threat to our continuity as a community from some criminal acts, but some crimes pose a greater risk than others. Murder is one such case. Indeed, murder victims have not just their right to life taken from them, but their capacity to exercise all rights. Therefore, we can gain an understanding of how some rights are more central than others, how some violations of certain rights are of more concern than others, and how the centrality of rights violations against the background of viewing rights as part of a system of law permits us to discern different penal tariffs for different crimes.

Note further the end of Seth's statement: 'The measure of punishment is, in short, the measure of social necessity; and this measure is a changing one' (Seth 1907: 305). There are two further features worth highlighting. First, laws are necessary for societal maintenance, but this does not mean all laws share in this necessity. In fact, British Idealists were liberals and opposed burdensome bureaucracy or what we might call today 'Big Government'. The view that we should oppose criminalization unless genuinely necessary is inherent in British Idealist legal thought – indeed, this is perhaps attraction enough for those of us who believe criminalization has reached dizzying and even troublesome heights (see Husak 2007).

Secondly, the measure of social necessity 'is a changing one'. The British Idealists opposed the idea that the philosophy of punishment offered any eternal tariffs. That is, persons holding opposing theories of punishment might argue that murder *ought* to be punished by death. Or perhaps there is a set range of penal options for someone who is an arsonist. The British Idealists disagree strongly. For them, the degree to which we punish a crime depends upon the centrality of the right violated. How central certain rights will appear to us will change over time. For example, the crime of being (or being perceived to be) a wizard or witch was once punished by death. The British Idealists would explain this on the grounds that wizardry or witchcraft could have been perceived as a direct challenge or attack on pivotal rights held by people at the time. This is no longer the case because we do not find wizardry or witchcraft a threat to our current system of laws. (Indeed, many of us may be looking forward to the next Harry Potter movie.)

Likewise, sodomy was also once punished by death. What explains why it has been decriminalized? Again, the British Idealist explanation – inherited from Hegel – is that there is a changing relation between crime and punishment (see Hegel 1991: §218). This changing relationship is the perceived threat by the community from a criminalized act (see Hegel 1991: §218R). The British Idealists' innovative view is that crimes should be understood not simply as threats to 'civil society' *a la* Hegel, but as threats to particular rights within a wider context of a system of laws. Thus, homosexuality was decriminalized because people no longer viewed it as constituting a threat to their rights. On the contrary, the rights violation became the failure to recognize the lawfulness of homosexuality in the first place. This brings us to the conclusion that there is no eternally fixed punishment for any crime. Instead, we should revise (and revise often) how we perceive the relationship between crime and punishment.[12] Therefore, as Hegel argues, 'a criminal code cannot be valid for every age ... A penal code is therefore primarily a product of its time and of the current condition of civil society' (Hegel 1991: §218A, R). We should never think the question of how to punish a crime is ever settled: it must always be open to revision.

This project of punishment as a reaction to crime often has the Hegelian characteristic of 'annulment' or, in other words, of punishment as an attempt to 'cancel' the crime in some meaningful sense. Thus, for example, Bernard Bosanquet argues:

> if the evil rule is not in this sense to stand and persist, then the act or fact must be cancelled, annulled, undone. This, I take it, and not the infliction of pain, is the essence of punishment.
>
> (Bosanquet 1918: 190–1)

When we punish, we punish in proportion to how a crime threatens a protected right. We do not punish actions because they may or may not be immoral, but only because they are deemed criminal. Our understanding of what is criminal and how severely any criminal action should be punished are historical perspectives and given to change over time. Nevertheless, when we inflict punishment, its purpose is to address the crime as crime and attempt to negate any positive effect it may have possessed: it aspires to reset the world as if the crime had not taken place. Of course, the law can never hope to bring the dead back to life. It would be a mistake to think crimes, such as murder, work against this view of criminal law. On the contrary, while law can never hope to bring back murder victims, it can 'resurrect' the centrality of the right to life through punishing those who have denied this right to others.

This then leads us to a final major position adopted by British Idealists. This position is that punishment can take a variety of forms as a response to crime. The British Idealist critique of punishment theory-as-usual is that it is too often one-sided and non-inclusive. The definitive statement is offered by Green, who claims that '[i]t is commonly asked whether punishment according to its proper nature is retributivist or preventative or reformatory. The true answer is that it is and should be all three' (Green 1941: §178; see Bosanquet 1965: 216; Mackenzie 1924: 430–2; Ritchie 1902: 221; Seth 1892: 236). This position is very similar to what we saw much earlier in Hegel's analysis of the ground of punishment in his *Science of Logic*.[13] The view there was that retribution, deterrence, and rehabilitation were unified in a single theory of punishment, but retribution served as a 'ground'. Thus, in the words of Bosanquet, the truth in the *lex talionis* is no more than that 'wrong demands negation' (Bosanquet 1918: 197). The retributivist feature is weak: it is merely that a person must have committed a crime to warrant punishment.

British Idealists are committed to the view that how we might punish persons who perform crimes may take various forms. For example, Bosanquet argues that

> The true place of deterrence and reformation in punishment is simply to determine the method and degree of details which no estimate of moral guilt can supply.
>
> (Bosanquet 1918: 203)

One implication of this view is that the determination of 'the method and degree of details' is not a given in any particular case. However, it is also true that – in some sense – non-retributivist features play a crucial role in British Idealist theories of punishment. For example, Bosanquet says: 'Deterrence and reformation are subordinate aspects implied within it; not consequences beyond it to which it is a mere instrument, and by which, therefore, it could be determined without limit' (Bosanquet 1918: 207). Thus, the warrant for punishment cannot be that it makes society happier, but because it is deserved on account of its being performed. The subordination of deterrence and reformation (or rehabilitation) is only to the 'retributivist' element that all criminals should have at least performed a crime at a bare minimum.

For British Idealists, deterrent and rehabilitative features are only 'subordinate' to the act of desert understood here as no more than having performed a criminal activity. A further illustration is offered by Green:

> In the crime a right has been violated. No punishment can undo what has been done, or make good the wrong to the person who has

suffered. What it can do is to make less likely the doing of a similar wrong in other cases.

(Green 1941: §193)

Punishment cannot change what has happened, but it can focus itself on preventing such behaviour in the future. The form that punishment takes can be flexible in its effort to best address and prevent repeated criminality. Such decisions must be made on a case-by-case basis. In some cases, more rehabilitative punishments are most appropriate. In others, different forms of punishment are most appropriate. Punishment can take retributivist, deterrent or rehabilitative form depending upon the best manner of protecting the right violated by the particular crime.

The form that legitimate punishment may take is fairly endless. For example, R. G. Collingwood says:

> The most perfect punishment involves no 'incidental' pains at all. The condemnation is expressed simply and quietly in words, and goes straight home. The punishment consists in expression of condemnation and that alone; and to punish with a word instead of a blow is still punishment. It is, perhaps, a better and more civilized form of punishment.[14]

(Collingwood 1989: 131)

Punishment may take any number of forms, including a stern word. This statement is particularly useful as it reminds us that British Idealists opposed the view of punishment as pain in return for pain. Our focus is also the system of law and the rights it attempts to protect. If a stern word rather than prison is best at addressing a particular crime to this larger end, then it is the most justified form of punishment in that case.

British Idealists adopted several positions that together offer a highly interesting and compelling theory of punishment. A system of law is necessary to maintain the continuity of society. Some laws are more central to this system than others. The centrality of any laws – and their corresponding violations as crimes – is historical and may change over time. We punish crimes to the degree that they threaten the rights protected within our system of law. This theory of punishment is 'retributivist' insofar as it demands that a crime must have first taken place.[15] However, its outward form is flexible given what is the best means to address any deterrent/prohibitive or rehabilitative framework. Thus,

British Idealists offer us a coherent, single, unified theory of punishment. Punishment can be retributivist, deterrent, and rehabilitative at once.

2.3   Conclusion

Today, British Idealism is too often understood to be a minor philosophical movement deserving little more than historical interest. I believe this is a serious mistake. British Idealists grappled with many of the same problems that continue to trouble us today. A closer consideration of their ideas may help us to re-examine our philosophical commitments and positions from a different perspective. Our efforts to engage in such a re-examination is richly rewarded on many issues, not least that of punishment. The British Idealists have offered us a perspective that sheds some light on how seemingly opposed philosophical camps may be brought together within a coherent, unified theory of punishment bringing together elements of retributivism, deterrence, and rehabilitation.

Of course, there is far more to be said about this project. I have only offered a brief outline of positions held by British Idealists on punishment. Nevertheless, I hope that what I have outlined will excite a greater interest in the work of the British Idealists and how it may be appropriated to help us better address issues of contemporary concern.

Notes

1. On theories of punishment generally, see Brooks (forthcoming).
2. Perhaps one example is the mixed theories of punishment offered by Hart and Rawls (see Hart 1968 and Rawls 1955).
3. Most commentators on Hegel's theory of punishment wrongly argue that it is retributivist and not a unified theory. For further explanation of this debate, see Brooks 2007.
4. I will highlight key features of the theories of punishment generally held by most British Idealists. While I would claim there is a general position held by most, I would not want to claim that all British Idealists were the same or held the exact same views on all matters pertaining to punishment. On further individual details concerning British Idealists and punishment, see Brooks 2003b.
5. For a defence of this view, see Stephen 1907: 106.
6. Otherwise, our condition, for Hobbes, is a 'warre of every man against every man' in a life that is 'solitary, poore, nasty, brutish, and short' (Hobbes 1996: 90, 89).
7. This is captured well by J. D. Mabbott: 'The only justification for punishing any man is that he has broken a law' (Mabbott 1939: 158). While he was not himself a member of the British Idealists, he had known and had been educated by several who were during his many years at the University of Oxford.

The universities of Glasgow and Oxford were the leading centres of British Idealism during the movement's peak.

8. Part of the reason for this position is that they believed it important for the moral development of individuals that they possessed a space in which to make mistakes and, in turn, learn from them, but free from the coercive power of the law.

9. For example, Green argues that 'crime should be punished according to the importance of the right which it violates' (Green 1941: §198).

10. I do not suggest that the only crimes that are not straightforwardly immoral are drug offences and traffic offences. Other such crimes might include prostitution and treason. Of course, some crimes may appear straightforwardly immoral, such as theft or murder. However, if we would want a criminal law that criminalized traffic offences *and* murder, then we could not claim immorality as a ground for our theory of criminalization where immorality was not a feature of all the crimes we would criminalize, should this include traffic offences.

11. See also Muirhead 1910: 27 [§9]: 'the judgement that theft is wrong is not explained by merely referring it to a moral sense or feeling ... but by showing that disregard for other people's property is inconsistent with that system of mutual relations which we call social life'.

12. I cowardly note within the endnotes the simple truth that this position is both highly attractive and problematic at once. It is highly attractive in offering a genuinely compelling explanation about why we change the penal tariffs of so many crimes over time. Or at least this is compelling to my eyes. However, there is a serious concern, namely, that it is not a falsifiable position.

13. I find it striking to compare the fact that Hegel uses the example of punishment he does in the *Science of Logic* with the position held by the British Idealists. I do not believe this is coincidental. Most British Idealists (and not least Bosanquet, Bradley, and Green) have an interest in Hegel's logic and his political philosophy. Furthermore, if a Hegelian dialectic brings together three positions into one unity, then one might expect – even if not expect the particular shape of argument to come – that a Hegelian position on punishment might be much like, say, a Hegelian position on the state. With the state, we find Hegel trying to bring together monarchy, aristocracy and democracy into one unified system of governance (see Brooks 2007). We should not be surprised to find Hegel offering the same three-fold relation in the case of punishment. Indeed, perhaps we should have been surprised if Hegel did not oppose retributivism, deterrence and rehabilitation as separate, distinct theories and attempt to offer an alternative for bringing them together. I have elsewhere argued that Hegel does, in fact, do this (Brooks 2007). I believe it is particularly striking that Hegel did this and it was apparently picked up by his most enthusiastic nineteenth-century readers, the British Idealists. Of course, this would suggest that Green et al. were more careful Hegel scholars (at least on punishment) than many today. I'd readily agree.

14. See Dewey and Tufts 1909: 417: 'That punishment is suffering, that it inevitably involves pain to the guilty one, there can be no question ... whether the punishment is externally inflicted or is in the pangs of conscience'.

15. Of course, there would be no violated right to protect if no crime had first taken place.

Bibliography

Beccaria, C. (1986), *On Crimes and Punishment*, trans. David Young. Indianapolis: Hackett.

Bosanquet, B. (1918), *Some Suggestions in Ethics*. London: Macmillan.

Bosanquet, B. (1965), *The Philosophical Theory of the State, 4th edn.* London: Macmillan.

Bradley, F. H. (1894), 'Some Remarks on Punishment', *Mind*, 4, 269–84.

Braithwaite, J. (2002), *Restorative Justice and Responsive Regulation*. Oxford: Oxford University Press.

Brooks, T. (2003a), 'Kant's Theory of Punishment', *Utilitas*, 15, 206–24.

Brooks, T. (2003b), 'T. H. Green's Theory of Punishment', *History of Political Thought*, 24, 685–701.

Brooks, T. (2007), *Hegel's Political Philosophy: A Systematic Reading of the Philosophy of Right*. Edinburgh: Edinburgh University Press.

Brooks, T. (2010), 'What Did the British Idealists Ever Do For Us?' in Thom Brooks (ed.), *New Waves in Ethics*. Basingstoke: Palgrave.

Brooks, T. (forthcoming), *Punishment*. London: Routledge.

Collingwood, R. G. (1989), *Essays in Political Philosophy*, ed. David Boucher. Oxford: Clarendon Press.

Cooper, D. E. (1971), 'Hegel's Theory of Punishment', in Z. A. Pelczynski (ed.), *Hegel's Political Philosophy: Problems and Prospects*. Cambridge: Cambridge University Press, 151–67.

Cottingham, J. (1979), 'Varieties of Retribution', *Philosophical Quarterly*, 29, 238–46.

Cunningham, S. (2008), *Driving Offences: Law, Policy and Practice*. Aldershot: Ashgate.

Dewey, J. and J. H. Tufts (1909), *Ethics*. London: George Bell and Sons.

Duff, R. A. (2001), *Punishment, Communication, and Community*. Oxford: Oxford University Press.

Feinberg, J. (1970), *Doing Deserving: Essays in the Theory of Responsibility*. Princeton: Princeton University Press.

Green, T. H. (1941), *Lectures on the Principles of Political Obligation*. London: Longmans.

Hampton, J. (1987), 'The Moral Education Theory of Punishment', *Philosophy and Public Affairs*, 13, 208–38.

Hart, H. L. A. (1968), *Punishment and Responsibility: Essays in the Philosophy of Law*. Oxford: Oxford University Press.

Hegel, G. W. F. (1991), *Elements of the Philosophy of Right*, trans. Allen Wood. Cambridge: Cambridge University Press.

Hegel, G. W. F. (1999), *The Science of Logic*, trans. A. V. Miller. Amherst: Humanity Books.

Hetherington, H. J. W. and J. H. Muirhead (eds) (1918), *Social Purpose: A Contribution to a Philosophy of Civic Society*. London: George Allen and Unwin.

Hobbes, T. (1996), *Leviathan*, ed. Richard Tuck. Cambridge: Cambridge University Press.

Husak, D. (2007), *Overcriminalization: The Limits of the Criminal Law*. Oxford: Oxford University Press.

Kant, I. (1958), *Critique of Pure Reason*, trans. Norman Kemp Smith. London: Macmillan.

Kant, I. (1991), *Groundwork of the Metaphysics of Morals*, ed. and trans. M. J. Gregor. Cambridge: Cambridge University Press.

Kant, I. (1996), *Metaphysics of Morals*, ed. and trans. M. J. Gregor. Cambridge: Cambridge University Press.

Mabbott, J. D. (1939), 'Punishment', *Mind*, 48, 152–67.

Mackenzie, J. S. (1924), *A Manual of Ethics, 5th edn*. London: University Tutorial Press.

Muirhead, J. H. (1910), *The Elements of Ethics, 3rd edn*. London: John Murray.

Rawls, J. (1955), 'Two Concepts of Rules', *Philosophical Review*, 64, 3–32.

Ritchie, D. G. (1902), *Studies in Political and Social Ethics*. London: Swan Sonnenschein.

Ritchie, D. G. (1905), *Philosophical Studies*, ed. Robert Latta. London: Macmillan.

Seth, J. (1892), 'The Theory of Punishment', *International Journal of Ethics*, 2, 232–9.

Seth, J. (1907), *A Study of Ethical Principles, 9th edn*. Edinburgh: William Blackwood and Sons.

Stephen, L. (1907), *The Science of Ethics, 2nd edn*. London: Smith, Elder, & Co.

Wood, A. W. (1990), *Hegel's Ethical Thought*. Cambridge: Cambridge University Press.

3
Punishment and Restitution

David B. Hershenov

The debt/atonement model of punishment seeks to reconcile the criminal with his direct victim, as well as the larger community, through restorative mechanisms of restitution and atonement.[1] As a result, it has certain advantages over better known rival models.[2] Unlike retribution, reform and deterrence, the approach does some good, first and foremost, for the victim of the crime. But it can also benefit the victimizer and indirectly victimized members of the larger community. Competing theories usually profit but one of the three. They also fail to do as well in removing the tension between justice and mercy. Yet even when mercy is not an option, retribution, reform and deterrence can dictate punishments that are intuitively excessive. But the problem isn't just that of excess. At others times, it seems they will endorse inappropriately lenient responses to crime.

I will argue that a properly construed debt/atonement approach, despite its stress on punishment taking the form of restitution, can handle three common objections that it is incapable of providing appropriate punishments. The first is that it cannot justify punishing murder for the dead cannot be compensated. Even if this turns out to be true, surprisingly, it bestows no relative advantage upon rival accounts for if the dead cannot be benefited, then they cannot be *harmed*, and thus punishing killers who did not harm those they killed will be difficult for any theory to justify. The second objection is that it cannot accommodate our practice of punishing failed attempts where there appears to be no harm done and the target didn't even know the attempt transpired. Ironically, it turns out that *only* the advocated approach can justify our practice of punishing failed attempts less severely than successes. The third objection is that the theory sometimes advocates making criminals suffer in order to satisfy the vindictive desires of their victims. I'll argue that so harming criminals is a defensible way to extract the debt payment they owe their victims. However, I'll conclude that if it were wrong to ever intentionally harm criminals, it would still be necessary to excuse the practice given the failure of the most plausible alternative to the institution of punishment: a system of restitution that repudiates intentionally harming lawbreakers.

3.1 Why punish?

The most common response is that the criminal *deserves* it. But what good does it do to make him suffer? Well, perhaps it satisfies the public's sense of justice. But that just returns the question to what good does justice deliver when giving the criminal what he deserves? It can't be an *intrinsic* good if it isn't good in the first place. The retributivist seems to cut off explanation prematurely. Rival theories like deterrence do some good for society as a whole, while reform can do the criminal some good. Yet the immediate victim benefits little. Of course, it might be claimed that improving the lot of the victim is a civil matter. However the line between torts and crimes is not set in stone.[3] I will argue that there are good reasons to treat restitution as a form of punishment, although there will be (rare) situations in which it can replace punishment, understanding the latter to necessarily involve intentionally harming the criminal.[4]

The debt/atonement theory places a priority upon aiding the direct victim, so the debt payment is more important than the debtor's atonement. But the approach aims to restore the criminal and victim to their status as equal citizens as they were before (or should have been).[5] The victim is brought as close as possible to his appropriate status through some form of restitution. In fact, the criminal's contrition and belated recognition of his victim's worth can play a role in the latter's restoration. And a remorseful criminal, who accepts his debt payment and the accompanying suffering as a form of penance will both be able to alleviate his guilt and prove to himself and others that he has learnt his lesson and thus ought to be restored to society as an equal.[6]

Alas, it will often happen that the criminal is not contrite and there will be times when the victimizer can't render restitution. In the former, the criminal can still provide restitution. In the latter, the wrongdoer can still atone. A situation where neither can be appropriately provided no more sinks the debt/atonement theory than the occasional failure to maximize crime prevention scuttles the deterrence approach, or the inability to make a particular criminal virtuous wrecks reform, or the impossibility of giving a very elderly criminal the decades in jail that he deserves torpedoes the rationale for retribution. All theories, on some applications, will fall short of their own ideal.[7] The degree of the failure, the frequency at which it occurs, and how poorly the theory accords with broader moral principles will be far more decisive in evaluating the approach.

3.2 Justice and mercy

One of the broader principles is mercy. There is considerable tension between justice and mercy. If justice is a virtue, and mercy means not bestowing justice, then it would seem that mercy is a vice. Such an unwelcome conclusion usually assumes as a premise a retributivist account of justice where the criminal deserves a certain level of punishment, and anything less is a miscarriage of justice. If the premise is replaced with one that claims the rationale for punishment is to reform criminals, mercifully releasing them prior to rehabilitation would undermine justice. And if the purpose of punishment is taken to be deterrence, then it seems the possibility of mercy will reduce the deterrent effect. However, if punitive justice is determined by what restitution requires, then the forgiving victim (or her judicial/executive representative) is free to mercifully accept less compensation as a means to restoration and reconciliation than that typically demanded by the law. She can claim the apologetic and remorseful criminal owes her nothing else, his debt either paid or forgiven, and he can thus be restored to society as an equal. Justice as restitution allows both x amount of compensation and x minus n compensation. Justice doesn't demand either. It depends upon what the victim requires to be restored and reconciled to the release of the criminal. Perhaps this involves having his moral worth recognized, peace of mind regained, and material wealth recovered. What brings about the first two may legitimately vary with the behaviour of the criminal and the character of the victim, while the material debt can be forgiven without rendering the reconciliation corrupt. So the higher restitution might be the norm enacted in law but mercifully accepting the lower is not incompatible with justice. Therefore mercy in a restitutionist account is not internally at odds with justice. There is no need to invoke a value external to justice in order to trump considerations of justice.

3.3 Inappropriate punishment

The principles governing restitution in the debt/atonement model not only fail to provide an internal obstacle to merciful early release but they don't demand sentences of inappropriate lengths as do reform, deterrence and even retribution. These problems have been well rehearsed in the literature so I will be brief and thus able to spend more time highlighting the appeal of restitution and dispelling misconceptions about the approach.

In the case of deterrence, it could be obtained by punishing innocents or through excessive punishments of the guilty. On the other hand, a deterrent approach could sanction responses that are too lenient. Deterrence might also be obtained by faking someone's punishment. In other cases it might not be possible to deter certain crimes or perhaps punishment of the much admired will inspire copycat crimes or other lawbreaking. Nevertheless, our intuitions are that punishment is still warranted even if there is no deterrent value in doing so. The debt/atonement approach captures our belief that the victimizer should compensate the victim and undergo a change of attitude – and often have this brought about by his own suffering. Such suffering may satisfy the victim as it teaches the criminal how the victim felt, symbolically defeating the criminal and thus vindicating the victim's worth.

The most likely problem for reform is that it will require excessive punishments. Imagine someone whose crimes are minor but due to a character flaw can't be easily reformed. Society shouldn't keep say a small-time thief in jail for decades because he is likely to shoplift again. The debt theory can make better sense of our intuitions here than reform. Reform entails atonement and restitution but the converse isn't the case. It is not that restitution and atonement take up where reform leaves off, as Garvey suggests.[8] Someone could be genuinely remorseful, penitent and willing to make restitution, nonetheless, he is so disposed to commit such crimes again. This may be because of weakness of the will or some other character defect or merely the ineffectiveness of prison as a setting for moral improvement. However, from the perspective of the debt/atonement theory, if the criminal has paid his debt and genuinely atoned, then he ought to be released. The debt/atonement theory demands remorse and restitution, not sainthood.

Retribution will also punish inappropriately. This is most obvious in the case of Morris-style retribution which aims to offset the illicit gains of those criminals who don't restrain themselves as law abiding citizens do.[9] But the lawful may have felt no compulsion to rape or murder and thus don't resent the liberties of such criminals. Or the difficulty some people have restraining themselves from one crime (tax fraud) as opposed to another (raping geriatrics) may not be correlated with the degree of harm of the respective crimes. The natural response is to defend a form of retribution where the greater the intended harm, the greater the deserved punishment. However, this account will still have a problem with punishing those who are contrite and forgiven by their victims. It intuitively seems that they ought to be punished less but the harm they caused or intended is as great. There are also some just and reasonable laws that are violated without wrongdoing on the part of the lawbreaker. The classic case is when a life is saved at the expense of someone else's property. Surely the lawbreaker doesn't *deserve* to suffer but is merely required to render restitution, any harm in doing so being foreseeable but unintended. There is also the concern that the retributivist concept of desert falsely assumes the criminal was free to do otherwise than he did. However the absence of such libertarian free will is not an obstacle to maintaining that those who intentionally harm others ought to atone and render restitution.

3.4   Failed attempts

A common complaint directed at restitution based accounts of punishment is that they can't account for our intuitions concerning penalizing failed criminal attempts.[10] Let me first remind readers that the theory advocated here is a debt *and* atonement approach so someone could initiate a wrongful attempt and warrant punishment, even if there is no harm that needs to be offset by restitution. The criminal still needs to atone and punishment could provide the place and time for atonement. Of course, society can't force someone to atone, for its components of remorse, apology and penance must be freely undertaken to be just that.[11] But society can, given the proper account of forfeiture of some rights, place the criminal in a setting that makes atonement more likely.

That said, I would still argue that there is harm in failed attempts. There is obviously a harm where an attempt leaves the target petrified, sleepless, and in therapy. But what about when the intended victim doesn't even know the failed attempt has transpired? Why punish such a criminal? The advocate of moral education will insist that the criminal needs to be reformed. The retributivist will stress that the criminal is evil for he intended harm and thus deserves punishment. The deterrence theorist has his own argument for punishing mere attempts, even though no one aims to fail, and that is because the knowledge that one won't be punished if one's attempt fails will likely increase criminal endeavours for it lowers their probable costs.[12]

David Boonin claims that a restitutionist can account for punishing failed attempts of which the intended target is ignorant on the grounds that such attempts raise the probability that he will be victimized.[13] One is harmed if put in an objectively more threatening situation, even if one is unaware of it. This may often be true but it isn't necessarily so, and we will want to punish in scenarios where it is not. It is even possible to imagine a case where the attempted crime not only fails to increase the probability of harm, but actually produces an *overall decrease* in its likelihood. This hypothetical would involve a known criminal under constant surveillance. Wherever he went, more law enforcement and associated public health and safety agents (paramedics, firemen and so on) would be found than otherwise. Thus if he attempts to commit a crime against you, he will fail because there are so many law enforcement agents blanketing the area. Even if it is illegitimate to claim the criminal's *inevitable* failure, nevertheless, we can still plausibly claim his attempt makes you safer overall although the risk of harm from him increases an infinitesimal amount. The reason you are better off overall is that a consequence of the presence of so many public safety agents protecting you from the known criminal is that they will then also render you safer from other sources of harm. For example, any other criminal in the vicinity who views you as an easy mark will have his chances of success dampened by the many agents already in the area protecting you from the attempt by the criminal under surveillance. Or if you were to be struck by a reckless driver, fall on a slippery sidewalk, or suffer a heart attack, you would receive quicker and better care than you would in the absence of the person who engaged in a failed criminal attempt. Thus your targeting in the failed attempt increases your overall safety. You are better off as a result of his intention to prey upon you. Yet intuitively, such an unsuccessful criminal still ought to be punished.

What those who deny that the restitutionist can handle attempts have in common is a failure to appreciate non-experiential harms. It may indeed be true that there aren't posthumous non-experiential harms but there had better be non-experiential harms for the existent. It is hard to make sense of harm if it is due only to its experiential impact. For instance, the reason that infidelity is upsetting is that it is bad to be so betrayed. The harm is there before the recognition of it. There would be nothing to be indignant about if there were not first a non-experiential harm.

The intended victim who is ignorant of his being criminally targeted has still been treated in an undignified manner. He was not thought to have sufficient value to make him immune to such an attempt. So there is an offence, an indignity that he suffers. When he finds out that he has been targeted he is justified in being outraged because the criminal's assumptions degraded him. He could rightly demand amends be made for the contempt expressed. He might not only want an apology but need proof of the victim's remorse, such as that given by a willingness to accept the hardship of punishment. And he might be vindictive as well, wishing to hurt the criminal whose contempt for him removed any obstacles to his being mistreated. So if there are non-experiential harms, then there can be a reason to demand punishment in the form of restitution for the failed attempt.

The debt/atonement account provides a better justification than its rivals of our practice of punishing failed attempts less severely than successes. The criminal whose attempt fails due only to luck needs to be reformed as much as the criminal who succeeds. If reform involves some hardship to sensitize the criminal, the same degree would be called for in punishing the perpetrator of the unsuccessful attempt as the successful crime. The retributivist is likely to claim that the person whose attempt failed is just as deserving of punishment as the successful criminal for they aimed at the same harm. And we have noted that even though no one attempts to fail in a criminal endeavour – rather everyone attempts to succeed – there is still a deterrence-based reason to punish attempts, for the criminal will be more likely to make an attempt if failure is not costly. There may even seem to be deterrent-based reasons to punish attempts more severely than successes to give the perpetrator an incentive not to try again. The second attempt would seem to require a punishment more severe even than that for a success which, obviously, failed to deter.

David Lewis claims that there isn't a need to punish second attempts more severely than successes, just second attempts more severely than first attempts. But his overall theory will actually justify punishing attempts more severely than any successes.[14] He describes a penal system that is a lottery in which the citizenry allow the chance-drawing of straws to determine which attempts are to be punished. Or if all criminal attempts are to be punished, which are to be punished more severely. He insists that given the equal chances, the lottery 'does, in some sense, punish all attempts alike, regardless of success'.[15] Lewis claims that our penal practices are justified if such a penal lottery would be. 'If not, not.'[16] The two systems are allegedly equivalent, for instead of drawing straws what our society actually does is allow the luck distinguishing successful from unsuccessful crimes to determine the distribution and severity of punishments. Real events thus stand in for drawing straws.

Lewis is wrong to assert that our system of punishment is justified only if such a lottery is. While our system of punishment is more or less acceptable, a lottery is not. Suppose the lottery worked by always punishing failed murder attempts more severely than successes, where instead of drawing the short straw for the shorter punishment, we used successful crimes as the stand in for short straws. Let us assume that in such a system there would be no loss in deterrence and that individuals who attempt crimes, successfully or not, are equally in need of reform or retribution since they are equally evil. Still, most people would be unsatisfied with this system since individuals who do much greater harm would be punished much less severely than those who bring about much less harm. It appears that we are willing to tolerate a lottery only if chance brings more misfortune, or at least as much, to individuals who have actually killed our loved ones than to individuals who try to kill them or others but fail. But if we are ready to accept a lottery, we have to be willing to allow luck to punish failures more than criminal successes. Accepting the legitimacy of such a lottery means accepting the legitimacy of all its possible outcomes.

While most theories of punishment suggest that attempts should not be punished less severely than successes, most people believe that punishments for successes should be greater than attempts.[17] If punishment is punitive restitution, as maintained by the debt/atonement theory, then it is possible that the public's intuitions can be justified as well as explained. The victim has suffered more harm if the crime succeeds, thus there needs to be more restitution. There was the disdain expressed by the attempt *and* the loss due to the success. To see that luck doesn't invalidate differences in restitution, consider two vandals who, by chance, do different amounts of damage. People generally don't find there to be anything intuitively wrong with making one vandal pay more compensation than the other because the artworks he deliberately disfigured turned out, unbeknownst to him, to be more valuable art than that destroyed by the other wrongdoer. So if punishment and restitution are not distinct, but the former involves the latter, then it is unsurprising that successes will be punished more severely than (failed) attempts. Thus it seems that the restitutionist can not only account for punishing attempts, but can do so in a way more in accordance with our intuitions and practices than rival theories.

3.5 Restitution and murder

At first glance, restitutionists have an obvious problem with murder. Public Reason will not permit a policy to be based upon theistic claims that the deceased still exist or the crime was an offence against God to whom the criminal must make amends. So working with only assumptions that the secular will find reasonable, it might seem difficult to imagine how the deceased can be compensated and restored to their pre-crime state of well-being. Since our intuitions and practices reflect a belief that murder is one of the worst crimes and deserving of punishment, restitution would seem to fail woefully here as a form of punishment or replacement for punishment. I think this line of thought, embraced by so many authors, is a bit hasty.[18] Moreover, even if it is correct, restitution is not the only response that will be in trouble because the victim no longer exists – retribution, deterrence and reform will likely fare no better.

It is commonly held that the deceased have interests that can be fulfilled or thwarted posthumously even if death brings about the nonexistence of the subjects of those interests. For example, it is thought that the deceased may have an interest in their property being distributed in a certain way, in their projects being fulfilled, their value acknowledged, their reputations vindicated, their achievements recognized, and the flourishing of their surviving relatives and so on. Now if this is true, it would seem the deceased can be compensated somewhat for their wrongful deaths. The crucial point is that it is difficult to claim that death harms the deceased by frustrating their interests without also claiming that the deceased have interests that can be satisfied to their benefit which could amount to restitution. Of course, the deceased can't be restored to the level of *experiential* well-being they possessed when alive since they can't be restored to life, but they may still have interests that can be promoted if not fulfilled. Some of these interests could be satisfied in a manner that could be described as restitution. The deceased may have an interest in their murderer suffering even if they can't savour the experience, or in their murderer compensating their surviving relatives, or furthering some project of theirs through financial contributions or labour. The victim may even have a posthumous interest in their murderer being brought to recognize their worth, to express that and demonstrate remorse. So unless there is a compelling argument that restitution requires the recipient to experience the compensation, restitution is compatible with punishing murder.

If it is instead maintained that benefits to the deceased is a category mistake for being benefited involves states and only existing subjects can be in beneficial states, then the same reasoning would entail that the deceased couldn't be in harmful or deprived states. That is, their being dead couldn't be a harm to them. If that is so, then it is not just restitutionists offering their alternative to the existing system of punishment that will find themselves in philosophical hot water when dealing with murder. The leading theory of punishment, retribution, and the runners up in popularity, reform and deterrence, will all share in any embarrassment that restitution suffers.

The retributivist punishes because the criminal *deserves* punishment. Punishment is deserved because the criminal wrongfully and intentionally caused or attempted to cause harm. But if the murderer didn't cause the murdered any harm, then why does he deserve punishment? Surely, a satisfactory answer is not going to be that he caused the survivors grief or made his fellow citizens anxious. The restitutionist could easily make a parallel move and claim that the restitution be directed to these people instead. It won't work to say the criminal deserves punishment because he had evil intentions even if he didn't do any harm. It is hard to flesh out what could be evil about an intention that if successfully carried out is not harmful. Or at least, it isn't easy to see why the immorality of intending what is wrongly thought to be a harm deserves a great harm in response. And if it is merely the intention or the morally flawed character behind the attempt that warrants punishment, then the typical difference in severity of punishment between successful murder and attempted murder will not be justified.

If death is not a harm to the dead, the remaining rationale for deterrence is likely to be to prevent certain unwelcome feelings in those still alive. But the feelings of some survivors will be unreasonable if based upon beliefs that the dead are harmed or that the living will be harmed by their own deaths. And their *reasonable* lament for losing their cherished companions will still fail to provide a rationale for punishing those who kill people (hermits, loners, orphans and so on) who will not be missed.

Advocates of reform believe that the criminal should be punished in order to improve his character. But if the murderer didn't harm the deceased, then it isn't clear what is wrong with his character. Well, it might be thought that his character is flawed because he *attempted* to harm the deceased, he was just oblivious of the Epicurean-style argument that death can't be a harm. But then it seems that reform of character isn't really called for, just some additional knowledge. It is probably true that those willing to murder are also willing to do many other bad things like inflict pain. But that correlation is only contingent and seems to be committing society to reforming people for what they *might* have done rather than did do. Moreover, if that is all that reform can offer to justify punishing murderers, then it seems a slim advantage over the restitution advocated by the debt/atonement account.

So it appears that the problem of restitution for the murdered has parallel manifestations plaguing retribution, deterrence and reform. As a result, there is no relative advantage gained by restitutionists' main rivals, and thus restitution can't be undermined if its competitors are in the same leaky boat.

3.6   Restitution and revenge

It is frequently declared that the victim has a debt to society.[19] Retributivists rarely do justice to such talks which seems more at home in the restitutionist framework. However, a problem for the debt/atonement approach is that it often seems that the criminal is too poor, uneducated and unskilled to make restitution. But restitution fails less often, and to a lesser degree, than might be expected despite the impoverishment and lack of restitution-making skills typical of many criminals. This is, in part, because restitution can involve vindictive satisfaction as a debt payment. Victims can 'get even' with the person whose denial of their value made the initial transgression possible. They can receive psychic compensation when the criminal realizes his punishment is undertaken for their sake and at their urging. The victim may be pleased that the suffering criminal is made to feel bad, forced by such suffering to acknowledge the significance of the victim's pain and anger, as well as the esteem in which he is held by the supportive society that carries out the punishment for him. So it isn't just that the criminal's well-being will be lowered, but the victim's well-being is raised in response as the tables are turned on his tormentor.

It is important to distinguish revenge for the sake of restitution from sheer sadistic revenge where the goal is not getting *even*, nor accompanied by a recognition that the criminal should be restored to society as a citizen with equal rights and duties after having paid his debt.[20] Furthermore, where there is a punitive role for revenge, the suffering it can endorse is restricted by norms determined by both the degree of the initial harm and deontological constraints that protect the criminal's dignity.

The taking of revenge can even satisfy the criminal that is contrite. If a criminal feels guilty, he might be angry at himself for what he did, just as the victim and the rest of the society will be angry at him.[21] Such a criminal may want to make himself suffer. The penance gives expression to this self-directed anger. The contrite criminal might be especially willing to suffer if doing so makes his victim feel better. He may want his victim to get his vindictive fill. The macho version of this attitude is displayed by the cowboy in the Hollywood Western when he allows a party he wronged to punch him in return. There is something egalitarian and restorative about taking and accepting such revenge.

Philip Montague and Dennis Klimchuk claim that the vindictive account of restitution isn't applicable to murder for the victim, even assuming his possession of posthumous interests, is not alive to *relish* the suffering of the criminal.[22] Vindictiveness seems to involve enjoying the misery of one's victimizer. However, I harbour some doubts that *enjoying* revenge is essential to it. Consider first what seems to be a case of the living taking revenge. A person sets a trap to retaliate for some earlier wound. Even if he is later unaware that the trap has been sprung and his enemy injured, it seems correct to describe him as having taken revenge. It may be that a sufficient condition for vindictiveness is that the person desires those who wronged him to suffer for he believes their doing so will improve his own well-being. If well-being can be enhanced by interest satisfaction, then provided there are posthumous interests, there can be a posthumous increase in well-being and hence posthumous revenge. It doesn't strike my ears as wrong to hear that the dead can take revenge from beyond the grave. For example, if we change the previous case slightly to where a person makes use of a device triggered by his death that painfully injures or kills his murderer, it again seems appropriate to speak of his taking revenge.[23] So it might not be incorrect to speak of the dead receiving vindictive satisfaction even if they can't experience it.

However, no restitution, vindictive or otherwise, may be required if the criminal is contrite and the victim(s) forgiving. Even in the case of murder, one can imagine a slow death that allows, however unlikely, the victim and criminal to reconcile. Someone may maintain the forgiving victim is 'a deep problem' for the debt/atonement theory.[24] I don't find it an embarrassment for the approach that punishment may sometimes not be needed. The ideal served by the debt/atonement account is restoration and reconciliation and this can be met, on rare occasions, without punishment.

It is worth keeping in mind, especially in the vast majority of egregious crimes, that there are usually indirect victims in the greater community, the large numbers of which make it less likely that they will all be forgiving. That will ensure few quick releases of the criminal and the resulting loss of deterrence power – the avoidance of the latter being a welcome but unintended side effect. Members of the direct victim's community may also be victimized by being made to feel less safe, burdened with the costs of the criminal justice system, or insulted through the criminal's disregard of the victim's value, a value that they too possess in virtue of sharing properties with the victim. Although the latter is most evident in how hate crimes offend others in the group of the victim, a similar vicarious offense can occur when it is just someone's dignity or humanity that is ignored in crimes that don't involve targeting members of historically maltreated groups. Therefore, a forgiving or deceased victim need not mean that the criminal goes free. The vindictive feelings of the larger, indirectly victimized community will see to it that he suffers. Moreover, the compensation to the larger society need not take the form of vindictive satisfaction, it could just involve the peace of mind gained by knowing that a predator is forced to keep his distance, or an increase in public safety financed by payments extracted from the criminal.

A related misconception is to think that a forgiving victim automatically means less punishment. The victimizer need not always compensate each victim separately, the total compensation increasing with the number of victims. The same punishment or debt can simultaneously benefit the criminal's direct and indirect victims. So even if the direct victim is without vindictive feelings, the large number of indirect victims may mean the same amount of suffering as a debt payment as would be the case if the direct victim sought revenge. The harm inflicted upon the criminal need not rise or fall depending upon the number of unforgiving victims. Since the same burden inflicted upon the criminal can do 'double duty', compensating different people, there'll be many cases where even the direct victim's forgiveness won't mean any less punishment.[25]

The idea of legitimizing vindictive feelings will be anathema to many. Revenge will be seen as pointless, or even disruptive to the practice of reform, retribution and deterrence. Perhaps the distinction which I have made between sadistic vindictiveness on the one hand, and egalitarian and judicial vindictiveness on the other, will make it somewhat easier to accept. The place allotted for revenge allows the satisfaction given to a victim from the suffering of the criminal to be considered a debt payment. Such a non-financial payment will likely be needed when the victimizer is either very poor or very rich; otherwise their contempt for their victims would have little impact on their own well-being, one being unable to make financial restitution, the other unfazed by it.

The role I envision for revenge may also seem more palatable when compared to that played by the desire to make the criminal suffer in the retributivist scheme. My contention is that if it is not objectionable, or not very problematic in the retributivist framework, then there is even less reason to find it so in the restitutionist account. The retributivist *believes* the criminal ought to suffer and so *desires* that he suffer. This is not a thirst for revenge since the retributivist need not delight in the prospect of the victim suffering, even though he desires it, nor aim to have his well-being increased by the decrease in the criminal's. It would be a mistake to conflate retribution and revenge, even though the vindictive will *very* often disguise their real motivation with apparently high-minded calls for retributive justice. The paradigm case of non-vindictive retribution would be when parents regretfully turn in their own law-breaking son to the police so that justice can be done. The parents take no delight in their grown child's suffering, but nevertheless, recognize that he deserves to suffer. Their wishing they didn't have to bring their own son to justice does not mean they lack a conditional desire that he suffer. The vindictive on the other hand, not only desire someone to suffer, but relish the prospect, believing their well-being will be raised as a consequence of the other's misery.

Since retributivists and vindictive restitutionists both desire others to suffer, the former have little grounds for criticizing the latter. In fact, the desire for the criminal's suffering seems pointless in the retributivist framework and thus more suspect. Retributivists desire suffering but not so it betters the criminal or satisfies his victim. As Bradley says in his endorsement of retributive suffering: 'The destruction of the wrong, whatever be the consequence, and even if there is not consequence at all, is still a good in itself.'[26] The vindictive restitutionist claims the suffering can play a restorative role for the victim, increasing his well-being and enabling him to later reconcile with his victim after the debt is paid. Moreover, such suffering can even assuage the guilt of the victimizer who is angry with himself, who wants to compensate his victim, and whose acceptance of his debt and penance proves his worthiness to be returned to society. So the restitutionist bestows upon the criminal's suffering a purpose that the retributivist does not, one that benefits the victim, and ideally the criminal.

The effects of vindictive restitution support my claim that restitution should replace retribution as the model for punishment. However, Klimchuk makes the interesting claim that restitution, vindictive or not, cannot replace retribution for it presupposes its notions of desert and proportionality.[27] He argues that restitution will need to be guided by retributivist norms to be appropriate. The fear is that restitution-governed punishment could be inappropriately lenient in the absence of vindictiveness or excessive where such feelings are intense and unabated. One can indeed imagine victims who are not satisfied with virtually any amount of suffering others have undergone. We can also imagine hypersensitive people for whom what would be a minor slight to others is devastating to them and thus the required payment for full restoration would be immense. But none of this follows from the principles of the debt/atonement approach. The law frequently works with norms of what a reasonable person should do and feel. For example, the neurotically hypersensitive plaintiff won't be entitled to receive more in a defamation case. Likewise, the sadistic or the hypersensitive won't be entitled to more restitution, whether in the form of their victim's suffering or otherwise. The guiding norm for the debt/atonement approach is what it would take to restore the reasonable person who was so wronged. So it is a mistake to claim that the debt/atonement theory lacks the resources to 'measure objectively' loss and compensation.[28] The theory is not committed to the wrongdoer's punishment being determined by the victim's assessment of misconduct. Restitution need not reflect the vices or character flaws of the victims. So no wild variations need to be tolerated, and no appeal made to a *deserved* punishment other than in the nonretributive sense of what level of compensation the victim deserves in order to be restored.

This is true even in the case in which the victim's forgiveness is corrupt. Forgiveness is not genuine when the victim just wants to forget the crime or has such low self-esteem that she thinks there was little wrong done to her. It is not, as Klimchuk believes, that retributivist norms must be appealed to in order to reject any early release of the criminal or to make sense of our outrage at the lack of punishment. The problem is really that there hasn't been any restitution and reconciliation. The criminal has not atoned and the victim has not been compensated and had her worth recognized. Of course, society can't force the victim to recognize her value or desire compensation; however, it can refuse to facilitate her degradation. Thus it can reject the release of the unrepentant criminal whose contempt for the victim is unabated. The victim is thus (perhaps unwillingly) provided with the compensation of being protected from such a predator and her well-being somewhat restored. Her well-being has an objective component. This phenomenon is illustrated by the case of domestic violence in which the repeatedly abused refuses to press charges or do much to protect her dignity. If the abuser is released, he is likely to prey again upon his victim or someone else who shares her attributes, the value of which he disregarded earlier. It may be paternalistic, but she is made objectively better off by his prolonged incarceration. And keep in mind it is the shared attributes that make the offended members of the larger community indirect victims of the earlier crime. So they are unlikely to forgive prematurely.

3.7 Restitution without punishment

David Boonin ends his recent book on the problem of punishment by arguing for replacing punishment with restitution.[29] Following Barnett, he calls this 'pure restitution' in order to distinguish it from an account like mine that considers restitution to be punishment. Boonin argues that since all theories of punishment advocate intentionally harming the criminal, none of them can be justified. He believes that people have rights, such as to their property, and so a right that their wealth be restored if illicitly taken. But Boonin insists that no one has a right that bad people suffer.[30] He claims that restitution is only for what one was *rightfully* entitled. The satisfaction of vindictive feelings is not something a crime victim has a legitimate claim to even if the criminal caused such feelings to arise.

To argue that Boonin is wrong about harm would involve mostly restating the claims that I have made above and adding a little about forfeiture of rights. So I would rather end the paper arguing that even if intending to harm criminals can't be justified, punishment has to be excused for society can't do without it. And if the debt/atonement theory is superior to rival accounts of punishment, then it is the system that should be tolerated even if it can't be justified.

Boonin is aware that many readers will claim that society can't function without punishment. He writes: 'Punishment, on this understanding, is necessary, either as a condition for the existence of a social order at all or as a condition for the kind of social order that makes possible just relationships among its members.'[31] So Boonin considers the possibility that even if punishment cannot be justified, it might have to be excused out of 'an appeal to necessity'. His response is that this won't be the case for pure restitution can ensure a just social order. Pure restitution can involve far more than garnished wages and seized assets. It can include even incarceration, monitoring devices, house arrest, restraining orders, compulsory counselling and preventive detentions. These are not punishments when undertaken without the intention of harming the criminal, instead implemented for the purpose of providing restitution to his victims. Boonin is well aware that criminals will suffer harm in a system of pure restitution, but argues that this is morally acceptable for the harms are merely foreseen rather than intended.

However, I very much doubt the mandated fines, preventive detentions, restraining orders and the like can work without the threat of intentional harm and so harm-induced restitution will be as morally suspect as imposing punitive harm. If a person has been placed under a restraining order, house arrest or compelled to work off a debt incurred, the threat of harm will be needed to make him fulfill his obligations. If not facing the subsequent harm of incarceration, he will be likely to ignore his bill and violate his travel restrictions. And to ensure that the criminal works in prison to pay off his debts, he will have to be threatened with the harm of solitary confinement or the loss of some other prison 'privileges'. Moreover, the criminal will likely repeatedly try to flee any holding centre if not for the threat of harm that keeps him there. It is not just guards armed with tasers, nightsticks, guns and trained to apply painful pressure by hand, but the electric fence, barbed wire and snarling dogs that represent an intention to harm the criminal, to inflict pain in order to prevent flight. A society without some of these measures is likely not to be a minimally safe and just one. Thus it seems that the pure restitution approach will fail to meet the necessity condition.

Boonin can't maintain of the above harms that they are unintended side effects rather than deliberately imposed. To borrow Anscombe's phrase, that would amount to *double talk about double effect*. To claim that barbed wire or solitary confinement is not intended to harm the criminal but merely to induce payment of restitution is like claiming in the famous case imagined by Philippa Foot that intentionally blowing up the fat man stuck in the cave's exit doesn't involve the intention to kill him.[32] If one knows that death consists of the loss of a certain bodily integration and that the explosive device will rip a person apart, then intending the latter when one knows that it necessitates the former, is also intending the former. The metaphysical impossibility of intending one without the other is not relevantly different from the impossibility of claiming to intentionally order a glass of water but not a glass of H_2O when one knows they are necessarily the same. Likewise, the connection between barbed wire, solitary confinement and pain is too tight (probably lawful necessity), and too well known, for it to be claimed that such measures are not intended to harm, merely intended to bring about restitution.

Nor will it help Boonin to appeal to the counterfactual that if officials could obtain the restitution without the threat of harm, they would, while the advocates of punishment don't want a substitute for inflicting harm upon the criminal. This is like saying someone who killed his victim for money didn't do so intentionally for if he could have obtained the money without killing, then he would have. The harm is still intended despite the wish that a harmless alternative was available.

So the only difference between the harm that law enforcement will provide in order for Boonin-style restitution to occur and the harm in my debt/atonement account is that in the former it is intended as a means to subsequently obtaining restitution, while in the latter it is intended to be a part of the restitution. Therefore we see that Boonin's restitutionist scheme will require intentional harm and he thus joins the punitive restitutionist in the same boat which is taking on water.[33] But those who view the debt payment as a punishment will see the water pouring in not as harmful leakage but as a requirement to cool the engines to ensure the proper operation of the ship of state.

Notes

1. Restitution can occur without atonement but it can also be a component of atonement.
2. I have argued this previously, see David B. Hershenov (1999), 'Restitution and Revenge', *Journal of Philosophy*, 79–94, and (2000) 'Punishing Failed Attempts Less Severely than Successes', *Journal of Value Inquiry*, 34, 479–89.
3. S. Garvey (1998–9), 'Punishment as Atonement', *UCLA Law Review*, 46, 1801–58.
4. For an account that punishment necessarily involves intended harm, see D. Boonin (2008), *The Problem of Punishment* (New York: Cambridge University Press) 12–21.
5. 'The should have been' is added, for perhaps the victim suffered misfortune or mistreatment prior to the crime and so it would be inappropriate to merely restore him to his pre-crime status.
6. More needs to be said to provide a full justification of punishment. For instance, why are certain wrongs punished and not others? How do we make sense of wrongdoers forfeiting rights? Why does the state have a monopoly on punishment? But answers to these questions will not be distinctive to the debt/atonement approach and need not concern us here.
7. Boonin 236–7.
8. Garvey 1849.
9. H. Morris (1968), 'Persons and Punishments', *The Monist*, 24, 477–501. For a more extended critique see Hershenov (1999), 82–3 and Boonin 119–14.
10. R. Dagger (1999), 'Restitution: Pure or Punitive', *Criminal Justice Ethics*, 10:2, 33–4. F. Miller (1978), 'Restitution and Punishment: A Reply to Barnett', *Ethics*, 88:4, 359 and D. Klimchuk (2001), 'Retribution, Restitution and Revenge', *Law and Philosophy*, 20, 92.
11. See Garvey for an illuminating account of secular punitive atonement involving remorse, apology and penance.
12. Hershenov (2000), 81–2.
13. Boonin 251–3.
14. D. Lewis (1989), 'The Punishment that Leaves Something to Chance', *Philosophy and Public Affairs*, 18:1, 58.
15. Lewis 58.
16. Lewis 62.
17. P. Robinson and J. Darley (1995), *Justice, Liability and Blame: Community Views and the Criminal Law*, 206.

18. Klimchuk 96–8. P. Montague (2002), 'Recent Approaches to Justifying Punishment', *Philosophia*, 5. Even Boonin claims that the 'murdered cannot be even partially restored to well being', 240. But he argues that their debt can be transferred, though it apparently does them no good.
19. Hershenov (1999) 80–1.
20. Hershenov (1999) 90.
21. Garvey provides an intriguing discussion of the guilty identifying with their victim, being angry at themselves, and consequently willing to suffer a penance (1999) 1823.
22. Montague 5; Klimchuk 97.
23. It may also be that prior to their death they relished the knowledge that the person who harmed them would suffer. So the intention to harm someone might have provided some vindictive pleasure ante-mortem even though the harm would occur posthumously.
24. Klimchuk 97–8.
25. Of course, there will be scenarios where this is not the case, for the indirect victims are few or the harms they incur are insubstantial.
26. H. M. Bradley (1935), *Ethical Studies* (New York: Oxford University Press) 27–8.
27. Klimchuk 98–101.
28. Klimchuk 99.
29. Boonin 213–75.
30. Boonin 271–3
31. Boonin 2.
32. P. Foot (1978), *Virtues and Vices and Other Essays in Moral Philosophy* (Los Angeles: University of California Press), 21–2.
33. Boonin could claim a system of intentional harm for the sake of restitution is preferable to intentional harm for the sake of punishment. But given that suffering in the form of punishment can enhance restitution and facilitate atonement, it would seem preferable to excuse punishment.

4
Punishment and Rehabilitation

Christopher Bennett

The dominant view in the academic literature on punishment over the last thirty years has been that penal rehabilitation has had its day.[1] Rehabilitation, the reader would gather, is over, and in its wake 'just deserts' theory vies with a new utilitarianism based on risk-management technology to take its place as the dominant penal philosophy of modern societies. Yet despite its much-heralded death, there is clearly a good deal of rehabilitative work going on in the criminal justice systems of modern Western states.[2] Furthermore, there has been increasing interest in the case for the abolition of punishment, and some of the alternatives to punishment being canvassed have a strongly rehabilitative element.[3] For this reason, now seems a good time to attempt an assessment of the moral value of penal rehabilitation. We will be asking about the proper role of rehabilitation in the criminal justice system, and looking at the extent to which it deserves to be resuscitated. In particular, we will be concerned with a moral critique of rehabilitation: namely, that rehabilitation is incompatible with a proper respect for the moral agency of offenders. Our key question will be: is rehabilitation a welcome antidote to the condemnation or control offered by the other main penal philosophies; or should it be rejected as a condescending and disempowering approach to offenders?

4.1 Setting up the debate

Rehabilitation aims to change the offender for the better. It sees criminal activity as symptomatic of a problem with the offender, and seeks to resolve that problem. Hence there are reasons to favour penal rehabilitation when one looks at the offender from a purely humanitarian perspective (that is, when one is concerned solely with the welfare of the individual offender); and rehabilitation can also have a place – for instance, for medium-risk offenders – if one takes up a utilitarian view (aiming to promote the general welfare of some population by reducing the risks posed by dangerous offenders). However, there has also been principled opposition to rehabilitation. The strand of opposition that I am interested in here does not simply reject rehabilitation on the grounds that doing the offender good is incompatible with giving the offender the punishment he deserves. On that sort of view, rehabilitating the offender would prevent us, say, from doing justice to the claims of the victims. Rather the view in which I am interested has focused on the idea that rehabilitation is incompatible with some important ethical ideals associated with the rights or moral status of offenders themselves. The claim is that seeing the offender as the proper object of rehabilitation is intolerably *condescending*. Rehabilitating the offender would violate the moral claims of the offender to be treated as an equal, as a moral agent in his or her own right. Thus the debate that I am interested in is over the question whether the respect we owe to the offender as 'one of us' rules out rehabilitation.

We can illustrate the debate by considering the following quote from a UK government White Paper from 1990:

> [M]uch crime is committed on impulse, given the opportunity presented by an open window or unlocked door, and it is committed by offenders who live from moment to moment; their crimes are as impulsive as the rest of their feckless, sad, or pathetic lives. It is unrealistic to construct sentencing arrangements on the assumption that most offenders will weigh up the possibilities in advance and base their conduct on rational calculation.[4]

In its original context, this passage is arguing about the likely ineffectiveness of deterrent punishments on the conduct of offenders whose lives are not subject to much rational calculation. However, the view of offenders that it expresses leads naturally to a conclusion favourable to penal rehabilitation – at any rate, as opposed to retribution or condemnation. For retribution and condemnation focus on the thought that what happened was the agent's *fault*; that he was in *control* of what he was doing; that he didn't have to act that way; and thus that he has brought ignominy *on himself* by what he did. By contrast, the point of view quoted above stresses how difficult it is for offenders to behave lawfully, given their 'moment to moment' existence. On this view, criminal activity is seen as an, if not inevitable, at any rate unsurprising, result of the chaotic lives of offenders. Most offenders, it suggests, are not the kind of people who exercise much control over their lives. Of course, it can be true in some minimal sense that criminal acts are the agent's own fault: offenders act intentionally, and with the relevant degree of knowledge. But meeting these conditions is compatible with a high level of personal disorganization and incapacity for any significant degree of rational deliberation, planning or control. Offenders might be quite capable of acting deliberately – but at the same time be altogether incapable of taking up a broader perspective on their impulsive course of action. Given what we know about typical criminal lifestyles, this view suggests, we cannot fairly or appropriately hold such offenders responsible and punish them for what they do.

When we take everything into account, this approach suggests, offenders deserve pity rather than condemnation. However, while there is something admirably sympathetic in this perspective – after all, it focuses on the conditions that make it more difficult for some citizens rather than others to obey the law – it is not difficult to detect a hint of superiority in the tone taken in this passage. There is no concern here to see offenders as equals. In the use of the epithets 'feckless', 'sad' and 'pathetic', the writer makes it clear how he evaluates the lack of such capacities for planning and control. The passage adopts the perspective (and makes the reader complicit in this perspective) that 'we' know what we are doing, and 'they' cannot be expected to; therefore (we can conclude) 'we' have no alternative but to find ways to manage 'them'. The writer has an unspoken assurance in his possession of the capabilities that he is denying to the offenders with whom he is dealing. And it is not too great a leap to see in this passage the assumption that the writer is part of an elite which has the right to govern these unruly masses.

The opposition to rehabilitation in which I am interested emerges in reaction to this perceived condescension. This opposition claims that such pity as is expressed here shades into contempt – and that it is a contemptuous view of offenders that is being expressed when one suggests that we should 'make allowances' for offenders and that we 'cannot expect more of them'. Pity and contempt are clearly related. After all, one expression of contempt is to call someone 'pitiful'. While pity, compassion or fellow-feeling (in German, *mitleiden*: 'suffering with') are important virtues in many circumstances, the counter-argument to rehabilitation claims that pity goes too far if it leads us not to hold the offender responsible. On this view, there is something valuable about treating someone as a responsible agent: one thereby grants the agent a certain kind of dignity or respect. When one withholds such respect one insults the agent. Thus, while he acknowledges the temptation to exempt some offenders from retribution, Michael Moore argues that we should examine our reluctance to blame carefully to see whether contempt for the offender is not at its root.

> It is elitist and condescending towards others not to grant them the same responsibility and desert you grant to yourself … To refuse to grant him the same responsibility and desert as you would grant yourself is thus an instance of what Sartre called bad faith, the treating of a free, subjective will as an object [...]. It is a refusal to admit that the rest of humanity shares with us that which makes us most distinctively human, our capacity to will and reason – and thus to be and do evil. Far from evincing fellow feeling and the allowing of others to participate in our moral life, it excludes them as less than persons.[5]

This passage asks us to look at the way we view ourselves, and compare that with the way we think about offenders. Do we not assume that we have control and authorship over our own actions? Is this assumption not indeed a necessary condition of acting? If we refuse to view offenders as being in control of their actions in the way we view ourselves, are we not treating them as mere objects who cannot really act and choose for themselves? Of course, it is true that human beings act in circumstances not of their own making. No one chooses the situations to which they will have to respond. But when we come to act, do we not take it for granted that it is fundamentally *up to us* how to respond to the situations we face? When we make a decision, it seems to us that we have the options before us, and these options present themselves as open to us and awaiting our decision. In confronting such situations we assume that we have the power to think about our options from various perspectives and come to a conclusion about what we should do. We assume that we have a reasonable amount of self-control and that (largely) we act on our better judgement. If we take these things for granted in our own case, but are tempted to treat offenders as mere creatures of impulse, aren't we treating offenders as less than ourselves? Indeed aren't we denying them the basic possession of moral agency? Isn't our apparent fellow-feeling a mask that hides a failure to take the offender seriously as one who is essentially like us?

We now have the battlelines drawn between the two sides of the debate. On the one hand, we have rehabilitation motivated by an attempt to understand the offender's situation sympathetically, and take into account the difficulties that might stand in the way of lawful behaviour.

This 'sympathetic' approach involves playing down the importance of individual culpability, and looking through the offender to the conditions in which he acts. However, as suggested by the passage from the White Paper, it might seem that what makes this 'looking through' possible is a view of the offender as 'pathetic' and in some way insignificant. Does that involve a failure of due respect to the offender? If the offender realized that this was how he was being treated, would he be comforted by the fact that someone was viewing his plight sympathetically? Or would he be insulted at not being taken seriously as an agent who decides his own fate?

4.2   Rehabilitation, responsibility and respect for persons

Let us begin by elaborating the moral attack on rehabilitation. One central claim that opponents of rehabilitation sometimes make is that to treat someone with rehabilitation is to treat their behaviour as the result of a 'condition' to be cured rather than something for which they are responsible; and that this is to treat them as an object rather than a subject, as part of the natural world rather than as a free agent.[6] The crux of the case against rehabilitation is that this way of dealing with a person leaves out of consideration much of what we take to be valuable about being a person, and therefore constitutes a severely impoverished and even insulting way of relating to her. We have a deeply rooted intuition that human beings are more than parts of the natural world: they can control and direct their actions in line with their understanding rather than simply watching them unfold as natural processes. Furthermore, this sense that we are capable of rising above 'mere nature' is one of the sources of the intuition that humanity has a special dignity or status. It is the fact that we have 'minds of our own', our ability to control and direct our lives, that marks us out and makes us valuable. If this is the view that we take then it is clear that a rehabilitative approach that denies that we can be the authors of our own actions will be taken as a denial of what is really of value in human existence. Human action, on this view, cannot be seen simply as a symptom of an underlying condition that calls for a cure: it must rather be seen as a product of the free decision of an agent who freely authors her own life.

However, one way of responding to this critique of rehabilitation is to accuse it of *hubris* about the human condition. The central intuition underpinning the critique is a Kantian view that many have found ultimately implausible. It sees humanity as distinct from the natural world in having a freedom to transcend the limitations of preceding causal influence. What makes humanity special, on this Kantian view, is that no matter what our past we are capable of deciding freely on the matter at hand. However, this view is notoriously difficult to understand, let alone defend. Human actions, whatever else they are, are events in the natural order. This suggests that they must be subject to whatever laws determine all the other events that occur in the natural order. We cannot escape the natural order unless somehow we can suspend the laws of nature each time we act. Theorists of a broadly naturalistic frame of mind have therefore been sceptical about whether we could have such an ability – and hence whether it could really give us much in the way of dignity.

However, there is a more promising understanding of the Kantian intuition. This is to adopt something more like the Kantianism of P. F. Strawson.[7] Strawson does not take the heroic line of denying that human behaviour can be understood in terms of antecedent causal influence. Rather he claims a) that explanations in terms of antecedent causes do not exhaust our interest in human behaviour and b) that such explanations are not always the appropriate ones to guide our interactions with people. On Strawson's view, human behaviour is capable of being understood in terms of an 'involved' as well as an 'objective' attitude. The involved attitude is the one we take when we see human beings as potential participants in a range of characteristic human relationships and hence as being the subjects of certain demands or normative expectations.[8] As Christine Korsgaard has elaborated:

> To hold someone responsible is to regard her as a person – that is to say, as a free and equal person, capable of acting both rationally and morally. It is therefore to regard her as someone with whom you can enter the kind of relation that is possible only among free and equal rational people: a relation of reciprocity. When you hold someone responsible you are prepared to exchange lawless activity for reciprocity in some or all of its forms. You are prepared to accept promises, offer confidences, exchange vows, cooperate on a project, enter a social contract, have a conversation, make love, be friends, or get married. You are willing to deal with her on the basis of the expectation that each of you will act from a certain view of the other: that you each have your responses which are to be respected, and your ends which are to be valued. Abandoning the state of nature and so relinquishing force and guile, you are ready to share, to trust, and generally speaking to risk your happiness or success on the hope that she will turn out to be human.[9]

To adopt the involved attitude is to see someone as subject to meaningful *demands* that they are capable of appreciating and meeting. The objective attitude, on the other hand, is the one we adopt when we see human behaviour as the deterministic result of an (exceedingly complex) system of outputs. When we let our interaction with a person be guided by the involved attitude, we engage in certain forms of behaviour – from the expression of reactive attitudes to reasoning together – that require us to see the person as sensitive to the normative demands of a situation. Seeing a person as at least potentially sensitive to normative demands seems, at least on the face of it, incompatible with seeing their responses as determined by antecedent causal factors Yet while the engaged and the objective attitudes are in some ways incompatible, Strawson's claim is that they are both valid perspectives. The truth of either perspective does not rule out the truth of the other. The fact of our successful engagement in interpersonal relationships does not show the objective attitude to be false: at best it shows it to be incomplete when taken on its own. On Strawson's view there is more that can truly be said about human behaviour than is captured by the objective perspective: to restrict oneself to the objective attitude would be to neglect various important and salient aspects of human behaviour.

On this alternative reading of the Kantian claim, the thought is that, since involvement in human relationships inevitably involves being subject to the moral demands constitutive of such relationships,[10] being condemned or criticized when one fails to live up to those demands is an essential part of being treated as a potential participant in a range of valuable human relationships. Being a potential participant in a range of valuable human relationships is a valuable type of status that ought, at least *prima facie*, to be respected. Although the details will vary with particular circumstances, the minimum implied by this *prima facie* duty to respect a person as a potential participant in a set of valuable human relationships is that it is at least sometimes inappropriate to adopt the objective attitude and to allow our interaction with a person to be guided by a view of them 'as an object to be managed or treated or cured': it is inappropriate when this involves treatment that conflicts with whatever, substantively, is involved in 'proper respect' for our status as potential participants. Thus we can understand the claim that to treat someone simply as an object to be re-programmed or cured would be to violate their status. It would be inappropriately to adopt the objective attitude in such a way that it excludes or violates the view of them as someone with whom we could have this valuable set of relationships. What is wrong with this is what is wrong with any violation of a person's status: it involves treating them as less than they are. It is condescending, insulting, incompatible with the offender's dignity. This suggests a more social, less metaphysical understanding of the value of being a responsible agent.

These considerations illustrate Moore's claim that when one is not held responsible one is treated as a mere object. One is treated as a mere object in the sense that one is viewed as a system of inputs and outputs to be managed and controlled rather than a someone who is 'one of us', a participant responding intelligently to the demands of the moral life. If there is something problematic in treating a person as an object, Moore claims, the corollary is that there is something positive about being held responsible, and hence something positive about retributive responses. This 'involved' perspective of which the practice of responsibility is part is a necessary condition of the existence of such interpersonal relationships, and such relationships are an important part of what is valuable in human life. Holding someone responsible is in an important way to *include* them in the moral life we share with others, whereas adopting the objective attitude involves *excluding* them from it by seeing them in a way that denies that they are really moral actors at all.

4.3   What is penal rehabilitation?

In the previous section we made some headway in understanding why someone might claim that being treated as a person involves being held responsible, and that not being held responsible involves being treated as an object. In order to assess the implications of this critique for our overall view of the role of penal rehabilitation in criminal justice, we need to know in more detail what penal rehabilitation involves. Rehabilitation can be understood to involve a wide variety of interventions. A range of examples might include the following:

a) Attempts to change the offender's attitudes or personality by deep intervention: for instance, by electric shock therapy or partial lobotomization.
b) Moral (re-)education that gets the offender to reflect on the human consequences of his actions.
c) Attempts to make the offender remorseful for the crime, perhaps through a meeting with its victim.
d) Required programmes of, for example, drug rehabilitation, anger management or Cognitive Behavioural Therapy (CBT).

e) Optional programmes of, for example, drug rehabilitation, anger management or CBT (for example, while the offender is 'doing time').
f) Literacy or work education aimed at increasing the offender's chances of getting a job on returning to normal life after imprisonment and/or punishment. Participating in such educative activities can be made required or optional. Other support with re-settlement or re-integration can involve encouragement to keep up family ties while in prison, and so on.

These interventions differ drastically in their ambition and intrusiveness, and in the methods they use to effect behavioural change. Furthermore, some are conceived as *offers* of support to offenders while others are coercively imposed. And these differences will clearly change our moral assessment of them. Some of the 'therapies' on this list involve the kind of treatment seen in films like *A Clockwork Orange* and *One Flew Over the Cuckoo's Nest.* They involve wholesale attempts to re-cast the offender's personality by medical means – against his will if need be. If this is what rehabilitation involved, many would be concerned that it does indeed treat the offender as a mere object to be changed as we see fit. However, other items on the list have more limited and attractive ends. They can be seen as attempts to prevent punishment from inflicting disproportionate damage on an offender's life and prospects; and/or as attempts to recognize that offending behaviour has its causes, and that there are personal and social problems that can make it difficult for some people, even though ultimately responsible, to obey the law. In general, we can distinguish different accounts of penal rehabilitation by their differing answers to questions such as the following.

4.3.1   What is the end-state at which rehabilitation aims?

Rehabilitation sees criminal activity as a symptom of some underlying problem, and seeks to resolve that problem. Resolving the problem can involve more or less ambitious interventions, depending on what end-state is being aimed at. For instance, on the most ambitious version, criminal activity might be seen as symptomatic of some problem with the offender's ability to lead a good or worthwhile life, and the rehabilitative intervention would be aimed at increasing the offender's ability to lead a good life or worthwhile life. This version is ambitious both in the scope of the imagined intervention itself and, perhaps, in the claim to know what constitutes a good or worthwhile life for the offender. (It might invite scepticism about the claim that the authorities know the offender's good better than he knows it himself.) Less ambitious versions would substitute 'productive' or 'law-abiding' for the 'good or worthwhile' life: rehabilitation would simply aim to help the offender to become a useful member of society or to avoid harmful or anti-social behaviour. Related to these differences in approach there are distinctions in the depth of intervention that is envisaged. Some of the items involve ambitious 'deep' interventions that aim to change the offender's attitudes, character or personality. Some on the other hand aim only to change behaviour; while some do not aim to change the offender as such, but rather to enable her better to meet goals that she already has but which might have been frustrated by a lack of education or opportunity.

4.3.2   What is the ultimate reason for seeking to influence the offender?

Rehabilitation can be adopted for different reasons, and that can affect its moral quality. Fundamentally, the distinction here is between interventions that are aimed at the offender's own good, and those that are aimed at the general social good. On the former branch, we might think of rehabilitation as aiming to enable the offender to live a good, worthwhile, productive or at least law-abiding life as an expression of individual concern for him as a human being. On the latter, we can think of rehabilitation as aiming to enable the offender to live a good, productive or at least law-abiding life because treating offenders in that way is the most cost-effective way to reduce crime or reduce risks of harm. The latter invites the concern that the offender is being treated as a mere means to an end.

4.3.3   What are the means by which rehabilitation is carried out?

Rehabilitation aims at behavioural change. Some have worried about the extent or intrusiveness of the change being aimed at. But others have thought that even radical change in an offender's personality might be acceptable as long as it is brought about in the right way. Thus some writers have stressed the difference between, on the one hand, interventions that appeal to the offender's understanding and seek to change his behaviour by changing the way he thinks, and, on the other, interventions that seek to bypass his understanding. The latter type of interventions may be vulnerable to the charge that they do not treat the offender as a rational agent; they treat the offender as an object to be re-programmed rather than someone with whom we can enter into a rational discussion about the considerations that count against offending behaviour.

Furthermore, this 'bypassing' of the offender's understanding can come about in different ways. The most drastic is when the offender's personality is changed by some physical intervention such as a lobotomy. But another way is when the offender is engaged in discussion, but then given manipulated reasons for not offending. For instance, an offender might be offered 'talk' therapy rather than a more intrusive therapy, but that therapy may not be an open and honest discussion about what is wrong with such offending: it may rather amount to manipulation by discursive means. For this reason, Duff has argued that offenders should be dealt with by methods of 'transparent persuasion': that is, by an attempt to persuade the offender to accept that offending behaviour is wrong by offering him good and relevant reasons against acting in that way.[11] Transparent persuasion could be a method of rehabilitation, and would be compatible with treating the offender as a rational agent, not a mere object. For when we enter into a discussion with someone, we treat them as having the capacity to grasp and assess good reasons: that is the characteristic of a rational agent.

4.3.4   Is rehabilitation something *offered* to offenders or something they can be *required* to undergo?

Rehabilitative treatments can vary depending on whether they are thought of as being options that are made available to the offender or treatment to which the offender is subjected regardless of consent. However, being *required* to undergo some treatment can mean different things. There are some 'medicalized' treatments that the offender might be forced bodily to undergo. On the other hand, there can be treatment programmes that an offender can be required to attend in the sense that he will be punished or subjected to some more drastic intervention if he fails to attend.

4.3.5   Is rehabilitation thought of as the fundamental societal response to offenders, or rather as a goal subsidiary to retribution or deterrence?

This question is a fundamental one for the debate that we looked at above. For it is clearly one thing to say that rehabilitation is something that should *replace* retributivist responses, and quite another to say that it should *accompany* them. If rehabilitation is merely thought of as *tempering* deserved punishment then we might question Moore's claim that rehabilitation necessarily involves a failure to hold the offender responsible. One possibility is that offenders could be held responsible for their actions but *also* given support to address the problems that led to their offending.

This brief discussion makes it clear that there is a multiplicity of possible rehabilitative responses to offending. Let us draw up three broad strands in order to focus the debate.

- First of all we can imagine a form of rehabilitation that accompanies but does not replace retributive punishment. Its role is to help the offender address the factors that led to his offending, help him avoid re-offending, and to prevent his punishment from having a disproportionate impact on his life. Such rehabilitation could be optional or required.
- Second, we can imagine a form of rehabilitation that would replace retributive punishment for medium-risk offenders, and that aims to reduce the risks of their causing harm to others. The crucial thing here is to change the offender's behaviour in order to prevent its bad effects; any 'deep' change of the offender's personality would only be necessary if that was the most effective way to reduce risks of harm. Again, there may be reasons for making this optional rather than required, but, on this consequentialist approach, which it is will depend on the ultimate effectiveness of either approach in reducing risks of harm.
- Third, we can imagine a form of rehabilitation that is thought of as replacing both retribution and risk-management as the dominant societal response to wrongdoing. It involves an explicit rejection of the view of the offender as a responsible agent who deserves punishment for wrongdoing. Rather this view sees offenders as products of their circumstances who cannot be fairly blamed for what they do. It recommends that the offender be given whatever support is practicable to make it possible for him to live a better life.

The first option is important since it makes it clear that retribution and rehabilitation are not mutually exclusive approaches to the offender. Retribution need not exclude a concern for the wrongdoer, or a recognition of obstacles to law-abiding behaviour. The second option does not involve 'deep' rehabilitation, and therefore can escape the charge that rehabilitative strategies are intrusive. But in treating the offender as a 'risk' to be managed rather than an agent whose free choices can be assessed by normative standards, it might also be vulnerable to the charge that it fails to give the offender respect as a responsible agent. The third option seems the one that Moore has in his sights. Putting aside questions of who should judge what the offender's good consists in, it is clear that this option leaves no room for holding the offender

responsible for his actions. This view *might* involve manipulative therapies or intrusive interventions – or on the other hand it might restrict
itself to what Duff calls 'transparent persuasion'. (And this distinction
will be important below.) But the crucial thing is that it will not involve
the condemnation or punishment of the offender for what he has done.

How do these options stand with respect to the retributivist arguments
of the previous section? These retributivist arguments stressed the value
of treating one another as moral agents rather than as malfunctioning
objects to be put right. If we accept the arguments, however, we don't
have to reject rehabilitation of all sorts. For instance, the first type of
rehabilitation does not exclude retributivist responses: it condemns but
at the same time offers the offender assistance. Thus this seems quite
compatible with the retributivist's concerns. Indeed, the impulse to help
the offender that is manifested in such offers of assistance might appear
a necessary part of a retributivism that claims to be grounded in respect
for the offender as a participant in the moral life. However, there are
grounds for thinking that the retributivist arguments should lead us to
reject rehabilitation of the second sort, which, although it need not
actively deny that offenders are responsible, treats offenders as 'risks'
to be neutralized rather than as agents capable of engaging with the
demands of moral life. This second approach eschews rational engagement in favour of risk-management and, while it might be foolish to
deny that the authorities can sometimes be justified in treating people
in that way, offenders surely have a right to complain that their indi-
viduality is not being recognized.

What of the third type of rehabilitation? It might look as though anyone swayed by the arguments of section two will reject rehabilitation of
the third sort, since it actively denies that it is appropriate to see offenders as responsible for what they have done. However, whether this is
the case depends very much on how those arguments are interpreted,
and what is taken to be involved in being 'responsible'. Thus far, we
have interpreted the arguments of section two as showing that there
is something demeaning in treating a human being as though she was
incapable of grasping moral reasons, and therefore no more than an
object to be controlled or managed. That might be a justified objection
to certain sorts of rehabilitative intervention. But, as we have seen, one
possibility for the third type of rehabilitation is that it involves transparent persuasion. Transparent persuasion doesn't involve treating offenders as mere objects; rather it *assumes* the offender's ability to grasp moral
reasons. It engages with the offender in discussion about the reasons
why they shouldn't have acted as they did. Therefore if the objection

is only to rehabilitation that treats offenders illegitimately as objects to be managed, transparent persuasion escapes that objection. As far as we have established so far, therefore, there is nothing condescending about rehabilitation as long as it is conceived as rational argument with the offender about the reasons against acting as he did.

At this stage of our discussion, the conclusion that we have reached is therefore that, although we should be uneasy about some of the more radical forms of rehabilitation, there is an important place for rehabilitation alongside retributive purposes. Furthermore, as long as rehabilitation sticks to rational means, there is no moral issue regarding treating the offender as a mere object. Nevertheless, the retributivist might think that we have still not got to the bottom of the objection that there can be something condescending about treating someone with rehabilitation rather than retribution. What we have learnt, however, is that, if there is a valid point to be made in this area, we cannot make it as Moore does, in terms of treating a free subjective will as an object. In the next section, we will look at a better way of articulating the impression that something condescending is going on.

4.4   Full participants in the moral life?

This next step in the argument opens with the observation that transparent persuasion *by itself* cannot be the right approach to use with all offenders. Transparent persuasion seeks to engage the wrongdoer in a discussion about the reasons why it was wrong to act as the offender did. Reference to these reasons does not enter the picture as a justification of the condemnation of the offender, and as something acknowledged on all hands; rather, when rehabilitation is the aim, the reasons are being communicated to the offender with the object of changing the offender for the better by helping him to grasp their significance. This kind of educative communication will be appropriate for offenders who have not yet grasped those reasons, or who could not be expected to have grasped them for themselves. But it will not be appropriate if there are agents who can be expected to know that such acts are wrong, and who would properly regard themselves as responsible for knowing that. The point is not simply that some offenders already know that the acts they perform are wrong. If the retributivist's case rested on this claim, assessing it would entangle us in issues about whether the very fact that one acts wrongly shows that one does not fully grasp that it is wrong (requiring us to reject the Socratic thesis that no one knowingly acts wrongly). But this is not the point. It is rather that, whether a particular offender has the requisite knowledge or not, it is their *responsibility* to make sure that they have it and that they act accordingly. Therefore the point is that, for some agents who *can* be expected to act well, it is not our *place* to engage with them in transparent persuasion about the reasons against acting as they did. That is something that they can be expected to grasp for themselves, and should be let alone to do so.

The claim is therefore that it can be condescending to treat offenders as though it is necessary to explain to them that their act was wrong, and to do so without any condemnation of their failure to recognize its wrongness, since in doing so one would be treating them as though they couldn't have been expected to understand this for themselves. This is condescending because it impugns a capacity that we properly regard as an important source of dignity or status, namely the capacity to be a full and independent participant in the moral life, an agent who is capable of playing her part in moral relationships, and is in possession of at least a minimally functional moral compass. This argument slots neatly into a different way of understanding the Strawsonian view that we looked at in section two. While up till now we understood the argument of section two to rest on the wrongness of treating offenders as mere objects, it is now obvious that it will require more than that to explain what, if anything, is problematic about rehabilitation. Strawson's concern is to contrast the objective attitude, not just with the perspective in which we engage with one another in rational discussion, but rather with a more fully social perspective in which we treat one another as fellow participants in interpersonal relationships. To engage with someone in some interpersonal dealings requires, not just that she would be able to grasp the reasons for acting in certain ways if this was explained to her; rather it requires that she be able to see this *for herself*, without external assistance. In any actually existing moral relationship, participants operate on the basis of normative expectations that they have of one another; an understanding of this basis is usually taken for granted as shared implicit knowledge. Thus in order to operate even minimally within such a social scene one will need the capacity to grasp and assess, for oneself, the demands under which one finds oneself. To treat someone as though they are incapable of *this* is to say something rather serious about their moral standing: when a person cannot operate independently in the moral life, he cannot take a place in relationships based on trust,[12] and hence has, as Strawson says, to be controlled and managed.

We are now in a position properly to explain the charge of condescension. The proponent of rehabilitation separates herself from the offender, regarding him as lacking in a vital capacity that she herself possesses: the capacity to operate autonomously in the moral life. As we said about the superior tone of the passage quoted at the start (a tone exaggerated by the use of terms like 'pathetic'), the proponent of rehabilitation remains secure in her possession of these qualities that the offender lacks. She therefore comes to the conclusion that, while she can be self-governing, offenders have to be governed from without if they are to share a society with us. Of course, this attitude is not condescending in itself. It is not condescending when it is directed towards those who *really do* lack the capacity for self-governance. Treating someone as incapable of self-governance is only condescending when its object is someone who *does* have these capacities, when such treatment amounts to a *misrecognition* of the offender.[13] The opponent of rehabilitation can, of course, allow the existence of some people who are genuinely incapable of self-governance. But not all are: there are many who, like the proponent of rehabilitation herself, have to be regarded as autonomous. The debate between the two camps is therefore how extensive we should regard the category of people lacking moral autonomy to be.

This interpretation of the arguments of section two also has the advantage of giving us a better interpretation of the position taken by proponents of rehabilitation. Proponents of rehabilitation need not think that offenders lack moral capacities *altogether*; their claim is rather that many offenders do not have the developed moral capacities (say for independent participation in the moral life) that are necessary for full moral responsibility. The criminal law, on this view, sets the bar too high for people who live the chaotic lives of many offenders; this is not because offenders are not moral agents at all, but rather because moral agency admits of degrees. Some people who meet the conditions to be considered as Moorean 'free, subjective wills' nevertheless do not meet the conditions to be considered as independent participants in the moral life. As we noted above, the proponent of rehabilitation cannot think that it is merely a few offenders around the edges of the criminal justice system to whom this description applies. Rather, if she argues that rehabilitation should, to a considerable extent, replace retribution, she must think that a large number of offenders fall into this category. The retributivist argument, she might say, overplays the degree to which moral agents possess independent moral capacities. Classical liberalism may be founded on the image of the separate, sovereign and morally independent agents. But that is not the way people really are. Offenders in particular are often damaged and vulnerable people. They do not spring fully formed into existence with the capabilities that make them fully responsible for their actions. Rather they have to have to have a degree of luck if their moral capacities are to develop and remain undamaged. But not all of us are so lucky. One motivation for rehabilitation that we have overlooked so far is therefore that retribution demands too much of the vulnerable.

This represents the final turn in the argument that I want to consider in this paper: the charge that the critic of penal rehabilitation overlooks the fact that reasoning about normative considerations is a skill that we have to learn, and the product of a fortunate process of social development of which some, perhaps many, offenders may have been deprived. The capacity autonomously to participate in the moral life, this line of thought proceeds, is not a natural quality: it is rather a kind of expertise that is the product of inculcation in a way of life. This is a view that we might (following Charles Taylor) call the social thesis: the claim that the development of valuable human capacities depends on the presence of favourable social conditions.[14] Individuals, according to the social thesis, do not make their moral decisions in a vacuum, but rather draw on resources that are given to them by their social context. Though not mere *products* of society, individuals' decisions and characters are inevitably shaped by their social surroundings in countless ways. The social thesis rejects the 'atomist' view that individuals are naturally morally independent and self-sufficient. Though society does not simply determine what individuals think, the idea of a self 'unencumbered' by the sorts of attachments and commitments that we gain from being educated into a certain moral form of life is the idea of a self who has no ability to make meaningful decisions about how to live.[15] If this is correct, the proponent of rehabilitation concludes, then we cannot fairly assume that all offenders, regardless of the specific set of circumstances they have encountered in coming to be as they are, have an ability to think for themselves in the way that holding them responsible requires.

It seems to me that the retributivist can, and perhaps should, accept the social thesis (although a full assessment of its validity of course cannot be attempted here). The social thesis suggests that the ability autonomously to grasp, assess and apply moral reasons is socially acquired. If this is correct then it would mean that moral proficiency could be assimilated to the model of other sorts of proficiency in social practices. When one is being inculcated into a social practice, one has to pass through a stage in which one requires external assistance in order to be able to operate successfully. The distinction between being an expert and being an apprentice is familiar from many social practices. What distinguishes the two is the possession of an independent ability to grasp the reasons to do *this* rather than *that*, not just in artificially constructed and simplified cases, but in all manner of situations, and apply them proficiently to one's acts. It is the same ability that, according to the social thesis, underpins moral responsibility: proficiency in the social practice or craft of morality. However, what follows from this for the significance of rehabilitation? Although it seems clear that some agents may miss the forms of socialization that would allow the development of full moral agency, the question on which the debate rests is how extensive the failure to possess moral autonomy is. At this stage, we should note two points.

First of all, while it is of course true that there are some people who do not fully develop the ability to function independently as moral agents, there is no escaping the fact that this inability represents a serious deficiency, and that judging an agent not to have this ability has serious repercussions for the way in which we can relate to him. Secondly, we should be aware that judgements about whether offenders possess or lack the kind of minimal moral compass of which we have been speaking take place in a context in which certain conditions exist: (a) that those making these judgements are largely drawn from the middle and upper socio-economic classes of society, since these are the classes that largely run the institutions by which our societies are governed; (b) that those about whom the judgements are being made are largely drawn from the lower socio-economic classes; and (c) that we have reason to expect the existence of a tendency for the governing classes systematically to underestimate the moral abilities of those from the lower classes, since the view of the lower classes as morally helpless and incapable of governing themselves would legitimate the current inequalities of power and responsibility that result in rights to govern remaining the preserve of particular dominant social groups.[16] This suggests that we have to be very careful about making the charge of moral helplessness. After all, the criminal law does not defend fine moral distinctions: the kind of moral expertise that the criminal law demands is of a very minimal kind. It rather asks us to avoid certain well-defined acts that are widely known to be wrong, and whose wrongness is implied and confirmed by all manner of common social interactions, interactions in which one will participate regardless of the social group one belongs to. What motivates the more radical types of penal rehabilitation may be a concern that those who are already disadvantaged do not suffer more by their failure to operate the social system and play by the rules. However, at its best, the criminal law is not a bourgeois game or convention; it defends values that underpin decent communal life. Therefore failure to abide by such values cannot be regarded as a mere failure to keep to one's place. Penal rehabilitation may have good intentions, but arguments that it should replace retributivist responses on the grounds of moral helplessness have their own dangers.

4.5   Conclusion

In this paper I have been dealing with the question of whether a concern for the rehabilitation of offenders is compassionate or condescending. This is a complex question, and, as we have seen, any answer to it depends on what rehabilitation is taken to involve: whether it is offered or enforced; whether it uses rational or non-rational means to bring about change in the offender; and whether rehabilitation is taken to accompany or replace retributive purposes. In particular, we have seen that the retributivist should have no problem with the idea of rehabilitation that accompanies proper condemnation; but that there are significant arguments that it would be condescending to replace retribution with rehabilitation for many offenders. Overall, we have found reasons to be sympathetic to the retributivist view that some important status is connected with being viewed and treated as a responsible agent. Although we should not fall prey to the atomist view that individuals magically become fully responsible agents on reaching the age of majority, it nevertheless has serious repercussions for the way in which we can relate to offenders if they are labelled as lacking the basic autonomous grasp of the values underpinning the criminal law.

Notes

1. See for instance, F. A. Allen (1981), *The Decline of the Rehabilitative Ideal* (London: Yale University Press).
2. G. Robinson (2008), 'Late Modern Rehabilitation: The Evolution of a Penal Strategy', *Punishment and Society* 10, 429–45; P. Priestley and M. Vanstone (eds) (2010), *Offenders or Citizens? Readings in Rehabilitation* (Cullompton: Willan).
3. For the philosophical case for abolitionism, see, for example, D. Boonin (2008), *The Problem of Punishment* (Cambridge: Cambridge University Press); and D. Golash (2005), *The Case Against Punishment: Retribution, Prevention and the Law* (New York: New York University Press). For a strongly rehabilitative alternative to punishment, see J. Braithwaite (1989), *Crime, Shame and Reintegration* (Cambridge: Cambridge University Press).
4. Home Office (1990), *Crime, Justice and Protecting the Public* (London: HMSO). This passage is cited in M. Tonry and David P. Farrington (1995), 'Strategic Approaches to Crime Prevention', *Crime and Justice: A Review of Research* 19, 1–20.

5. Michael S. Moore, (1987), 'The Moral Worth of Retribution', in F. Schoeman (ed.), *Responsibility, Character and the Emotions* (Cambridge: Cambridge University Press), 179–219, at pp. 215–6.

6. H. Morris (1968), 'Persons and Punishment', *Monist* 52, 475–501.

7. See P. F. Strawson (1986), 'Freedom and Resentment', in G. Watson (ed.), *Free Will* (Oxford: Oxford University Press), 59–80.

8. Cf. , for example, the Strawsonian point of view developed in R. Jay Wallace (1994), *Responsibility and the Moral Sentiments* (London: Harvard University Press).

9. C. Korgaard (1996), 'Creating the Kingdom of Ends: Responsibility and Reciprocity in Personal Relations', in *Creating the Kingdom of Ends* (Cambridge: Cambridge University Press), 188–201, pp. 190–1.

10. For the idea that valuable relationships might be in part constituted by the demands they make on participants, see, for example, S. Scheffler (1997), 'Relationships and Responsibilities', *Philosophy and Public Affairs* 26, 189–209, esp. pp. 200–1.

11. R. A. Duff (2001), *Punishment, Communication and Community* (Oxford: Oxford University Press, 2001), p. 81.

12. For this characterization of trust, see K. Jones (1996), 'Trust as an Affective Attitude', *Ethics* 107, pp. 4–25.

13. On the notion of misrecognition, see, for example, A. Honneth (2007), *Disrespect: The Normative Foundations of Critical Theory* (Cambridge: Polity Press).

14. C. Taylor (1985), 'Atomism', in *Philosophical Papers* Vol. 2 (Cambridge: Cambridge University Press), pp. 187–210, esp., for example, 195.

15. M. Sandel (1982), *Liberalism and the Limits of Justice* (Cambridge: Cambridge University Press).

16. This perspective underpins much of the work of James Kelman. See, for instance, his novel: Kelman (1994), *How Late It Was, How Late* (London: Secker and Warburg).

5
Punishment and the Measurement of Severity

Jesper Ryberg

Should rape be punished more severely than other types of violent crime? Are white-collar crimes generally punished too leniently in comparison with other sorts of crime? And, if a prior criminal record should count when punishments are meted out, then how much harder should the recidivist be punished compared to a first-time criminal? Such questions concerning how we should respond to crimes of varying gravity occupy much space in public debate. They often prompt heated (though, unfortunately, less often thorough) discussion. Obviously, consideration of the relative severity of punishments also plays an important role, both when criminal laws are formulated by politicians and when punishments are meted out in criminal justice practice. Turning to academic discussion, the picture is no different. It is a fact that questions concerning the relative punishments of crime have attracted increasing attention over the last few decades. As a leading scholar has put it, penal theory has undergone a change in focus from 'why punish?' to 'how much?'.[1]

Given the comprehensive attention directed to questions of penal distribution, it is remarkable, however, how little is usually said with regard to the question of what is meant by one punishment being more harsh than another. In fact, it seems that most discussion, regardless of whether it takes place among penal scholars or in broader public debates, simply regards the comparisons of punishments in severity as an unproblematic issue not giving rise to problems of its own. At first sight this is not surprising. After all, the relative comparison of punishments usually seems fairly straightforward. For instance, the severity of a prison term seems to vary with its duration, while fines vary in gravity according to the quantity of money that is collected. However, little reflection is required to see that this may not be so simple as it seems. Since the mid-80s increasing attention has been directed to alternative types of punishment. With the contention, for instance, that a punishment system which offers only a relatively few punishment options will often punish perpetrators either too severely or too leniently relative to the crime committed, there has been a growing interest in intermediate sanctions – including, for example, home detention, community service, day fines, electronic monitoring and so on – as constituting the *tertium quid* between prison and probation.[2] However, once a criminal justice system is operating with several types of sanction, it is not plausible to assume that sanctions of one type are always more severe than the sanctions of another. It certainly makes sense to ask how a short prison term should be compared to a period of home detention, a large fine, or a long period of probation under onerous conditions. Now, though, a mere reference to parameters such as duration or quantity will no longer provide us with a sufficient answer. What this indicates is that the comparison of punishments in severity may not be as simple as we apparently often tend to believe. In fact, what I shall argue in the this chapter is that, on closer inspection, the measurement of punishment severity faces serious challenges.

The theoretical motivation for engaging in these considerations is simple. It is an often described fact that retributive theories of punishment – that is, roughly put, theories which regard the *desert* of the perpetrators as the cardinal concept with regard to how punishment is justified and should be distributed – have come to play a dominant role in modern penal theory. In contrast to the consequentialist approach which dominated most of the last century, the retributivist view on punishment has been revived over the last two or three decades. Today, penal theory is largely retributive theory.[3] Despite the fact that the retributive view on punishment has been interpreted in various ways, the different theories usually share the same overall view on punishment allocation, namely, that crimes should be punished more severely the more serious they are. However, this idea of proportionality in punishment presupposes that one is capable of measuring and ranking punishments in severity. If one cannot say whether one punishment should be regarded as more severe than another, then the whole idea of proportionality falls apart. Thus, the question to be considered in this article is whether retributivists have succeeded in delivering a plausible theory of punishment severity. Or, more precisely, whether a plausible theory of severity can be provided which makes it possible to apply the idea of proportionality in punishment as the governing principle of penal distribution. Even though the discussion of this chapter thus takes a penal theoretical point of departure it is, however, obvious that there is a clear practical side to it as well. Despite the fact that existing criminal justice systems almost never work on the grounds of one basic and consistent set of reasons for sentencing – in fact, it is typical to emphasize both consequentialist and retributivist aims as if these were fully consistent – there is no doubt that most criminal systems apply some degree of proportionality. Therefore, both penal law and penal practice to some extent presuppose the possibility of comparing punishment in severity.

What I shall argue in the following, as indicated, is that the measurement of severity faces challenges which have not been resolved by what retributivists have had to say on the matter so far. The first challenge – referred to as the challenge of differences in impact – concerns the fact that punishments may affect people differently. Though this challenge is not unfamiliar in traditional penal theory, it seems to me that the importance of the problem has not been fully recognized nor properly dealt with. The second challenge, which I call the challenge of delimitation, concerns the fact that it may not be as simple as we tend to believe to specify what we should take into account when the severity of a punishment is determined. The chapter is concluded with comments on the practical and theoretical implications of the presented challenges.

5.1   The challenge of differences in impact

As mentioned, the comparison of punishments in severity does not usually strike us as problematic. Comparing the punishments of one year or two years in prison seems a simple matter. We would have no doubts as to what would constitute the harsher punishment if it were to be inflicted on us. However, it is important to keep in mind what proportionality implies, namely, that if A has committed a crime that is more serious than the one committed by B then A should be more harshly punished. And if the crimes of A and B are equally grave they should be equally punished. It is precisely when we start comparing the severity of different punishments inter-personally that it becomes clear that this may not after all be so simple. The problem is that a punishment, say one year in prison, may affect people very differently. In order to clarify how a punishment may affect the person on whom it is imposed, and thus to depict a clear picture of how punishments may affect different individuals differently, it will be helpful to introduce distinctions between, first, the objective and subjective effects of a punishment and, second, the direct and indirect effects of a punishment. Let us consider each distinction in turn.

The distinction between the objective and the subjective effects of a punishment is simple. Roughly, we can say that the objective effects concern what a punishment does to an individual, while the subjective effects concern the way in which the individual is affected by what is done to him/her. Obviously, prison terms of respectively one year and two years or fines at 100$ and 1000$ differ in objective effects. The punishments do different things to those who are punished. This is what makes them different punishments. While this comes as no surprise, it is more interesting to consider that even punishments which are the same in name may vary in objective effects. If A and B are each sentenced to one year in prison they may nevertheless be affected very differently in objective terms. A may end up in a small ill-lit cell without a view, and in prison conditions which are terrible.[4] In contrast, B may be placed in a well-functioning prison, in a more comfortable cell with a window at eye-height, with easy access to different facilities, and so on. Of course, a society can make the effort to adjust prison conditions so that they are as uniform as possible between different prisons. But it is hard to imagine that there will not, to some extent, exist objective differences between punishments which are the same in name.

However, suppose that prison conditions are totally adjusted so that a prison term of one year has precisely the same objective effects on each individual who receives this sentence. Even if this is so, it may still be the case that the prison term affects those who are punished very differently: the punishment may have different subjective effects. Two individuals may react differently to the same objective effect. As Bentham – who considered the issue thoroughly – has put it: 'a punishment which is the same in name will not always either really produce, or even so much as appear to others to produce, in two different persons the same degree of pain'.[5] Bentham refers to the disposition a person has to feel a quantity of pleasure or pain upon the application of a cause of given force, as the degree of his or her 'sensibility'. That there exist significant variations in the sensibility of different people is hard to dispute. For instance, the suffering a person endures from spending time in prison obviously is conditioned by the affected person's psychological sensitivity. Some persons are easily frightened and become very nervous, while others are psychologically much more robust. Some get more bored or frustrated than do others if placed under monotonous life conditions, and so on. In fact, though we typically face such differences in the inter-personal comparison, they may exist even at the intra-personal level. A person may be less sensitive at the age of thirty than at the age of sixty. Criminal record may in this respect also make a difference. Criminologists report that the first custodial punishment is typically experienced as more traumatic than later but objectively similar punishments. Moreover, there may even be changes in a person's sensibility during a punishment. Some inmates adjust successfully to prison life, but the opposite may also be the case. What starts out as bearable may, if a person loses hope or the instinct for self-preservation, turn into a nightmare even if the prison conditions are unchanged. So much for the distinction between the objective and the subjective effects of punishment.

The second distinction to which we shall focus attention is that between direct and indirect effects of punishment. Though this distinction is also relatively simple to grasp it is, I believe, somewhat remarkable how often it is ignored in penal discussions. The direct effects of a punishment consist in the ways in which a person experiences the punishment imposed upon him/her. For instance, the direct effects of a prison term may consist in the suffering, frustration, unpleasantness or discomfort which a person feels at being placed behind bars. Though it is probably these feelings that many people typically think of, if they try to imagine what it would be like to go through such a punishment, it is nonetheless clear that such direct effects of being punished do not exhaust the ways in which a certain punishment may affect one's life for the worse. A punishment may also have indirect effects, in the sense that it deprives the one who is punished of something. For instance, the indirect effect of a prison term consists in the fact that it deprives the punished person of all the valuable experiences this person would have had if he or she had not been locked up. The prison term precludes the person from a daily life with wife/husband, children, friends, work, a hobby, or whatever this person regards as valuable in ordinary life. Of course, such indirect effects of a punishment may well have direct effects in terms of the sorrow which a person experiences from realizing what he or she is missing. But obviously this does not change the fact that we can distinguish between what a person experiences in being punished and what he or she is prevented from experiencing by being punished. In order to avoid misunderstandings, however, it should be underlined that the point of introducing this distinction is neither to suggest that all punishments have both kinds of effect nor that a certain punishment either has direct effects or indirect effects. Some types of punishment seem only to have direct effects. For instance, an obsolete type of punishment such as flogging does not deprive us of something. It affects us only directly in terms of the suffering it causes. In contrast, the death penalty only has indirect effects on the one who is punished. Though one may of course suffer severely prior to the punishment, it is obvious that once the punishment is carried out there no longer exists a person who is directly affected. But the death penalty deprives the person of all the things he/she would have experienced had he/she not been executed. Similarly, I believe that the main effects from receiving a fine are indirect. Though one may of course feel annoyed at being fined, the way a fine affects us consists first and foremost in the fact that it prevents us from something which we would have had or done, had we not been punished in this way. Finally, as we have seen, a custodial punishment usually has both direct and indirect effects on the one who is punished.

Having introduced the above distinctions between, respectively, the objective and subjective effects and the direct and indirect effects of a punishment, we now have a more informed background for understanding and sustaining the initial claim that punishments which are the same in name may nevertheless effect people very differently. By pairing the two distinctions we can see that even though a punishment may be the same in name, say one year in prison, it may affect persons A and B differently by having different objective and direct effects (if there are differences in the prison conditions); by having different subjective and direct effects (if A and B suffer differently due to differences in sensibility); by having different indirect and objective effects (if A and B are deprived of something different); and by having different indirect and subjective effects (if A and B, due to differences in sensibility, would have reacted differently to what they are prevented from experiencing). Or, to put the whole point another way and perhaps a little more clearly: Even if A and B are both sentenced to one year in prison they may be affected differently due to differing prison conditions. Even if the prison conditions are exactly the same – which is not very likely – A and B may still be affected differently due to their individual sensibilities. Even if their sensibility to these conditions is exactly the same – which is not very likely – they may still be affected differently for the worse by being deprived of different things. And finally, even if they are deprived of precisely the same things – which is not very likely – they may still be differently affected if there are differences in their sensibility to these things had they had the chance of experiencing them. All in all, I believe that this outlined picture of the possible effects of being punished provides reasonable support for the conclusion that differences in the way the 'same' punishment affects different persons for the worse are not rare exceptions. On the contrary, such differences are precisely what we should expect in most cases.

The interesting question to which this conclusion now leads us is what this means with regard to the measurement of punishment in severity and thus with regard to the idea of proportionality in punishment. If one holds that the punishment severity should be measured in terms of how much a punishment contributes to making our lives worse or, perhaps more precisely, that both direct and indirect effects must play a role in the computation of severity, then this has obvious implications for the application of the principle of proportionality. If A and B have committed the same crime we can no longer assume that proportionality is observed merely by imposing on the two the 'same' punishment, such as one year in prison. And if A receives two years in prison for having committed a crime that is more serious than the one committed by B, who is sentenced to one year in prison, then it may still be the case that B is more severely punished and that the demand of proportionality is violated. The same may also be the case if A commits the same crime twice in his/her life and receives the 'same' punishment in both cases. Thus, the way in which the idea of proportionality is usually thought to work, namely, in terms of types and not tokens of punishment – for example, that two years in prison is a more severe type of punishment than one year in prison – is inconsistent with the outlined view on punishment severity.

Now, how can a proportionalist, such as a modern retributivist, react to this challenge? Basically, there are two directions an answer can take. The first possibility is to give in and accept that it no longer makes sense to present the proportionality principle as being concerned with types of punishment. What this means is that one will, in the application of the principle, have to account for differences in impact and that the severity of punishment is determined for individual cases. This might imply that, in order to ensure that A and B are equally severely punished for having committed equally serious crimes, A may end up with one year in prison while B gets three years behind bars. The other possibility is to reject the suggested approach to punishment severity in favour of a model that allows the distribution of proportionate punishments to work in terms of types of punishment. What the implications are if the proportionalist cannot avoid the first possibility is a matter to which we shall return in the final section. For the present it is worth considering whether the second answer constitutes a genuine theoretical option. More precisely, I shall consider two ways in which the challenge of differences in impact has been met. As will be argued, neither answer seems to be plausible.

As mentioned, almost no theorist has taken up the issue of punishment severity. However, one of the few exceptions is von Hirsch. Though he has not fully developed his view on the matter, he strongly opposes what he refers to as a 'subjectivist view' according to which severity is determined on the ground of unpleasantness and the discomfort experienced. A problem with this view, von Hirsch contends, is that it has 'troublesome social implications'.[6] In so far as being inured to deprivation is related to social class, the view implies that 'the middle-class person is put on probation and the ghetto youth jailed for the same infraction'.[7] Now, given how the least privileged members of society in a historical perspective have been treated within criminal justice systems, it is not surprising if one regards this as a very dubious implication. However, it is hard to see that this constitutes a convincing argument against a view on severity which allows for inter-personal differences in impact.

The first thing to consider if one finds von Hirsch's argument appealing is that, if the punishment imposed on the ghetto criminal is one which in name is more severe than the one imposed on the middle-class criminal, this is not then unacceptable in terms of justice. It would strike many as clearly unjust if the ghetto criminal were to be punished more severely than the middle-class criminal. But this is not the case. On the contrary, the whole point of imposing on the two persons punishments which are different in name may be to ensure that they are equally severely punished for the same infraction. Thus, one should be careful to avoid the pitfall of accepting von Hirsch's argument out of justice considerations. This being said, is not von Hirsch right in emphasizing that this may nevertheless have troublesome social consequences? The answer might well be in the affirmative. However, what is important is that this is not sufficient to make the argument against the suggested conception of severity conclusive. Insofar as one accepts that the possible consequences of relying on one conception of severity rather than another should matter in the assessment of each conception, it seems arbitrary to focus *solely* on the social consequences to which von Hirsch draws attention. What one would have to do, in order to avoid arbitrariness, is also to consider whatever other consequences would follow from applying one conception of severity rather than another (for example, the possible consequences that might follow from a conception that does not allow for impact-relativity and which, therefore, implies that a young and strong criminal should be punished equally severely as an old and vulnerable criminal). It is not obvious in which direction such a comparison would point. What is more important, however, is that it is far from obvious that we should accept von Hirsch's assumption that conceptions of severity should be assessed on the grounds of social (or other) consequences. As a simple analogy, suppose that taking a bath in water at a temperature of 70 degrees Celsius has harmful consequences.

Such consequences would certainly count as a reasonable argument against bathing at this temperature, but they would hardly count as an argument against measuring temperature on the Celsius scale. Similarly, if it turns out that punishing the ghetto criminal differently from the middle-class criminal has undesirable consequences, then it is far from obvious why this should be considered as an argument against a certain conception of severity rather than against the sort of normative penal theory according to which the punishments are distributed. After all, a conception of severity does not in itself imply anything with regard to how different criminals should be punished. Thus, it seems that the von Hirsch argument is misdirected. At least, it has to be shown why this is not an argument against the penal theory – such as a retributive theory prescribing proportionality in punishment – rather than against theories of what basically makes one punishment more severe than another. Thus, all in all, von Hirsch's argument does not appear to be convincing.[8]

The second way in which one could try to avoid the challenge of differences in impact is also presented as part of von Hirsch's approach to gauging punishment severity. As mentioned above, von Hirsch rejects an account according to which severity is determined by how unpleasant a sanction is experienced as being. Following von Hirsch's scheme, severity should be gauged in terms of how a sanction impinges on a person's 'living standards' by which he means the 'means and capabilities' that assist persons in achieving a good life.[9] Now, though focusing on means and capabilities might seem to rule out what a person experiences in terms of unpleasantness or suffering (and which might vary due to differences in sensibility), this is not in itself sufficient to avoid the challenge of differences in impact. As we have seen, an important aspect of most types of punishment is that they have indirect effects by depriving a person of something valuable. However, since people lead different lives there may be major differences with regard to which *means* to a good life different people are deprived of by a certain punishment. There is, though, a further twist to von Hirsch's proposal. What he suggests is that severity should be gauged according to how a sanction 'typically' affects a punished person's living standards. In other words, severity should be determined on the ground of *standardized* estimates. If we accept this proposal then it follows – in fact, independently of whether one focuses on means and capabilities or experienced unpleasantness – that the challenge of differences in impact is blocked. Even if A is affected much more than B from spending a year in prison, A is not punished more harshly if the severity of the punishment is determined in terms of what the effects of this punishment characteristically are.

However, appealing as this may seem, the proposal still leaves one crucial question open: Why should severity be measured on the ground of standardizations? To suggest that this makes everything much easier will, obviously, not do. One cannot just redefine what matters in some practical but morally arbitrary way. Unfortunately, von Hirsch does not present an argument to this effect. The only argument I can think of is the following, which has some affinity to reasoning in certain parts of political philosophy. It is sometimes suggested that, in comparing broader political decisions which have an impact on the lives of very many people, it is simply impossible to rely on considerations as to how a decision improves or declines the actual quality of life for each and every individual who is affected by the decision. Rather, what we have to do, so to speak, is to employ another 'currency' which does not leave us paralysed from the outset but which is genuinely applicable in political decision-making. In other words, we have to rely on estimates of the *typical* impact. In the same vein, might it not be held that in order to have a well-functioning criminal justice system we have to apply a standardized account of punishment severity? I believe there are several reasons to be sceptical of this line of reasoning.

Firstly, it is not obvious that it actually constitutes an argument against what basically matters. Sometimes one has to make adjustments in order to apply a certain normative position in practice, but this need not change what basically matters morally. Secondly, and more importantly, the argument is based on a mistaken empirical premise. While one often does not know the identity of the individuals and thus the precise impact on those affected by broader political decisions, this is not the case when we are talking about the punishment of criminals. We know precisely who each individual is, and how he/she is punished. But this means that it will, at least to some extent, be possible to make estimates of the impact of a punishment in individual cases. In fact, as Kolber has recently pointed out, individual calibrations do to some degree already exist within the context of law.[10] For instance, detailed psychological evaluations even now take place within criminal justice systems (for example, in relation to disposition plans for juvenile offenders, in relation to certain mitigating factors or when it comes to judgements of dangerousness). And, as Kolber argues, such evaluations may be significantly improved in a not-too-distant future with the development of modern neuro-imaging technology. Obviously, developing systems for individual calibrated punishments may be expensive to administer and such procedures may be vulnerable to errors. But still, it remains premature to contend that we simply have to rely on standardizations.

Thus, this suggested argument in favour of introducing standardization does not seem plausible. However, in the absence of an argument to this effect it is reasonable to conclude that it is simply *ad hoc* to introduce standardizations in the account of what matters morally in the measurement of severity.

Now where does this leave us? As we have initially seen, there are strong reasons for claiming that punishments which are the same in name may have variable effects on different persons. Moreover, it seems reasonable to believe that the ways in which punishment affects our lives for the worse should figure in the assessment of punishment severity. Together this implies that one and the same sanction may punish different persons, or the same person over time, with different degrees of severity. Since neither the argument concerning social implications nor the argument concerning standardization seems plausible, we can conclude that the challenge of differences in impact remains intact. What precisely this means for the idea of proportionality in punishing is something to which we shall return later. For the present the purpose is limited to examining the problems concerning the comparison of punishment severity. As we shall now see, further challenges are lurking behind the next corner.

5.2   The challenge of delimitation

When a criminal is punished for his or her misdeed this may affect this person's life for the worse in many different ways. In fact, as we shall see, a person may be affected in ways which go far beyond what we usually think of when considering the impact of a punishment. The second challenge to the idea of measuring severity, to which we shall now turn, arises from the fact that it may not be a simple matter to specify how much of the suffering or deprivation which a certain punishment causes should be included in the assessment of severity of this punishment. There exists, I shall argue, a *challenge of delimitation*.

At first sight, this may seem somewhat strange. After all, is it not precisely the amount of suffering or deprivation which a punishment causes that determines the severity of this punishment – no more and no less? That it is not as simple as that can easily be demonstrated. A punishment may have various sorts of consequences affecting the punished person's life for the worse. That a person may seriously miss his or her wife/husband is, I believe, what we would probably regard as part of the unpleasantness of being in prison. This is something that should figure in the assessment of severity. But what if the wife or husband demands a divorce? Should the sorrow which this causes to the punished also figure in the assessment of severity? We can easily imagine that, in the same way as the experience of missing one's wife/husband is a result of being in prison, the demand for a divorce is a result of the stay in prison. It may be caused by the prison term and may not have happened had the punished person not been placed behind bars. Or, alternatively, consider the indirect effects of being in prison. That a prison term deprives a person of the pleasure he or she would have experienced from going to work will probably strike many as something that should figure in the assessment of the punishment. But what if the person is not only prevented from going to work but is also prevented from getting a highly-desired promotion which the person would have got had he/she not been in prison. Does this make the punishment even more severe? The point of these examples can of course be stretched much further. It is not hard to imagine cases where a prison term, or another punishment, triggers a series of events which reach far out into the future – for example, years after the punished person is released – and which all contribute to worsening the punished person's life. And, it should be noted, this is so independently of whether one holds that severity should be determined on the ground of experienced unpleasantness, deprivation of pleasant experiences, or in terms of the loss of the means to and capabilities of a good life. Thus, to put the question more generally, if a prison term, a period of probation, a fine, or any other punishment triggers a chain of events which are harmful to the punished person, then how many of these consequences should figure in the assessment of the severity of the sanction? The challenge of delimitation consists in providing a morally non-arbitrary answer to this question.

Meeting the challenge of delimitation is not a simple matter. As we have seen, it will not do merely to contend that severity should be measured in terms of standardized estimates. There may be many causal effects of a prison term or a fine which we do not usually regard as part of the severity of the punishment, but which would have to be included in the assessment even on a standardized account. Moreover, as we have seen, introducing standardization requires a moral justification. Probably the most promising answer is to engage in considerations of what should be regarded as a punishment in the first place. For instance, if the sorrow experienced from the demand of a divorce, or the fact that one has been deprived of a promotion, should not be considered in the measurement of severity of the punishment which has triggered both effects, then the explanation is not that these effects constitute particular types of experience or deprivation which are different from other experiences or deprivations and, therefore, should not count in the assessment of severity. Rather, the explanation is that these effects are not part of the punishment at all. This, I imagine, is probably the answer that many people would find appealing. However, if this is how one believes that the challenge of delimitation should be dealt with, then one is committed to delivering some sort of criterion for the distinction between, on the one hand, the punitive effects of a sanction and, on the other, the non-punitive side-effects of this sanction. Can such a criterion be provided?

The question as to what characterizes a punishment, that is how a punishment should be defined, is not uncontroversial. Luckily, though, there are many aspects of the definition question – such as whether a punishment must contain suffering, whether it must be imposed upon an offender, and whether it must be for an offence against a legal rule – which are irrelevant in the present context. However, there is also a condition which has been underlined in the definitions dominant since the 50s – such as the Flew-Benn-Hart definitions – and which appears more promising, namely, as Hart puts it: that a punishment 'must be intentionally administered by human beings other than the offender'[11]. Since we are not here considering the possibility of self-punishment the latter condition is irrelevant. But the former condition, that of intentionality, might seem to provide what it takes to answer the challenge of delimitation. The reason why the suffering of being divorced, of losing a job or an apartment, or other like collateral consequences which are triggered by a certain sanction, should be disregarded in the assessment of the punishment is that these effects are not *intended* by the sentencer. They are side-effects of the punishment – not part of it. Now, does this way of excluding much of the sanction-triggered suffering or deprivation from considerations on punishment severity constitute a plausible way of resolving the challenge?

As mentioned, this answer certainly has immediate appeal. However, it is important to make clear what the answer precisely amounts to. What we are considering is not whether some sort of accident which happens to a perpetrator while performing a crime – for example, the breaking of a leg – can count as a punishment for this misdeed. The idea of *poena naturalis* is not the issue. What is under consideration are cases where a perpetrator is imprisoned, fined or treated in another way which constitutes a standard instance of a punishment but where this has a number of harmful effects on this person's life. Thus, there is no doubt that what we are considering are intentional acts of punishment. In order to rule out the possibility that suffering resulting from the loss of a wife/husband, a job, an apartment or whatever, should be included in the assessment of punishment severity, what one will have to hold to is that only the suffering, unpleasantness or deprivation which is intended by the sentencer should count as part of the punishment. Or, more precisely, that the severity of the punishment is determined by the intended amount of suffering and deprivation. Taking this view, if the sentencer intends to inflict a certain amount of hardship on a criminal, then no matter what the collateral effects this may have on the one who is punished, this does not affect the severity of the punishment. Such effects may be regarded as most unfortunate and steps might even be taken to palliate them, but they are extraneous to the question of punishment severity.

Though it seems as if we have here found a way of dealing with the challenge of delimitation, the hope does not last long. The contention that severity should be determined in terms of intended suffering or deprivation is not only a much stronger position than claiming that punishment presupposes intention, it is also a much more dubious claim. The first problem is that a sentencer rarely considers a particular amount of suffering or deprivation while meting out a punishment. To this it might perhaps be replied that the sentencer might engage in purely comparative considerations of the sort: more suffering or deprivation should be inflicted on A than on B. Still, this does not answer the deeper problem, namely, that it becomes totally irrelevant what actually happens to the one who is punished if all that matters is what was intended. This becomes particularly obvious in cases involving mistakes or misinformation.[12] Suppose that a sentencer for some reason regards the death penalty and a fine as equally severe punishments and consequently imposes these punishments on two perpetrators who have committed equally serious crimes. According to the suggested answer it follows that the two criminals have been equally severely punished; and this is so despite the fact that the one has suffered the loss of some money while the other is executed. Now, this cannot be a plausible view. Admittedly, the example is extreme, but I nonetheless believe it manages to establish that the idea of basing punishment severity solely on intended suffering or deprivation is defective.

References to intentions cannot do the job of distinguishing between the effects which are part of a punishment and those which are not. Are there other ways in which we could provide the required delimitation criterion? The only other answer I can think of also relates to the question of how a punishment should be defined. However, it does not relate to the standard definitions. On the contrary, one of the objections that have been directed against traditional definitions is that they ignore that a punishment possesses 'symbolic significance'. As put by Feinberg, who was one of the first to stress this point, a punishment is a device for the 'expression of attitudes of resentment and indignation, and of judgments of disapproval and reprobation'.[13] But if this is regarded as a necessary condition for something to count as a punishment then we have, it might be suggested, a reason for disregarding from the measurement of severity some of the consequences that might befall a person as a result of a sanction. For instance, if a person happens to break his/her leg in prison, the pain which this may cause would not be part of the punishment because it does not mediate any kind of condemnatory messages to the punished. Likewise, if someone as a result of a prison term loses family, job, or apartment, this may of course be extremely painful for the person who is affected, but this is nevertheless not a part of the punishment. The pain, so to speak, is not a message-conveying type of suffering. Following this approach, have we found a satisfactory way of delimiting punitive and non-punitive suffering and thus a way of identifying what should and what should not count in the assessment of punishment severity?

The answer is that this is not the case. On closer inspection such a suggestion is not convincing. As indicated, theorists advocating the idea that a punishment conveys a condemnatory message also believe that it is the hard treatment inflicted on the criminal that delivers this message. However since, as we have seen, a sanction may trigger long chains of events involving hardship for the punished person, the requirement to answer the challenge of delimitation is a criterion for when hardship communicates a message and when it does not serve this function. At this point the expressionist approach to punishment unfortunately is not very well developed and, what is more important, it is hard to imagine what a plausible answer would look like. To suggest that it is only the hardship which is intended by the sentencer to deliver a condemnatory message which actually serves this kind of function is not a sufficient answer. It leads into all the same kinds of problems we have just considered in relation to the intentionality clause. As a somewhat grotesque implication it would follow that, if a sentencer intends a certain amount of suffering to communicate a message to the criminal, if the criminal then actually undergoes more suffering while in prison, then one morning when this person wakes up in the cell he/she is no longer being punished because the hardship is now of a non-communicative nature; and this will be so even if the person still has to spend a long time in prison until the full time is served. To suggest, on the other hand, that whether hardship has a message-delivering function somehow depends on what the criminal believes was intended by the sentencer is also a position which gives rise to problems and which may in some cases not even succeed in drawing a threshold in the series of harmful events which might be triggered by a sanction (that is, if the punished person believes that all the suffering that befalls him/her was meant to communicate a message). Of course, more can be said on the complicated question as to what constitutes the necessary and sufficient conditions for communication. However, I shall not here engage further in this discussion. The task of explaining what part of the suffering that a sanction triggers should – due to its communicating function – be regarded as punitive suffering and which part should be regarded as extraneous to the punishment, falls upon the shoulders of those who wish to suggest that the delimitation challenge should be solved along these lines. However, for the present no explanation to this effect has been provided and, as indicated, solving this task may not be easy.

In sum, the attempt to deal with the challenge of delimitation on the ground of considerations of the definition of punishment did not seem to offer any simple solutions. Lacking any other candidates for a solution, it seems that the challenge of delimitation remains intact.

5.3   The problem of severity

What we have seen in the foregoing sections is that the concept of punishment severity, which at first sight appears unproblematic and which is usually applied without any hesitation, is much more complicated once we start digging below the surface. Initially it was suggested that the suffering and unpleasantness as well as the deprivation which a sanction causes is part of the severity of this punishment. This seems morally plausible, it is consistent with how we assess the gravity of other calamities that might befall us in our lives, and it accords both with standard definitions of punishment and – though space does not permit me to show this – with the basic idea of versions of retributive theories of punishment. However, such a conception of severity gave rise to two challenges, namely, that one and the same type of punishment may affect people very differently and consequently punish them with different degrees of severity and that a punishment may trigger long chains of suffering and deprivation which, in the absence of a plausible delimitation criterion, would have to figure in the computation of severity. And furthermore, as we have seen, it is hard to see how these implications can be avoided. But if this is correct what does it imply?

The first obvious implication concerns the allocation of punishment in penal practice. Much of the reasoning which takes place in criminal justice practice and which follows a proportionalist scheme may well be mistaken. For instance, reasoning within a criminal justice system may well take the following form: B, who is standing before the court, should be punished more severely than A, because last week A was sentenced to six months in prison and the crime committed by B is a little more serious than the one committed by A; therefore, B should be sentenced to eight months in prison. As mentioned, reasoning in criminal justice practice does not always follow a strict proportionalist scheme and there exist variations between different criminal justice systems with regard to what is regarded as valid reasoning. But it can hardly be disputed that this type of reasoning often plays an important role in criminal trials. However, if the foregoing considerations are correct, then this reasoning may well be flawed. It is based on a naïve comparison of punishments in name (eight months is a more severe punishment than six months, and so on). Or, conversely put, in the absence of answers to the outlined challenges it seems that if a criminal justice system really wishes to live up to proclaimed proportionality standards it will have to undergo comprehensive revisions in the way in which punishments are meted out.

The challenges, however, also have implications at a more basic theoretical level. As mentioned, the requirement of proportionality constitutes the basic principle of penal distribution in modern retributivist thinking. Faced with the challenge of differences in impact, the retributivist will either have to present a conception of punishment severity that does not open up the possibility of inter-personal (and intra-personal over time) differences in severity of the same sanction – an option which, as indicated, does not seem viable – or he/she will have to abandon the standard idea of proportionality in favour of a conception of the principle that accounts for such differences and which might thereby imply that the hardboiled criminal A receives two years in prison while the thin-skinned criminal B receives one year for the same infraction. However, this step is not without drawbacks. One of the traditional points of criticism which retributivists have directed against the utilitarian approach to punishment is that this approach implies a high degree of *individualization*. For instance, insofar as a punishment is supposed to work as some kind of treatment, it would have to be tailored to the needs of the individual criminal. Likewise, in order to restrain potential recidivists, the punishment would have to be suited to the risk the individual criminal poses to the public. In contrast, retributivists have often presented the principle of proportionality as a way of avoiding the problems of individualization in penal distribution. However, for the retributivist who gives in and accepts individual differences in severity of the same sanction, this advantage no longer exists. Even though utilitarians would have their eyes on a different set of consequences, the retributivist will have to adjust the allocation of punishment to the ways in which each individual criminal is affected. Now, the point of emphasizing this is not to suggest that individualization *itself* constitutes a moral problem but rather to underline that the virtue of simplicity in application – often underscored by retributivists as a major advantage of the principle of proportionality, in contrast to a utilitarian approach to penal distribution – is no longer obvious.

A simple reply for the retributivist would of course be to reject that simplicity in application itself constitutes a theoretical virtue. However, this far from leaves the retributivist on firm ground. The implications of the challenges are more far-reaching than that. The first thing that should be noted is that the retributivist cannot just accept the implications of the challenge of delimitation. In order to avoid all those harmful consequences which, in a particularly unfortunate case, might be triggered by a minor fine being taken into account in the assessment of the severity of this punishment – or, in another admittedly extreme example, that we cannot, in a case where a certain punishment triggers a life-long series of harmful events, estimate the severity of this punishment until the punished person is dead and thus no longer affected – the retributivist will have to face the challenge of delimitating punitive suffering. Biting the bullet does not seem an option. And, when it comes to the challenge of differences in impact, even the revision-minded retributivist faces a more profound theoretical problem. To see this we will have to take a closer look at the idea of proportionality.

In order for the retributivist to provide genuine guidance with regard to how severely different crimes should be punished, it is not sufficient merely to maintain that a demand of *ordinal* proportionality should be observed. That is, it will not do merely to contend that more serious crimes should be more severely punished and that equally serious crimes should be met with punishments of the same degree of severity. For instance, if A has committed a crime that is more serious than the one committed by B, then ordinal proportionality is observed if A gets a $10 fine and B gets a $5 fine, but also if A receives the death penalty while B ends up in prison for life. In other words, insofar as we wish for guidance, with regard to the distribution of punishment, more is required than mere ordinal proportionality prescriptions: the retributivist will have to engage in considerations on how specific crimes and punishments should be paired. The answer that has been presented by retributivists who have taken up this challenge is that one should construct a scale of the gravity of different crimes and, correspondingly, a scale of the severity of different punishments and subsequently link the two scales. Different answers have been provided with regard to how precisely this linking should take place. According to one approach, the two scales should be linked at the poles (that is, the most serious crime and the most severe punishment as the upper anchor point, and the least serious crime and the least severe punishment as the lower anchor point). Following another suggestion, the two scales should be anchored only at a lower point determined on the ground of considerations on crime prevention. However, no matter which anchoring theory the retributivist advocates, the whole scheme is doomed to fail. What we have learnt in the foregoing discussion concerning differences in impact is precisely that it does not make sense to talk about *one* scale of punishment severity. One year in prison is not an equally severe punishment for different persons on whom this sanction is imposed. On the contrary, this sanction as well as any other sanction is most likely to have both subjectively and objectively variable effects on different persons. But if that is so, where does this leave the retributivist? As far as I can see there are only two answers available, neither of which seems convincing. The first possibility is to give in and accept that one cannot operate on a general scale of punishment severity and to admit that, for each criminal, one will have to work out an individual scale of punishment severity on the ground of which the anchoring can be carried out. This possibility, which basically amounts to constructing separate criminal laws for each criminal in a society, will not – I think – be regarded as attractive from a retributivist perspective. The other possibility is to maintain that one should employ a general scale of punishment severity and that this scale should be constructed on the ground of standardization; that is, on the ground of how severe the punishments on the scale typically are for the persons on whom they are imposed. However, as we have seen earlier, if what basically matters in terms of severity is something that allows for individual differences between different persons, then it will not do merely to adopt a scale measuring standard severity. This jump from what matters to something else certainly requires some sort of moral justification, which is not provided simply by the fact that this seems required in order to make the retributivist penal distribution scheme work in the first place. And, as mentioned, no argument to this effect has been provided. Thus, not only the challenge of delimitation but also the challenge of differences in impact seem to cause severe theoretical problems by apparently blocking the route to genuine guidance with regard to how different crimes should in the end be punished.

In sum, what has been argued in this paper is that the comparison of punishment in severity, which both in penal practice and penal theory is usually treated as almost unproblematic, gives rise to serious problems. Two challenges have been identified, the challenge of difference in impact and the challenge of delimitation. In the absence of morally plausible ways of dealing with these challenges, it follows that criminal justice systems operating with some degree of proportionality will have to undergo serious revisions and that the whole idea – strongly underlined in this retributively dominated modern area within penal theory – that the principle of proportionality constitutes an operational distribution principle that succeeds in closing the gap between penal theory and penal practice, falls apart. As mentioned, it is noteworthy how little has been said about severity in modern discussions on punishment. Even those theorists who have done most to explore the idea of proportionality in punishing have not provided anything close to fully developed accounts of severity. However, as the foregoing considerations establish, the time has come in which to start taking seriously the concept of punishment severity.

Notes

1. A. von Hirsch (1991), 'Proportionality in the Philosophy of Punishment: From "Why Punish?" to "How Much?"', *Israel Law Review*, vol. 25.
2. See, for instance, N. Morris and M. Tonry (1990), *Between Prison and Probation* (New York: Oxford University Press).
3. See M. Davis (1992), *To Make the Punishment Fit the Crime* (United States of America: Westview Press), p. 6; or J. Ryberg (2004), *The Ethics of Proportionate Punishment* (Dordrecht: Kluwer Academic Publishers), 'Introduction'.
4. See, for instance, A. Kolber, 'The Subjective Experience of Punishment', *Columbia Law Review* (January 2009), p. 6–7.
5. J. Bentham (1988), *The Principles of Morals and Legislation* (Amherst, New York: Prometheus Books), chap. 13, para. 14 (p. 182).
6. A. von Hirsch and A. Ashworth (2005), *Proportionate Sentencing* (Oxford: Oxford University Press), 147.
7. Ibid.
8. See also J. Ryberg, *The Ethics of Proportionate Punishment*, chapter 3.
9. A. von Hirsch and A. Ashworth, *Proportionate Sentencing*, p. 148.
10. A. Kolber, 'The Subjective Experience of Punishment', Part 3.
11. H. L. A. Hart (1968), *Punishment and Responsibility* (Great Britain: Clarendon Press), p. 5.
12. See J. Ryberg, *The Ethics of Proportionate Punishment*, 112ff.
13. J. Feinberg (1970), 'The Expressive Function of Punishment', *Doing and Deserving* (Princeton: Princeton University Press), 98.

6
Punishment and Forgiveness

Leo Zaibert

Among the different possible reactions to (perceived)[1] wrongdoing, two have monopolized philosophical attention: punishment and forgiveness. Reacting to wrongdoing with indifference, or with elation, may be interesting case-studies for psychologists, but not so much for philosophers. Punishment and forgiveness are, moreover, customarily taken to be mutually exclusive: you cannot punish and forgive simultaneously. It is quite possible to first punish someone, only to later forgive her. But it does seem difficult to argue that we can simultaneously punish and forgive the same person for the same action.

I think all of the above is fundamentally correct. If it is, however, then a problem immediately presents itself: whenever punishment is justified, forgiveness would *a fortiori* be unjustified, and vice-versa. To the extent that part, at least, of what justifies punishment is that it is deserved, it seems that then it would never be right to (synchronically) forgive someone who deserved punishment. But the suggestion that we can 'forgive' someone who did not deserve to be punished seems odd – for if the person is not guilty (that is, deserving of punishment) what exactly are we 'forgiving'?

There is, then, an interesting difference between the philosophical treatment of these two phenomena. However difficult – and difficult it surely is – the justification of punishment has always been taken to be at least a tractable problem; the justification of forgiveness, on the other hand, has appeared downright paradoxical.[2] Either what appears as a candidate of forgiveness is spurious (when in fact the 'forgivee' was not guilty, not deserving of punishment), or we are *unjustified* in forgiving her. For these reasons, some have argued that forgiveness is never justified.[3] I would like to explore here a hitherto unnoticed commonality between punishment and forgiveness which would allow us to see not only how forgiveness can sometimes be justified, but also how punishment and forgiveness are in closer conceptual proximity than typically recognized.

In what follows I will argue, first, that both regarding the justification of punishment and of forgiveness we need to pay attention to the notion of fittingness, in addition to the notion of desert. Second, I will argue that by admitting the existence of fittingness, we are forced to realize that the values that are important for the justification of punishment and forgiveness are more variegated than usually acknowledged. Third, I will suggest that the justification of punishment faces, in some cases, a difficulty which is quite similar to the so-called 'paradox' of forgiveness. Fourth, I will argue that both punishment and forgiveness bear structural resemblances to another famous problem in moral philosophy: the well-known problem of dirty hands. Finally, notwithstanding these resemblances, punishment and forgiveness seem to travel in the opposite normative direction from that exhibited by traditional dirty hands cases. Forgiveness and (at least some cases of) punishment constitute what I shall call problems of clean hands.

6.1   Fittingness and desert

In some ways, the discussion of punishment can be seen as a battleground on which the forces of deontological and teleological comprehensive ethical doctrines fight their wars. And just as it is difficult to reconcile deontological and teleological ethical doctrines in general, so it is in the case of punishment – or even more, since punishing a wrongdoer is causing her suffering, this is particularly difficult to justify. Famously, justifications of punishment break into two camps: consequentialist and retributive. Consequentialists justify the infliction of suffering on the basis of some expected consequences (say, deterrence, rehabilitation, or incapacitation) which would outweigh this suffering. Retributivists, on the other hand, seek to justify the infliction of suffering along the lines that the wrongdoer deserves to suffer. There, exist, too, and as one would have expected, all sorts of mixed justifications, which seek to combine the attractive aspects of each of the two camps – but I do not think that they fare well.[4]

Without taking sides regarding the different justifications of punishment, I would like to focus briefly on the notion of desert, which seems to play an inescapable role in the justification of punishment. Desert has been perceived by some to be so terribly mysterious that it cannot be of any use.[5] Despite the complications surrounding this notion most authors agree, however, that '[m]ost desert claims have moral force, in the sense that they are prima facie ought claims: the fact that someone deserves something means that she ought, other things being equal, to receive that thing'.[6] Thus, in many cases, desert is seen as very close to justice: to give people what they deserve is, other things equals, to treat them justly.

In fact, more than one author has suggested that the idea that punishment should only be inflicted on the deserving is so important that it should in fact be part of the very definition of punishment.[7] While I agree that desert is very important, and that whatever turns out to be the correct justification of punishment will have to include references to what wrongdoers deserve, I believe that including desert in the definition of punishment is inconvenient. For doing this renders punishment either justified by definition (if you have strong retributive inclinations), or else desert-based retributivism is problematically reduced to a merely semantic thesis concerning the meaning of the word 'punishment'.[8]

Something similar to desert, however, does belong in the definition of punishment: fittingness.[9] If you think that you should punish a wrongdoer, then, purely as a conceptual matter, you must believe that it is fitting that you do so. By calling a course of action 'fitting' we suggest that it is the appropriate thing to do, morally *or otherwise*. Admittedly, fittingness and desert are similar – some authors claim that desert is 'a sort of "fittingness"'.[10] But they are also importantly different. Desert claims are more likely to issue in action, that is, in the action of giving people what they deserve, than fittingness claims. An analogy with a famous discussion in the philosophy of mind may be helpful. Just as my intention to run a marathon is likelier to cause me to actually run a marathon than my mere desire to run a marathon, my belief that someone deserves punishment is likelier to *cause* me to actually punish him than my belief that it is fitting that he be punished.[11]

The justificatory force of fittingness is thus, in this regard, humbler than that of desert. Rarely fittingness alone justifies punishment (or any other action, for that matter), whereas desert, at least for many retributivists, is by itself capable of justifying punishment. Even non-retributivists would admit that desert plays an important role in justifying punishment. This is of course not to say that fittingness is utterly unimportant in terms of the *ultima facie* justification of punishment – I am discussing it here precisely because it is important, even if in some ways less important than desert. But in a different way fittingness is more far-reaching than desert. Fittingness is broader than desert in that desert seems to be wholly at home within the moral (or ethical – I use 'morality' and 'ethics' interchangeably) context, as opposed to other normative contexts, whereas fittingness spans a larger swath of the normative universe.

Consider examples of actions that are fitting without being deserved. Imagine you have a tennis match with a colleague who has a serious illness; you and your colleague were evenly matched until the illness. No one knows whether she will regain her earlier form in tennis. It seems fitting that you graciously (without making it obvious) play slightly less competitively, so as to not make her feel worse. But it seems equally clear that she does not *deserve* that you play less hard. One may want to argue that this is just to be kind, or polite, but then again, kindness and politeness would just be forms of fittingness. To be fitting is to be somehow appropriate, even if this appropriateness is not deserved, or even if we also have other names to this fittingness. Consider other cases. It is fitting that Susan, a very nice human being, wins the lottery, or that Kevin, a very nasty human being, has his car stolen. And I think it is again clear that neither does Susan deserve to win the lottery nor Kevin deserves to have his car stolen. And yet it is fitting when nice things happen to nice people, and bad things happen to bad people – independently of whether or not these things are deserved.

The ultimate justification of actions, in general, needs to take account not only of desert, but of fittingness as well; and the same applies to punishment and forgiveness in particular.

6.2 Taking values seriously

A sceptical reader may at this point object to my distinction between desert and fittingness by saying that it unnecessarily complicates matters. The distinction I have presented, the sceptic continues, is at bottom only a reminder that values can conflict, and that my using unusual names to refer to these values is not particularly helpful. In response, while I admit that this is a matter of different types of values, I still think that recognizing the existence of fittingness as such is of considerable importance. For it reveals that the *sorts* of values which can come into conflict when we justify our actions are more variegated than typically assumed. Fittingness' breadth entails that, as I will argue below, there could be conflicts between moral and other sorts of values, and sometimes these other values trump the moral ones.

The main other type of value I have in mind is aesthetic, though I am also interested in the unduly ignored class of charientic values. Over two decades ago, Joel Feinberg pointed to 'an astute but little known article by Peter Glassen', where Glassen coined the term charientic to refer to a class of values which were, in his opinion, neither ethical nor aesthetic.[12] Unfortunately, Feinberg's engagement with the charientic did not usher in significant work on this other type of value. According to Glassen, these sorts of judgments are related to vulgarity; his examples include picking one's nose and chewing gum.[13] But while Glassen admits that 'the problems of the general theory of value will require for their solution an understanding of charientic judgments just as much as of ethical and aesthetic judgments',[14] he seemed more concerned with proving that these other sorts of values exist, rather than with examining the conflicts between moral and non-moral values.

Similarly, even Feinberg, who discusses charientic values in the context of examining the moral limits of the criminal law, refers to them only when he discusses offences, and not harms. That is, Feinberg considers them 'miscellany', and not on a par with the more serious harms.[15] Like Glassen, Feinberg is above all interested in explaining how these different axiological realms exist, and not in examining conflicts between values belonging to these different realms. This is particularly interesting in light of the fact that Feinberg admits that, for example, while the term 'decent' has obvious ethical implications, it was originally a charientic term.[16]

In contrast to both Glassen and Feinberg, I would like to deploy the tension between fittingness and desert in order to shed light on a series of recalcitrant and difficult moral conundrums. The term 'decent' is particularly useful for my purposes, for, as Feinberg points out, its etymology links it to the idea of fittingness.[17] And I shall argue that, in some cases, not forgiving the guilty is indecent (unfitting) to such a high degree that the right course of action is to grant forgiveness. Focusing on the case of forgiveness is particularly helpful in that its justification is taken to be extraordinarily complicated – and complicated regardless of whether one is a consequentialist or a retributivist.

Imagine you are a consequentialist confronted with the case of a Mafia boss who has committed many crimes. If you punish him, however, his associates would wreak havoc in your city, thus causing immense suffering. As a result you decide to 'forgive' him. As Claudia Card has noted, freeing the Mafioso on these sorts of consequentialist grounds does not seem like forgiveness at all.[18] Similarly, to let a prisoner walk free hoping that she would lead you to a 'bigger fish', or, in war, to free a prisoner hoping that the enemy will free one of your comrades in return is not to forgive them.

Now imagine you are a retributivist; you justify punishing the Mafioso simply because he deserves it – you don't need anything more. What could possibly justify your forgiving him? Nothing, it seems. And this is of course the reason behind the sort of grandiloquent mystic talk which surrounds the discussion of the justification of forgiveness: 'there is only forgiveness, if there is any, where there is the unforgivable. That is to say that forgiveness must announce itself as impossibility itself'.[19] 'Forgiveness', Jacques Derrida continues, 'is thus mad. It must plunge, but lucidly, into the night of the unintelligible'.[20]

It appears, then, that whether you are a retributivist or a consequentialist you cannot possibly justify forgiveness. One option at this stage is to bite the bullet and admit that forgiveness is never justified (and in fact always wrong), say, as John Kekes says: '[r]easonable blame is incompatible with forgiveness'.[21] Since I believe that *some* instances of forgiveness are not merely justified, but downright admirable, I would like to resist this move.

But resisting is difficult, for when you forgive someone you simultaneously believe that the person should be punished for what she did, and that *you* should not punish her. But this seems paradoxical.[22] After all, if you believe punishment to be justified – and, moreover, if you would not mind it if someone (or something) else were to make this wrongdoer suffer to the degree that she deserves – it remains mysterious why you would forgive rather than punish. In other words, if you admit that punishment is appropriate, why don't you then go ahead and punish?

The careful reader will by now anticipate my answer to this question: the distinction between fittingness and desert explains how situations like the above are possible and even justified. In cases such as these, we do not consider *our* punishing the deserving to be fitting. These are cases in which desert and fittingness come into conflict; and these sorts of cases are not unfamiliar: I may be morally entitled to demand that you pay that small debt you owe me, and I may refuse to so demand it, simply because I find it unfitting to do so; you may in fact deserve that I publicly expose your arrogance, and I may still refuse to expose you, because I find it unfitting to do so. Cases of forgiveness are simply one form of this larger and familiar sort of situation. I forgive you when I refuse to punish you because I find it unfitting to give you the punishment that you deserve. And if I am correct in believing that in this case fittingness trumps desert, then I am, furthermore, justified in forgiving you.

6.3 Punishment and the political

Even if you agree with all of the above, however, you may still object to my position by arguing that at best it serves to clarify aspects of forgiveness, but not to show similarities between forgiveness and punishment, which is what I had set out to do. Conflicts between fittingness and desert when we forgive, the objector may continue, do not arise within the context of punishment. If such objection were correct, my appeal to the distinction between fittingness and desert, rather than showing a commonality between punishment and forgiveness, would reveal yet another difference between these two responses to wrongdoing. A brief answer to this reading of my thesis is simply to ask back why should punishment be conceived as immune to these sorts of conflicts – for, as noted above, the tension between fittingness and desert arises in many sorts of cases, not only in cases of forgiveness. But, of course, I would like to engage more substantially with the objection, by presenting cases in which these sorts of conflict occur in the context of punishment as well.

Consider an argument against the death penalty I have defended elsewhere.[23] There is something wrong about a state which kills people, even if all of this state's victims deserve to be killed. In other words, you do not need to deny that someone deserves to die for what she did in order to oppose the death penalty. To bolster my argument I appealed to the following thought experiment. Imagine a really heinous crime, say, Bob raping and killing a one-year-old baby; let us stipulate that Bob deserves to be punished by death. Now imagine John, who does the same thing as Bob, except that he rapes repeatedly, and then kills the baby slowly and in the cruelest way possible, all in front of the baby's parents, and so on. If Bob, *ex hypothesi*, deserved death, John deserves something worse than death. (I take it that it is obvious that some things are harder to endure than death – it seems hard to deny that the combination of great suffering and death is worse than death without the suffering.)

But agreeing that someone who commits a crime revealing unspeakable cruelty may deserve more than death, say, that he may deserve to be tortured, does not, I think, commit us to asserting that our criminal justice system should be reformed in such a way that people who deserve to be tortured should in fact be tortured. That is, we may cogently oppose torture even of those who deserve it. We may not want to have a perfectly calibrated system whereby for each degree of wickedness a criminal has displayed we would add a degree of severity to his punishment.

Quite clearly, the degree of wickedness humans are capable of showing is probably infinite. That is, whatever you can imagine as the most wicked action, you can also imagine adding something to it which would make it more wicked, *ad infinitum*. But increases in the severity of the punishment that we are willing to inflict on wrongdoers are not infinite.[24]

It follows, then, that even if you are a full-blown retributivist, you may in fact allow limits to your retributivism. In particular, I would like to argue that there are upward limits to what we should, in the final analysis, do to wrongdoers. To torture people, even if they deserve to be tortured seems beyond the pale. Of course, my argument against the death penalty is incomplete in the sense that I have not yet proven that death is beyond the pale – I have not proven that torture is beyond the pale either. But the argument is sufficient for my purposes here, in that it does suggest, strongly, that *some* things are beyond the pale.[25] And what, in our current context, does it mean to say that something is 'beyond the pale'? It means, among other things, that we will never want to do it, and that will refuse to do it, even if someone deserved to have this done to him. And why would we refuse to do it in a case in which we admit that the person does deserve to have this done to him? We would so refuse, I submit, because we find doing this sufficiently unfitting so as to effectively negate the desert judgment.

Still, some may, while agreeing that there are limits to what we would want the state to do to criminals, deny that we need to appeal to fittingness in the way that I have done so. For, they may argue, what explains our unwillingness to have state punishments which are too severe (even if they are deserved), is a series of other moral, and, above all, political principles. Thus, one could explain this unwillingness by appealing to the inherent dignity of human life,[26] or to a certain epistemological humility that even the most extreme retributivist should exhibit,[27] or to the idea that desert claims constitute only prima facie obligations.[28] More frequently we find appeals to principles of political philosophy which seek to curb the state's punitive power.

I do not doubt that these explanations are possible, and indeed important. But if appealing to them entailed excluding fittingness from consideration, then I would resist them. After all, if we examine what the ultimate bases for these principles are, we will encounter appeals to fittingness again. Just reflect on the myriad occasions in which, outside the political sphere, we refuse to do certain things to others, even if we are perfectly entitled to do them, and even when those others deserve that we treat them in the very way in which we refuse to act. (Think again about the examples mentioned above when we refuse to demand payment of a small debt, or when we refuse to publicly humiliate our showboating colleague even when he deserves to be exposed, and so on) It seems hard to appeal to political principles in these cases, since the context is clearly apolitical.

It is, then, precisely the distinction between fittingness and desert which explains, in part at least, the underlying structure of some of these dilemmas. They are not merely moral dilemmas, insofar as the notion of fittingness is not an exclusively moral notion. We sometimes refuse to remind an acquaintance of a small debt, because we find it *ugly* or *vulgar* or *indecent* or *disagreeable* to do it. We sometimes refuse to expose other people's vices, because we simply do not like being the sort of person who does that. Our refusal is the result of our thinking that doing this is aesthetically, or charientically, wrong, even if not morally wrong. Independently of whatever political or pragmatic considerations against the state inflicting too severe punishments, there exist considerations exclusively linked to fittingness.

The impasse between what is deserved and what is fitting has led many to suggest that forgiveness is either necessarily unjustifiable, or utterly mysterious. But, as it turns out, this impasse is visible in cases of punishment as well, even though the explanation as to why it is appropriate for the state not to punish with the full severity called for by desert has not been surrounded by a similar halo of mystery. Admittedly, in cases of punishment the tension between fittingness and desert is never resolved by fully trumping what desert dictates, although we do limit and curb what desert dictates we do to wrongdoers because punishing in full would be too unfitting. But although not to the same degree as in forgiveness, the tension is also present in cases of punishment.

If I am right in this, then punishment and forgiveness are much closer together than typically believed; they occupy different places along a continuum going from complete (or almost complete) coincidence between what is deserved and what is fitting to cases in which what is deserved is completely (or almost completely) at odds with what is fitting. And, as I wish to argue below, the distinction between fittingness and desert is also helpful in placing both punishment and forgiveness in close conceptual proximity with another famous type of moral dilemma: the problem of dirty hands.

6.4 Punishment, forgiveness, and dirty hands

The problem of dirty hands is commonly taken to be a problem of political philosophy or at least of political morality, characterized by the difficult choices politicians often face.[29] I do not wish to deny that, as Michael Walzer points out, the problem of dirty hands 'is frequently discussed in the literature of political action – in novels and plays dealing with politics',[30] or that it is, moreover, 'posed most dramatically in politics'.[31] Most of the philosophical literature on dirty hands indeed focuses on political contexts. As an empirical observation, it may, perhaps, be true that politicians are more prone to face dirty hands problems, or that the dirty hands problems that politicians face are more interesting (or 'dramatic') than those faced by private citizens in their private lives.

But, just as I suggested in the cases of punishment and forgiveness, we should, in the case of dirty hands resist the obscuring effect that political principles may have upon the existence of something as basic (and apolitical) as the tension between fittingness and desert. Walzer himself admits that 'we can get our hands dirty in private life also, and sometimes, no doubt, we should'.[32] As a matter of fact, Walzer is emphatic in that he does not 'want to argue that it [the problem of dirty hands] is only a political dilemma'.[33] Part of this obscuring effect is that if we situate the discussion entirely within the political context, the dilemma tends to too quickly transform into the tension between sticking to a moral principle and averting a great calamity.[34] Quite often the discussion of dirty hands is presented in the context of torture, by political actors, to attain political ends. And these ends tend to be extreme: say, ticking bomb scenarios somehow poignantly stacking the deck in favour of doing whatever is necessary in order to avoid a bomb going off and killing countless innocent victims.

One risk of this sort of approach is that it renders the conceptual contours of the problem of dirty hands too fuzzy. That is, this approach makes it harder to distinguish the problem of dirty hands from other sorts of situations in which choosing is (psychologically) very difficult, or cases in which deciding is painful. Consider paradigmatic moral tragedies such as 'Sophie's Choice' scenarios (where a person, at gun point, is forced to choose between the death of one of her two children), or 'lifeboat' situations (in which, in order to protect life, one is forced to throw innocent people overboard), or killing in self-defense.[35] Naturally, most people would feel bad about sacrificing an innocent person, or about choosing which one of their children should be killed – and even about killing in self-defense. But the awfulness of this feeling is not by itself constitutive of the sort of moral dilemma essential to dirty hands. Sophie, say, did not do anything wrong – and doing wrong as we do the right thing is the essence of dirty hands.

Non-dirty hands cases of this sort are akin to cases in which a doctor needs to amputate a limb, or abort a foetus, in order to save the patient's life. Sure, the doctor may regret that the limb had to be amputated, or that the foetus had to be aborted, but she would be just silly if she somehow felt, in a deep sense, guilt. And deep guilt is precisely what, in standard cases of dirty hands, those having done the right thing are supposed to feel. The person who gets her hands dirty should feel deeply guilty about having chosen to do the right thing.[36]

Of course there is here plenty of room for scepticism regarding the cogency of the standard case of the problem of dirty hands. If you did the right thing, why should you nonetheless feel guilty about it? A robust, sensible moral theory, the sceptic would insist, should make clear that if a given course of action is the right thing to do, this precludes feeling *guilty* about doing it. Merely as a matter of moral phenomenology, however, I think that dirty hands situations do exist (in and out of politics), and that their existence is not simply a matter of our not being mature enough to understand them, or about our moral theories being somehow defective.

In order to assuage the sceptic, however, we need to better explain the sense in which guilt is crucial for the dirty hands problem. To that effect, let us consider a couple of Walzer's examples. Walzer describes, first, a case of a decent politician running for office who nonetheless makes questionable deals with shady characters. Second, Walzer describes a politician who won an election on a platform of appeasing his country finds himself in a position whereby if he tortured a person, he would dramatically advance the noble agenda for which he was in effect elected, and who chooses to torture a man.

Referring specifically to the man in the first example (though the description is equally applicable to both men), Walzer tells us:

> Because he has scruples of this sort, we know him to be a good man. But we view the campaign in a certain light, estimate its importance in a certain way, and hope that he will overcome his scruples and make the deal. It is important to stress that we don't want just anyone to make the deal; we want *him* to make it, precisely because he has scruples about it. We know he is doing right when he makes the deal because he knows he is doing wrong. I don't mean merely that he will feel badly or even very badly after he makes the deal. If he is the good man I am imagining him to be, he will feel guilty, that is, he will believe himself to be guilty. That is what it means to have dirty hands.[37]

So, dirty hands is not just a matter of feeling bad, of regretting that some things had to be done, in the sense in which one can also feel sad and regretful that some things have simply happened. Dirty hands requires that one feels guilty – that one feels *really* guilty.

But Walzer puts this curiously, for he says that we 'want' politicians facing dirty hands dilemmas to make the choice; we 'want' them to have scruples, and thus we 'want' them to really feel guilty about doing what is right. I would like to unpack why Walzer talks about what *we* 'want' the politicians to do and feel. I think that it is precisely because he focuses so much on the political context that Walzer can get away with this oblique way of describing the choice of the politician. The political context attenuates the need to explain what we want politicians to do and feel – and why. Walzer writes from the perspective of the electorate, of those who are considering voting for these politicians, and thus he can focus on what we want them to do and feel, instead of focusing on the dilemma the politician faces in itself.

Similarly, Bernard Williams, in one of his characteristically penetrating articles, and while, like Walzer, admitting that dilemmas such as those posed by dirty hands are not the monopoly of the political, still seems to give political expediencies too much prominence. For as he discusses dirty hands he says 'only those who are reluctant or disinclined to do the morally disagreeable when it is really necessary have much chance of not doing it when it is not necessary'.[38] Not only do these words seem concerned above all with politicians, but they somehow seek to justify getting one's hands dirty by some sort of utilitarian calculus tied to political practicalities. We want politicians to feel bad about doing certain things, because doing these things is rarely the right thing to do; so, these feelings function, for Williams, as an insurance policy of sorts.

Still, the full import of saying that we 'want' people to do certain things in certain ways, or, with Williams, that we *'morally* want'[39] them to do certain things in certain ways, remains elusive. To say that we 'want' the politician to do so-and-so, it seems to me, is to say that this is the right thing to do; and when we say that we 'want' him to feel bad about doing the right thing, is because this is the right way of doing it. The beginning of wisdom regarding dirty hands cases – as well as cases of forgiveness and some cases of punishment – is that we are, in effect, simultaneously evaluating the action and the actor. Imagine, however, a doctor who enjoys amputating limbs; she only amputates them when it is medically obligatory to do so in order to save patients' lives, but when she performs these amputations, she does not feel any sadness at all – she actually laughs out loud, and makes fun of the amputee's new appearance. While we approve of the doctor's action, we disapprove of the way in which she did it. The doctor saved the patient's life but she evidently is a bad person. But even if we imagine a doctor who felt appropriate grief about amputating limbs, we will not thereby be in the presence of a dirty hands case. We can simultaneously evaluate the action and the actor in all sorts of situations. Cases of this sort, however, are helpful in delineating some neglected conceptual contours of cases of dirty hands, forgiveness and punishment.

The explanation afforded by the distinction between fittingness and desert makes it clear that whenever fittingness and desert are in (a certain type of) conflict, then we can say that one and the same thing is the right (in one sense) and wrong (in another sense) thing to do. The problem of dirty hands is but a type of conflict between desert (or justice) and fittingness, just as forgiveness and (some cases of) punishment are. In addition to speaking about the moral fibre of the person facing a dirty hands dilemma, guilt serves as a heuristic device, revealing the very existence of the dilemma. The dilemma obtains whenever fittingness and desert are in tension, whether or not the agent is aware of this tension. Of course, being alive to these sorts of tensions is a good thing, and perhaps particularly good for politicians to exhibit. But often lost in the shuffle of discussing dramatic cases in political decision-making is that the talk of our wanting' the politicians to feel guilty about doing precisely what we 'wanted' them to do anyhow, points to the fact that a *decent* person would realize that she is doing something which is simultaneously the right thing to do and the wrong thing to do. To have scruples, in Walzer's sense, is to exhibit decency.

The appeal to decency, with its etymological connection to fittingness, suggests a solution to the problem of dirty hands (and of forgiveness and punishment): once again the distinction between desert and fittingness comes to our aid, saving us from what would otherwise be too intractable a paradox. Dirty hands cases are such that desert (here understood in its connection to justice) and fittingness come into conflict. From the purely ethical perspective of desert, to win the election (via shady deals) and to attain peace (in part via torturing people), are the right things to do – but both are unfitting.

Consider the example of torture. I would like to suggest that torturing someone is *always* unfitting. There is no need, I hope, to provide details in order to argue that the inherent unfittingness of witnessing someone whose fingernails are being pulled out is not obliterated by anything else that you may know about the case. The scene, by itself, is disgusting – because it is unfitting.[40] Perhaps knowing that pulling out this person's fingernails is the only way of diffusing an atomic bomb in the heart of New York City, or that it is the only way to give this person his deserved punishment (say, for having himself pulled out millions of fingernails in the cruelest of ways), may affect our final assessment as to whether or not this specific man's fingernails ought to be pulled out. But the unfittingness of pulling fingernails, as such, would not disappear. The sight of a torturer causing unspeakable suffering to a helpless person is, by itself, repugnant – even if, given some rather unique and uncommon sets of circumstances, we may be willing to acquiesce with this repugnant act being done.

The emphasis on the political may make it difficult to see that, at bottom, what we have in cases of dirty hands is a conflict between desert and fittingness. Let us return to Walzer.

> Consider a well-known defense from Shakespeare's *Hamlet* that has often reappeared in political literature: 'I must be cruel only to be kind.' The words are spoken on an occasion when Hamlet is actually being cruel to his mother. I will leave aside the possibility that she deserves to hear (to be forced to listen to) every harsh word he utters, for Hamlet himself makes no such claim-and if she did indeed deserve that, his words might not be cruel or he might not be cruel for speaking them.[41]

Walzer at least entertains the possibility that if Hamlet's mother deserved to hear Hamlet's harsh words, then he would *thereby* not be cruel. Insofar as cruelty is always unfitting, Walzer's position may, perhaps, be taken to imply that to the extent that people deserved certain treatment, then, if we gave them what they deserved, no dirty hands problems would arise. It is possible, however, that even if Hamlet's mother deserved to hear these harsh words, it would be unfitting for Hamlet to utter them. If because of this unfittingness, Hamlet were to refrain from saying these words, we could say that he thereby forgave his mother. Of course, if Hamlet were to utter these words because he thought his mother deserved to suffer by hearing them, we could say that he thereby punished his mother.

In other words, both when we treat cruelly, or at least inflict suffering on, someone who deserves such treatment (punishment) and when we refuse to treat cruelly, or at least inflict suffering on, someone who deserves to be so treated (forgiveness), we would be in the presence of a conflict between fittingness and desert. And we would be, too, in the presence of a dirty hands problem. Punishment and forgiveness can thus be profitably seen as types of dirty hands problems – though as peculiar types, as I shall show next.

6.5   The clean hands problem and normative remainders

In traditional dirty hands problems the conflict between fittingness and desert is of the following sort: we sometimes do what we ought to do, even if it is ugly; or, in other words, we do what is deserved (or just) even if it is unfitting. That is, in all of the traditional examples of dirty hand problems, what is deserved (or just) trumps what would be fitting to do. Since the unfittingness of that which we do is not normatively insignificant, we have a dilemma – and since often we are aware of this dilemma, we may experience the guilt of which Walzer and others characteristically speak.

Now, it seems to me that in both forgiveness and the cases of punishment discussed above (namely, those in which even retributivists would accept limiting, because of considerations having to with fittingness, the amount of deserved punishment that will be meted out) we do what we find fitting, even knowing that we thereby disregard what desert entails. We know that our forgivee in effect deserves to be punished (and thus not justifiably forgiven). Similarly, when we refuse to punish to the full extent that people deserve, we are letting fittingness win out in its tension with desert. We do this because we find it just too unfitting to do otherwise.

Thus, both forgiveness and some instances of punishment share something important with traditional dirty hands problems: the tension between desert and fittingness. The main difference between these cases of punishment and cases of forgiveness, on the one hand, and traditional dirty hands problems, on the other, is that with the former fittingness holds sway, as it were, whereas in the latter desert (or justice) holds sway. In dirty hands problems we 'want' people to feel bad for doing the right thing; in forgiveness and some cases of punishment we 'want' people to feel good for doing the wrong thing.

I have of course not here attempted to indicate whether in this or that particular case fittingness or desert should hold sway. It would be, of course, an eminently worthwhile enterprise to investigate this point further, though I am rather sceptical that a fully effective formula could possibly be devised – for this is not, I think, a problem amenable to a formulaic solution. It was, in any case, not one of my goals to solve these normative dilemmas. What has been my goal here is to show

how, first, forgiveness and (some instances of) punishment have much more in common with each other than hitherto noticed, and, second, how forgiveness and these instances of punishment share quite a bit more than hitherto noticed with traditional instances of the problem of dirty hands. I believe that the distinction between fittingness and desert allows us to at least understand these problems better. While I suspect that this better understanding shall redound in progress regarding solutions to these problems, I still value the understanding in and of itself.

One particularly interesting consequence of taking fittingness seriously is that insofar as the normativity of fittingness is not limited to morality, it turns out that that in order to deal with dirty hands problems, and in order to justify punishment and forgiveness, we will by necessity have to appeal (in varying degrees) to non-moral forms of normativity, such as aesthetic and charientic normativity. Throughout his article, Williams eloquently talks about *moral* costs and *moral* remainders, and his discussion aptly suggests that morality really is a complex affair. But Williams did not engage with the possibility of aesthetic or charientic costs and remainders, or with the fact that these costs and remainders can cut across different normative realms. Some actions may be morally required and nonetheless have aesthetic and carienthic costs and remainders; some works of art may be aesthetically praiseworthy and nonetheless have ethical and carienthic costs and remainders, and so on.

Via the appeal to the notion of fittingness, I would like to expand Williams' talk of moral costs and remainders, and I would like to talk, more broadly, of *normative* costs and remainders. After all, the existence of conflicts between different types of normativity can hardly be denied; and if some moral dilemmas are, as Williams reminds us, not resolvable without reminders, the same is true of dilemmas involving different types of normativity. The appeal to fittingness may look just too bewildering, for, if I am right, to justify punishment or forgiveness we need to go beyond moral normativity, and things were already complicated enough within moral normativity. Still, I think the appeal to fittingness is on the right track.

Walzer and Williams believe, rightly in my opinion, that if a moral theory (say, utilitarianism) cannot account for the depth, or the very reality, of moral dilemmas such as dirty hands, so much the worse for this moral theory. Such theory fails to take into account the complexity of moral phenomena. I am suggesting something similar here, but placing special emphasis on punishment and forgiveness. Just as a moral theory which denied dirty hands dilemmas may be shallow, so a comprehensive value theory which presupposed that moral values could only conflict with other moral values appears shallow.

Punishment and forgiveness, traditional dirty hands cases, and clean hands cases, are all forms of conflicts between desert and fittingness. And if we wish to solve these conflicts, we need to move beyond a monomaniacal focus on moral normativity alone. We often make decisions based, in part at least, on the sort of aesthetic and charientic considerations with which fittingness is concerned. We often refuse to do certain things because 'this is not the sort of person that I am (or want to be or become), period'; some people do not ask for help when they need it, or do not assert all of their rights when they are (morally and legally) entitled to do so, and so on. And this is done in part for aesthetic or charientic reasons related to fittingness. 'I want to be able to look at myself in the mirror every morning' has obvious aesthetic and charientic dimensions. Why should these familiar sorts of considerations not be present when we deliberate about inflicting or refusing to inflict suffering on others?

I take it that not too many retributivists would want to be executioners, even if they only executed deserved prisoners: there is something inherently ugly about the life of an executioner. Similarly, there may be something ugly in punishing people always as they deserve to be punished: think of the oft-quoted passage by Seneca: 'it is a fault to punish a fault in full'.[42] Seneca's claim, too, can be fleshed out in terms of the distinction between fittingness and desert: it is unfitting, at least sometimes, to punish people to the full extent that they deserve. In fact, Seneca's famous dictum straddles the dirty hands problem, forgiveness, and punishment, in a way similar to the one in which I do it here. Doing the 'right' thing (the morally right thing) can sometimes be ugly, or vulgar, or, indeed, indecent.

One particularly sobering point Walzer made in his seminal paper is that the problem of dirty hands is really not a minor problem at all. For, Walzer claims, the problem of dirty hands 'relates not only to the coherence and harmony of the moral universe, but also to the relative ease or difficulty – or impossibility – of living a moral life'.[43] I agree with Walzer, and for the reasons expressed above, I believe that this remark applies equally well to the problems surrounding punishment and forgiveness. But just as I lament that Williams would stop at the talk of merely moral remainders, I lament that Walzer did not go further: these problems relate not only to the 'coherence and harmony' of the *moral* universe, and they do not merely affect our ability to live a *moral* life. They affect our world of values, broadly conceived – our lives are shaped by more than moral values. Punishment, forgiveness, and traditional dirty hands problems do put us in contact with non-moral (but still normative) aspects of our life. Terms such as 'harmony' and 'coherence', in particular, seem at least as much at home in the realm of aesthetic and charientic normativity as they do in the realm of ethical normativity.

Notes

Associate Professor and Chair, Department of Philosophy, Union College. With thanks to Felmon Davis, Ingvar Johansson, John Kekes, and Anna Schur.

1. Unless otherwise noted, when I refer to wrongdoing, I refer to *perceived* wrongdoing. Granted, the perceiver could be wrong, but this would not affect my views here. I wish to avoid epistemological discussions as to whether what we perceive as wrongdoing is really wrongdoing.
2. See references in Leo Zaibert (2009), 'The Paradox of Forgiveness', *Journal of Moral Philosophy* 6.3, 365–93.
3. See, for example, John Kekes (2009), 'Blame Versus Forgiveness', *The Monist* 92.3: 488–505.
4. See Leo Zaibert (2006), *Punishment and Retribution* (Aldershot: Ashgate), 16 ff.
5. See, for example, John Cottingham (1979), 'Varieties of Retribution', *Philosophical Quarterly* 29, 238–46.
6. Serena Olsaretti (2003), 'Introduction', in her *Desert and Justice* (ed.) (Oxford: Oxford University Press), 8.
7. The *locus classicus* of this move is F. H. Bradley (1967), *Ethical Studies*, (Oxford: Clarendon Press), 26 ff. For criticism of this position see Leo Zaibert (2006), *Punishment and Retribution*, 128 ff.
8. See Anthony Quinton (1954), 'On Punishment', *Analysis* 14, 133–42.
9. See Leo Zaibert (2006), 'The Fitting, the Deserving, and the Beautiful', *Journal of Moral Philosophy* 3.3, 331–50.
10. Serena Olsaretti, 'Introduction', 4.
11. For the difference between intentions and desires see John R. Searle (1983), *Intentionality: An Essay in the Philosophy of Mind* (Cambridge: Cambridge University Press); Michael Bratman (1987), *Intentions, Plans, and Practical Reason* (Cambridge, MA: Harvard University Press); and Leo Zaibert (2005), *Five Ways Patricia can Kill her Husband: A Theory of Intentionality and Blame* (Chicago: Open Court).
12. Joel Feinberg (1985), *Offense to Others: The Moral Limits of the Criminal Law*, (Oxford: Oxford University Press), 107 ff; Peter Glassen (1958), ' "Charientic" ' Judgments', *Philosophy* 125, 138–46.
13. Peter Glassen, 'Charientic', 138.
14. Ibid. 146.
15. Joel Feinberg, *Offense to Others* 1. See also Philippa Foot (1978), 'Are Moral Considerations Overriding', in her *Virtues and Vices and Other Essays in Moral Philosophy* (Berkeley: University of California Press), 181–8 where she admits that moral considerations need not be overriding.
16. Joel Feinberg, *Offense to Others* 110 ff.
17. Ibid. 110 ff.
18. Claudia Card (1972), 'On Mercy', *Philosophical Review*, 182–207.

19. Jacques Derrida (2001), *On Cosmopolitanism and Forgiveness* (London: Routledge), 33.
20. Ibid., 49.
21. John Kekes (2009), 'Blame Versus Forgiveness', 501.
22. See references in note 2, above.
23. See Leo Zaibert (2006), *Punishment and Retribution,* 198 ff. For a similar argument, see Jeffrey Reiman (1998), 'Why the Death Penalty Should be Abolished in America', in Louis J. Pojman and Jeffrey Reiman, *The Death Penalty: For and Against* (Oxford: Rowman & Littlefield), 67 ff.
24. An exception to this thesis is Stephen Kershnar who is in favour of using torture as a punishment. See, for example, Stephen Kershnar (2001), *Desert, Retribution and Torture,* (Lanham: University Press of America), 169 ff., and *passim.*
25. Ibid.
26. See Jeffrey Reiman, 'Why the Death Penalty Should be Abolished in America'.
27. See 'Study Questions', in Leo Katz, Michael Moore, and Stephen J. Morse (eds), (1999), *Foundations of Criminal Law* (New York: Foundation Press), 154.
28. See references in Leo Zaibert (2006), *Punishment and Retribution,* 153 ff. For criticisms of the prima facie obligation strategy see John R. Searle (1969), *Speech Acts: An Essay in the Philosophy of Language* (Cambridge: Cambridge University Press), 180 ff.
29. See, for example, Stuart Hampshire (ed.) (1978), *Public and Private Morality* (Cambridge: Cambridge University Press).
30. Michael Walzer (1973), 'The Problem of Dirty Hands', *Philosophy & Public Affairs* 2.2, 161
31. Ibid., 174.
32. Ibid., 174.
33. Ibid., 174.
34. See, for a similar distancing from the exaggerated emphasis on the political, Michael Stocker (1990), 'Dirty Hands and Ordinary Life', in Paul Rynard and David P. Shugarman (eds), *Cruelty and Deception: The Controversy over Dirty Hands in Politics* (Toronto: Broadview Press), 27–41, particularly at 32 ff.
35. I am assuming that in both these cases the choosers are being coerced, so there is very limited meaningful agency on their part.
36. Aside from Michael Walzer, *passim,* see also Michael Stoker's claim that the essence of dirty hands is that 'what is right to do is also, somehow, immoral' in Stocker (1990), *Plural and Conflicting Values* (Oxford: Clarendon Press), 54, and C. A. J. Coady's entry on the *Stanford Encyclopedia of Philosophy* (available at http://plato.stanford.edu/entries/dirty-hands/), where he asserts that the essence of dirty hands is that 'it is sometimes right to do what is wrong'.
37. Michael Walzer, 'The Problem of Dirty Hands', 166.
38. Bernard Williams (1981), 'Politics and Moral Character', in his *Moral Luck: Philosophical Papers 1973–1980* (Cambridge: Cambridge University Press), 62.
39. Ibid. 54, emphasis in the original.
40. For some of these descriptions see Elaine Scarry (1987), *The Body in Pain: The Making and Unmaking of the World* (Oxford: Oxford University Press), 27 ff.
41. Michael Walzer, 'The Problem of Dirty Hands', 170.
42. Seneca (2004), *On Mercy* (Cambridge, MA.: Loeb Classical Library), 318.
43. Michael Walzer, 'The Problem of Dirty Hands', 161.

7
Punishment and Dignity

Thomas S. Petersen

Torture, flogging, stoning, public shaming and the death penalty are *kinds* of punishment that several theorists of criminal justice claim to be morally unacceptable.[1] Furthermore, it is not only certain kinds of punishment that are ruled out as immoral, but also excessive *amounts* of the various kinds of punishment.[2] A. Von Hirsch, for instance, has claimed that imprisonment for even the most serious of crimes should not exceed 5 years,[3] while D. E. Scheid has suggested 15–20 years of imprisonment for such crimes as the absolute maximum.[4] But what are the arguments for these claims, and does close scrutiny of these arguments allow us to point out the difference between morally acceptable and unacceptable punishments? This distinction is necessary, since criminal justice ethics must be deemed deficient if it fails to guide us on questions about the kinds and degrees of punishment that are morally unacceptable.[5]

In this chapter, one central group of arguments for moral constraints on punishment will be challenged. These characteristically conclude that certain kinds of punishment (for example, torture, stoning and flogging) or amounts of punishment (for example, lifetime imprisonment) are immoral, and should not be used, because they *violate human dignity*.[6] The plan of this chapter is as follows. In section 7.2 the concept of dignity will be clarified. A distinction between common-sense interpretations of dignity and a Kantian interpretation will be described in detail. Section 7.3 presents a critical discussion of five attempts to identify and justify what kind, or amount, of punishment is immoral by means of a *dignity rationale*. Although it is easy to sympathize with the conclusions reached by advocates of the dignity rationale, it is concluded that the reviewed attempts to justify these conclusions are nonetheless implausible for various reasons. Most importantly, two themes run through the discussion in this section: it is shown (i) that all of the different versions of this rationale are rather vague and of little practical help when we want to identify which punishments are immoral; and (ii) that, where this identification is possible, the relevant justifications seem, at least, to be inconclusive. In section 7.4 some general problems for adherents of the dignity rationale are presented, including the observation that they have little to say when it comes to the maximum imposition of morally acceptable kinds of punishment.

Before we move on I wish to make a few comments on the importance of this chapter. First of all, and from a theoretical viewpoint, a theory of criminal justice that does not critically discuss which punishments are morally acceptable and which are not must be considered incomplete. However, there have only been few systematic discussions in the literature of the ways in which the notion of a violation of human dignity can be used to differentiate between moral and immoral punishments.[7] Secondly, and from a practical viewpoint, it is important for many people exactly what punishments their government will, or ought to, accept. What is accepted as the most severe punishment, for example, impinges on the welfare and rights of not only the offender, but his relatives as well as staff, in the criminal justice system, who will be required to impose the punishment. Equally, just how severely a state punishes its criminals may affect the way each of us evaluates the state we live in (or other states), as being fair, or either too mild or too draconian.

7.1 Dignity defined

To make progress in evaluating the dignity rationale we need, first, to know what we are talking about when we use the word 'dignity'. As a starting point, we can notice that it is beyond doubt that ascriptions of dignity *to a person* or *acts of a person* represent (psychologically, aesthetically or morally) positive appraisals. But apart from this general categorization the word 'dignity' can be used in a variety of ways. In the common-sense use of the word we can, for example, say that a person *has* dignity, meaning something like: this person has confidence or self-worth. Or we can say that a person who occupies an important position in society (for example, a Supreme Court judge or a general) enjoys dignity in virtue of his position; such a person can of course lose his dignity if he does not do the job well or is sacked. As another variation of this broadly profession-dependent use of 'dignity', consider the following headline in *TIME* magazine: 'California gives gay couples the matrimonial dignity they have long sought for'.[8] If people can have a matrimonial dignity, the sky is the limit so far as ascribing people dignity goes. In other words, there are no limits. Furthermore, the word 'dignity' has a variety of common-sense usages in which we say that people *act* in a way that gives them dignity. Thus, a person can 'speak with dignity' or 'grow old with dignity'.[9] However, in the identification of immoral punishments it is, as we shall see, clear that these interpretations of the word 'dignity' are not relevant. As a starting point, all adherents of the dignity rationale take 'dignity' to mean something other than what is mentioned above. What they have in mind will be critically discussed in section 7.3.

In the philosophical literature, since at least Kant's time, there seems to be a consensus that every person has dignity in the sense that every person has *unconditional* and *incomparable* worth.[10] This notion of dignity clearly differs from all of the familiar, common-sense interpretations mentioned above. For, according to many of these common-sense interpretations, dignity is *not* something everybody has; and when 'dignity' is identified with certain types of actions, these are not the types of act that everybody does. The idea that personal dignity is *unconditional* surely means that dignity is something which everybody has, no matter what condition she is in or how she acts. Furthermore, I take the assertion that dignity has *incomparable worth* to mean that the dignity of a person cannot be sold or gained in exchange for something else, such as money, gold or human organs. Again, the idea here is that dignity is something that every human being has.

In this chapter, my point of departure is this interpretation of the concept of dignity – that is, what I shall call the *Kantian* interpretation of dignity. Embedded in this interpretation of the concept of dignity is also the idea that dignity is more than a description of what characterizes humans; it is also a moral concept. According to the Kantian interpretation, dignity is a moral concept that functions as *the* central element in the moral principle that one should *respect* the dignity of people. According to this principle, acts which do not respect the dignity of people because they involve the denial, or violation, of human dignity are prohibited (or almost always prohibited).

What it means to *respect* the dignity of a human being is far from easy to establish. On one interpretation, I respect such dignity if I bring it about that a greater number of people are treated with dignity. This we could call the *consequentialist interpretation*. For instance, I could try to minimize numerous violations of dignity by violating the dignity of one person – for example, it could be that by enslaving one person I can prevent five others from being enslaved. On to the consequentialist interpretation, I should (everything else being equal) enslave that one person. On another interpretation, I respect the dignity of people by *honouring* their dignity. This might involve refusing to violate the dignity of one person – even for the sake of achieving fewer or less serious violations of the dignity of, say, five other persons. This we could call the *deontological interpretation*. In what follows I will focus on the deontological interpretation, as this is in keeping with the self-understanding of most defenders of dignity; it certainly seems to be the concept used by those who appeal to dignity to identify morally unacceptable punishments.

Apart from these categorizations, there is no doubt that dignity is an important and often-used moral concept. It is at the centre of one of the main branches within ethical theory, namely deontological ethics.[11] And, apart from research within pure ethical theory, it plays a central role in applied ethics, in connection with such topics as euthanasia,[12] the commodification of human body parts,[13] and post-humanism *versus* bio-conservatism,[14] also, as we shall see in detail later on, in the ethics of punishment. Finally, it is worth noting that dignity plays a central role in many constitutions, and in much legal and regulatory material: for example, the Universal Declaration of Human Rights.[15]

So far so good; but defining 'dignity', and identifying it as a central moral concept, is only a preliminary, though necessary, step in our investigation. What we should now be concerned with is whether, and if so how, respect for a person's dignity can give any precise guidance on the question of which punishments are morally acceptable and which are not. In what follows I will critically discuss five attempts to delimit immoral punishment using the concept of dignity. Let me begin with Kant – one of the most famous and influential philosophers to take the view that all humans possess dignity.

7.2 Dignity applied

7.2.1 The Kantian approach

According to Kant's well-known second version of the Categorical Imperative – also called 'the dignity principle'[16] – man should always treat a person as an end in itself and never merely as a means. However, although the dignity principle does offer some guidance when it comes to the ethics of punishment, it is clear that this principle does not provide us with an answer to the question we are dealing with. The reason for this is the following. First, note that the dignity principle can be used to deal with the question of *why the state should punish*. According to Kant the state should not punish with preventative aims, because this would be like treating the person as merely a means to the ends of others. Instead, as most readers will know, according to Kant we should only punish when, and because, an offender deserves to be punished. Where this rationale applies, according to Kant, we do not treat the criminal as a mere means to somebody else's interests.[17] Second, however, this principle cannot deliver an answer to our question about what kind and amount of punishment is immoral. For whether or not an offender is treated merely as a means does not depend on the kind or the severity of his punishment. It depends on the intentions of those who make the criminal law and eventually also those who execute the punishment. If the intention is to deter and prevent further crime, every type of punishment must be abandoned according to the dignity principle. So according to this kind of reasoning every type of punishment could, in theory, conform with this principle – as long as the offender gets what he deserves. So we still need an answer to our question of when and why some punishments are immoral.

7.2.2   An intuitive approach

Fortunately, some modern, Kant-influenced criminal justice ethicists have tried to explain how one can identify immoral punishment. According to J. G. Murphy, a punishment that violates someone's dignity should in principle be banned.[18] But when does a punishment violate someone's dignity? Murphy gives several examples of such punishment. For instance, he writes: 'sending painful voltage through a man's testicles to which electrodes have been attached, or boiling him in oil, or eviscerating him, or gouging out his eyes'.[19] And when it comes to the question of how we can *know* whether a certain punishment violates the dignity of the offender Murphy relies on our intuitions. This is apparent in the counter-thrust following his acknowledgement that he cannot:

> prove that it is wrong to treat people in this way [different kinds of torture]; for the wrongness of doing this is more obvious than any premises which could be given to justify its being wrong. Anyone who did not see this could not be made to understand anything else about morality.[20]

First of all, why is the wrongness of such punishment *more* obvious than *any* premises which could be given to justify its being wrong? It is a little curious that Murphy asserts this when he himself provides two premises in favour of one of his conclusions that it is immoral to punish people by boiling them in oil: 'punishments that violate people's dignity ought not to be executed' and 'boiling a person in oil violates a person's dignity'. Again, why is it that the moral wrongness of certain kinds of punishment is *more obvious* than an argument in favour of the wrongness? Sometimes we are in doubt about the wrongness of a punishment; and in such situations an argument might persuade us that the punishment in question is wrong. It is difficult here to see why not proving something and instead using your intuition makes things more obvious.

Secondly, although it is obvious that torture, say, is wrong when seen in isolation, this does not prove that torture is always wrong. Some utilitarians do argue that, in very specific situations, we could accept torture – for instance, if the purpose is to minimize the amount of associated torture. And some retributivists accept torture where, and because, the offender (in their view) deserves it. Furthermore, to claim that these retributivists and utilitarians 'could not be made to understand anything else about morality' is, as Jesper Ryberg has observed, too harsh.[21] If one cannot see that such treatment is terrible for the person who undergoes it, then Murphy seems to be right. However, to claim that theorists, for example utilitarians, who might in principle accept torture where it maximizes welfare, do not know anything about morality is simply wrong. People like Jeremy Bentham, John Stuart Mill, Henry Sidgwick and Peter Singer were or are utilitarians – of course they understand something about morality.

Thirdly, the existence of these philosophers also demonstrates that we tend to have very different intuitions when it comes to moral questions about punishment. How would Murphy deal with these differences? Is he always morally right on this subject, while his opponents are morally wrong or blind? This is hard to believe. It might, of course, be true that we have some common intuitions, and that these are true – for instance, that is it morally wrong to torture an innocent baby for fun. But when it comes to, say, capital punishment, the academic literature and the public debate about the subject show that we are quite some distance away from sharing the same intuitions.

Murphy seems to make his view clearer when he says that it is against the dignity of a perpetrator to *treat him as an animal* rather than a human being.[22] Although humans are animals, I believe that Murphy means by the word *animal* non-human animals. Apart from this comment, it is very difficult to apply this further description of what constitutes an act that violates dignity in order to mark out punishments that are immoral. Certainly, there are factual differences between humans and non-human animals that make it obvious why it is morally wrong to treat a human like a non-human animal. If, for instance, you served cheap dog food to your children when you could easily afford to serve them a healthier and appetizing food, it would be a wrong to do that. But serving such food for your dog would be perfectly all right. But, taken at face value, it cannot always be morally wrong to treat a person as an animal. I play with my turtle and my dog and I play with my children. Sometimes I stroke my turtle, but also my children and my wife; and when it comes to our question, the principle 'don't treat humans as animals' does not deliver the tool that we need. Do we treat a serious criminal as an animal if we lock him up in jail, or if we run high-voltage electricity through his testicles? How can Murphy use the further description of dignity to argue in favour of his view that we should accept the former punishment, but regard the latter as morally unacceptable? It is difficult to see how this can be done in any plausible way.

Of course, one explanation would be that, because we do not put dogs in prison, this is also not acceptable for humans. Doing this, we do not treat humans like animals. But, by following this kind of reasoning, nor should we abandon the practice of running high-voltage electricity through the testicles of a perpetrator of crime, as this is *not* how, from a moral point of view, we would punish a dog. So, obviously, treating humans as animals is sometimes morally acceptable, and not treating humans as animals is sometimes morally unacceptable. Fortunately, others have tried to make it clearer when a punishment is contrary to the dignity of a human being. Among these is the philosopher John Kleinig, to whose views I now turn.

7.2.3   The capacity for autonomy approach

According to Kleinig, dignity can be defined as follows: 'The capacity to frame for oneself the choices one makes, the paths one treads, and the goals one pursues is the foundation for human dignity.'[23] Applying this formulation to answer our question, Kleinig would hold that any punishments that deprive the offender of the capacity he characterizes are degrading and therefore morally wrong.[24]

For the sake of convenience, I shall call Kleinig's view *the capacity for autonomy approach*. I use this name because many definitions of autonomy focus on the capacity to frame for oneself one's choices and goals without undue influence. However, I am not convinced that this approach makes it any clearer than the last two how we should identify immoral punishment. As we shall see in the following paragraphs several challenges come to mind when one begins to think about the capacity for autonomy approach.

The first challenge, and one mentioned by Kleinig himself, is that his approach seems to imply that imprisonment, or any other kind of punishment, is inherently immoral: plainly, imprisonment deprives the prisoner of control over the terms of his life. Kleinig's own response to this objection is to emphasize that the person who has committed a crime has *chosen* to take the risks carried by his law-breaking behaviour – including the possibility of having his liberty drastically curtailed. There is therefore nothing wrong with imprisonment as such when a person knows what the consequences of criminal conduct are. But this, following Kleinig, does not mean that liberty ought to be curtailed in any which way: 'though choices within a prison environment are constrained, they need not be so constrained that the prisoners are deprived of the kinds of choices that manifest their human standing and self-respect.'[25] However, this answer can be challenged for a number of reasons. If determinism is true we cannot say that a person has literally chosen to commit a crime. Furthermore, if determinism is false, and if you know that your liberty will be constrained in a way that causes you to lose your self-respect, then it follows from Kleinig's reasoning that the offender has chosen to take the risk of losing his self-respect. If the latter is true, Kleinig has not described a justified difference between moral and immoral punishment. (I shall elaborate on the last point here at the end of this subsection.)

This brings us to the second challenge. What kinds of constraint or punishment are morally acceptable, and what kinds are not, is not explicated in a precise manner by Kleinig. For, unfortunately, he only gives us a single, and not very illuminating, example of immoral punishment:

> A prisoner who is expected to get up at a certain hour each morning is not deprived of dignity, whereas a prisoner who is expected to forgo the expression of his political opinion or religious observances in exchange for basic needs (for example, sanitary conditions or association with others) is being expected to sacrifice his dignity.[26]

An initial criticism here is that it is not obvious that you would sacrifice your dignity – that is to say, in this context, your capacity to frame for yourself the choices you make – were you to forego the expression of your political opinions. Literally you are not being deprived of the capacity to frame your political or religious views for yourself. What you are being deprived of is the *possibility of expressing* these opinions for a period of time; you still have the relevant capacity to form and express religious views. This is no different from saying that you still have the capacity to drive a car or play soccer when you are sentenced to a spell in prison during which you are not given the opportunity to drive a car or play soccer. This observation shows that the example does not make it any clearer how to identify the acceptable limits of punishment that Kleinig takes to follow from respect for dignity. To make this matter clearer, Kleinig should at least make a distinction between the *capacity* 'to frame for oneself the choices one makes' and the *possibility of expressing this capacity* in some kind of action.[27]

So, Kleinig is confronted with the following dilemma. If dignity is only violated if one's capacity to frame for oneself the choices one makes is removed, his example will be of no help. For most kinds of punishment will not ensure that the convicted loses his capacity for goal-setting and choice-making. On the other hand, if violating dignity stops a person from expressing or pursuing his goals, imprisonment, contrary to Kleinig's view, should be abandoned. It should be abandoned because most kinds of imprisonment do deprive the incarcerated individual of the possibility of acting according to his capacity to frame the choices he makes.

A third challenge is that Kleinig's example is not convincing when used to support the more concrete view that to forgo the expression of one's political opinions is a morally prohibited deprivation of dignity. Imagine the following situation. What would, and should, people choose if they have the choice between forgoing the satisfaction of their basic needs or losing the opportunity to express their political opinions? It is not obvious that you would, or should, choose to speak up or otherwise express your political views (for example, by voting for your preferred party at a national election) if the alternative is to thwart your basic needs. There are many situations where it seems obvious that you ought to choose to satisfy your basic needs instead of expressing your political views – at least, if the basic needs include access to food, water and medicine. Imagine a father of four who will be sentenced to death if he expresses his communist views in public. His execution will involve denying him food and water in such a way that he will die within a few days. This is, of course, a very harsh punishment for an act that ought to be legal. However, in such an unfortunate situation it seems reasonable to say that, because his family stand to suffer (everything else being equal), the father ought to sacrifice his dignity and choose to satisfy his own, and his children's, basic needs.

Fourthly, Kleinig's explanation for the view that imprisonment as such is morally acceptable because the criminal *knows* that his behaviour can result in the deprivations of freedom, and his simultaneous claim that certain kinds of imprisonment are immoral, are unconvincing. Why not say that a person who commits crimes has also chosen to take a known risk that he will be prevented from expressing religious views, or checking his email, or whatever else one counts as conduct that violates the dignity of the prisoner? To make my point clearer, let us say that we have two kinds of imprisonment: mild and severe imprisonment. In the former you can watch TV, use computers, get an education, visit your wife and children, and so on. In the latter none of this is possible, and you get poor food and bad sanitation. If imprisonment as such is justified because the offender has chosen to take the punitive risk associated with his offence, this justification can be applied to both kinds of imprisonment. It cannot be right to claim that the choice to commit a crime makes mild imprisonment morally acceptable because the criminal knows what to expect, but does not make severe imprisonment similarly morally acceptable. We need an explanation for this asymmetry, for without it we cannot identify the types, or conditions, of punishment that are morally unacceptable. Furthermore, what if the criminal (for example, because he is a juvenile) does not know that a certain act is illegal, or does not know what the punishment for that kind of illegal act is?

Finally, Kleinig is surprisingly silent about what kinds of choice, path and goal it is morally relevant to respect when it comes to punishment. But this needs to be spelled out in detail, since it is obvious that it is *not* always good that a person has the capacity to pursue his choices, paths and goals. Let me describe a case in which it appears to be morally right to violate a person's dignity. Most people would approve, morally, if a potential serial killer is deprived, by means of intense psychotherapy, of his capacity to live in the homicidal way he wants to live. The deprivation is morally good, although it violates the potential serial killer's dignity, because it will prevent people from being killed and prevent a person from being a perpetrator. One could, of course, claim that a person like this has lost his capacity for autonomy; and if this is the case, we do not violate his dignity by depriving him of his capacity to pursue his immoral choices and goals. So, in order to apply the capacity for autonomy approach, we need to spell out in more detail when, exactly, it is morally right (or wrong) to respect the capacity in question. And, furthermore, if a person may lose his capacity for autonomy, we need to know when this is the case. In sum, using Kleinig's approach we are left with a solution to our question that fails to provide a clear account of the difference between morally acceptable and morally unacceptable punishment. Kleinig's solution also seems to be inconsistent with the intuitive view that, in certain cases, it is morally right to violate a person's capacity for autonomy by means of a punishment.

7.2.4   The capacity for a sense of justice approach

Another way to explain how certain kinds or amounts of punishment infringe upon the dignity of humans is posed by R. S. Gerstein.[28] According to Gerstein the idea of human dignity is given content when it is explicated in terms of *the capacity for a sense of justice.* In his account of this capacity, Gerstein refers to John Rawls' use of the phrase. According to Rawls, a person with a sense of justice has the desire to act according to the right moral principles.[29] Applied to our question, then, Gerstein's answer is that: 'any punishment [is regarded as immoral] which would be inconsistent with the criminal's status as a member of the community whose capacity for a sense of justice (a capacity of which he did not make use [of] when he committed his crime) is worthy of our respect.'[30]

To begin with, we should note that this approach is different from the capacity approach we dealt with when looking at Kleinig's views. For you may have a capacity for autonomy without having a capacity for a sense of justice, and vice versa. If we accept that a person who acts autonomously must not be coerced or manipulated, we can think of a rational person who is free from undue influence but nevertheless does not have a sense of justice – someone, for example, who will not feel guilty after committing a serious crime. Equally, you may have the capacity for a sense of justice without being an autonomous individual: you might, for example, be a slave with a fully developed capacity to judge your situation as a case of injustice. However, despite these differences, the challenges these two capacity approaches face are very similar.

First of all, how should we apply this approach when it comes to the moral evaluation of specific punishments? Gerstein does not explicate in any precise manner what kinds of punishment are morally acceptable and what kinds are not. So, once again, we are left with the vague notion that any punishment that impairs the capacity in question could not be justly imposed. Gerstein only discusses whether capital punishment for a murder is immoral, and he concludes that 'It is not the suffering which *might* lead the retributivists to regard capital punishment as cruel and unusual, but its dehumanizing character [or violation of dignity], its total negation of the moral worth of the person to be executed'.[31] Again, such a vague answer is not of much help to the criminal justice ethicist who wishes to identify immoral punishments other than the death penalty. For if the dehumanizing character of capital punishment *might* lead retributivists to *abandon* capital punishment, it will follow that it *might* also lead to the *acceptance* of capital punishment.

Let me explain. First, then, how do we determine whether or not capital punishment is dehumanizing? Gerstein says that what counts as dehumanizing 'depends on attitudes that change over time'.[32] I will not critically assess this answer; I shall just mention that Gerstein, at least, needs to respond here to two issues: (i) *Whose* attitudes are we talking about? (ii) What should be done if, at a certain point in history, there is *no convergence* in the relevant people's attitudes? Again, what if there is consensus of approval on the death penalty? However, a more obvious way to answer the moral question about capital punishment would be to ask: How can one respect a person's capacity for a sense of justice by killing him? If you are dead, you have lost your capacity for anything. So if the offender is against capital punishment, and has expressed his view that capital punishment is morally wrong, it is difficult to see how you, after his death, can respect his capacity for a sense of justice. Capital punishment also seems to be contrary to Gerstein's view that we ought to use punishments in order to *preserve* and *stimulate* people's (or criminals') capacity for a sense of justice.[33] So there seems to be a way to answer that question without relying upon consensus.

Secondly, suppose we agree, with Gerstein, that capital punishment is dehumanizing. According to Gerstein, we can still, as retributivists, accept capital punishment.[34] Thus, the retributivists can argue that although capital punishment it is dehumanizing, it is morally more important that the murderer be executed because he *deserves* to be executed. However, Gerstein says nothing about how retributivists should balance these different considerations, that is, about how we should weigh the fact that an act that is dehumanizing and violates dignity against the proposal to give the offender what he deserves.

Quite apart from this interpretation of Gerstein's view on capital punishment, it is difficult to see what follows from his view if, for example, imprisonment is believed to be at the top of the punishment scale. What should be the maximum period of imprisonment? How many years in prison does it take, for instance, to preserve and stimulate a murderer's capacity for a sense of justice? Unfortunately, Gerstein does not say anything that brings us nearer to an answer to these questions.

This brings us to another challenge that Gerstein is confronted with. What kinds of individual is Gerstein referring to when he speaks of a person's capacity for a sense of justice? Does he, like Rawls, mean to refer to a rational and informed person? Or is he referring to an individual who is irrational and/or uninformed about the laws and ethics of society? There is no doubt that people's actual sense of justice varies according to their level of rationality and how well they are informed and understand the information they receive. But despite these differences, they may all have the capacity for a sense of justice – and this brings us to the next challenge for Gerstein.

What kind of capacity for a sense of justice is Gerstein talking about? Like Kleinig, he does not seem to be aware that we can interpret the capacity for a sense of justice in at least two different ways. On one interpretation, a person *has* a capacity for a sense of justice. On another interpretation a person can *act* according to his capacity for a sense of justice. Let us take for granted that you can have the capacity for a sense of justice without acting on it – say, as the result of weakness of will. But which of these two interpretations Gerstein's view is based on has implications for how one can *respect* the capacity for a sense of justice. You can respect a person's capacity on the first interpretation (not destroy a person's capacity for the sense of justice) without respecting it on the second (nevertheless hindering a person's conduct in some way). Thus, imagine a person who does not want to violate another's capacity for a sense of justice, but does find his expression of this capacity (for example, an invitation to violent behaviour) morally wrong and not worthy of moral respect. Gerstein appears to have the second interpretation in mind. He says: 'Just as we justify punishment as a response to those who abuse this capacity, so we shape and limit punishment out of the desire to preserve and stimulate it.'[35] So, following Gerstein, a perpetrator of crime abuses his capacity to a sense of justice when he acts in a way that violates the law. But the perpetrator nevertheless has the capacity for that sense of justice, or else he cannot abuse it.

A further challenge for Gerstein is that of specifying the kinds of punishment which, when inflicted on the offender, stimulate and preserve the right use of the offender's capacity for a sense of justice. Again, it seems clear that capital punishment is out of the question, since it is impossible to stimulate and preserve a person's capacity for anything when he is dead. But also, how can we respect an offender's sense of justice when, say, a judge imprisons him for a year for shoplifting, if the offender firmly believes that it is absolutely wrong to imprison people for such minor crimes? Suppose an offender is a utilitarian who believes that imprisonment for minor crimes is morally wrong and has only a negative effect on rehabilitation and the prevention of further crime. Then it is obvious that, according to the offender's sense of justice, it is unjust to punish him with imprisonment. But if such situations sometimes occur, it is difficult to see how a year of incarceration for shoplifting could be seen as something that will stimulate and preserve the inmate's capacity for a sense of justice. Through the imprisonment of the shoplifter, the state can, of course, express its own sense of justice, but that will not preserve or stimulate a person's sense of justice: it will change it.

Naturally, this might not be the most plausible sense of justice, since we all know that states can be morally wrong; and according to the shoplifter, at least, the state is not respecting his sense of justice when it imprisons him. This may also hold true of the murderer who believes that he is punished unjustly when he is imprisoned for life. So, again, it is difficult to see how one should be guided by Gerstein's proposal. How do we know when to respect a person's capacity for a sense of justice? One obvious answer is: when the person in question is acting according to the right sense of justice. But what is the right sense of justice when it comes to the moral question of how severely the state should punish criminals? To answer this question, as Gerstein does, by saying that any punishment which fails to respect the criminal's capacity for a sense of justice is unacceptable is simply to beg the question.

7.2.5 The self-respect approach

Several philosophers have argued that punishments depriving the criminal of self-respect should not be regarded as morally acceptable.[36] As far as this approach goes, Gerstein also has something to say when he writes: 'An affliction which undermines a man's self-respect ... could not serve as just punishment.'[37] According to Herbert Spiegelberg we can obtain a clear idea of what the moral value of dignity involves if we start to identify forms of punishment that are clear cases of indignity. As examples of such indignities he mentions torture, being forced to make confessions and being packed into overcrowded prisons.[38] Spiegelberg believes that such violations of dignity are morally wrong – not only because they cause great suffering, but because they 'break down the personalities of the victims and deprive them not only of the respect of others but of self-respect'.[39] Martha Nussbaum, follows roughly this line of reasoning in her objection to the use of public shaming as punishment.[40]

This approach to dignity is obviously not identical with either of the two capacity approaches that we have already been dealing with. You can have self-respect even though you have lost some important capacities, and you can lose your self-respect even though you still have the capacity for autonomy and a sense of justice. When this is said, self-respect is usually rather casually related to the capacity for autonomy or the capacity for a sense of justice. If, for instance, you have lost your capacity for autonomy, or the opportunity to express this capacity, it might be very difficult to maintain your self-respect.

However, if we are to exploit this approach to make a distinction between morally acceptable and morally unacceptable punishment, we need to know what, exactly, the view implies. At a first glance, it seems to imply that the state must never punish in a way that nullifies the criminal's self-respect. However, almost all kinds of punishment may cause a perpetrator of crime to lose his self-respect; and from this it follows that criminals should not be punished at all. This does not fit well with the work of any advocate of this approach to dignity, and it is out of keeping with most research efforts in the field of criminal justice ethics. We know that criminals who are punished are affected by the punishment in very different ways. Some are very sensible and may lose self-respect, at least for a while, after 10 days in prison; others will not lose self-respect in that way. Some will even gain extra self-respect, because their self-worth is boosted by so-called the 'street respect' of their peers.

Such an implication may point to a more acceptable interpretation here – namely, that it is only punishments that deprive the criminal of self-respect for a long period, or permanently, that violate dignity. Momentary loss of self-respect, due to punishment, is on this inter-pretation acceptable. But again, this is of little help if we are trying to classify immoral forms of punishment. For, again, people are sensible of the effects of punishment in different degrees. For how long must a so-called long-time loss of self-respect last? Furthermore, how do we measure not only the length of time during which one loses one's self-respect, but also the *depth* of that loss? Self-respect is not, apparently, a binary, black or white concept: normally, I lose my self-respect super-ficially or to some deeper degree. (Certainly, we can imagine someone saying that she has lost her self-respect entirely, or has none, but it is unclear what this would imply as an accurate remark.)

Finally, this interpretation of dignity has some rather implausible implications. At least, it does if the above-mentioned interpretation of dignity is the only moral value that we are required to respect. Following this interpretation, we would be prevented from saying, for example, that the imprisonment of Nelson Mandela was wrong *if* during his time in prison he never lost his self-respect. I am well aware of the fact that most adherents of dignity refer not only to dignity, but also to the suf-fering of the perpetrator when they argue that some kinds of punish-ment are immoral.

7.3   Further challenges

Apart from the challenges presented in the last section, all dignity approaches seem to have some further challenges in common. First of all, we can note that when criminal justice ethicists refer to dignity in our context, they usually attempt to mark out immoral *types* of punishment (boot-camp routines, public shaming, torture, capital punishment, *et hoc genus omne*). If there were a consensus on the types of punishment that violate human dignity, this would of course be an easy way to apply the dignity approach. But as there is no such consensus, we are left with no more than a range of different and poorly defended intuitions. However, worse is to come. Adherents of the dignity approach are conspicuously silent when it comes to questions about different amounts, or severities, of punishment. Let us accept that imprisonment – at least, if certain things are provided, such as a fair trial, sufficient food and educational opportunities – is a morally acceptable type of punishment. But what are the upper moral limits of imprisonment? Five years? Thirty years? And in answering this question, what would the rationale be for saying five years rather than thirty? It is difficult to see how a simple reference to dignity would solve this problem.

Even if advocates of the dignity approach were able to draw a clear line between morally acceptable and unacceptable punishments, other questions would become pressing. First of all, should we always respect a person's capacity for autonomy? What if we could increase the well-being of a person or others by disrespecting a person's capacity for autonomy, perhaps for a short time? How should we balance these concerns? Do we only have instrumental reasons to respect the capacity for dignity, or does respect for dignity have value in itself? On the one hand, if dignity only has instrumental value in relation to well-being, we might just as well talk about well-being (or its privation: suffering) instead of dignity. To define well-being is, of course, no easy task. But it would be less complicated than defining the two different values of autonomy (dignity) and well-being.[41] On the other hand, if dignity has value in itself, is it then the only moral factor that has value in itself? If not, we need to ask how, if well-being has value alongside dignity, these two values should be weighed against one another. Should we also respect a person's capacity for autonomy if his well-being will be increased by not respecting this capacity? (A case in point, here, would be one in which a punishment would disrespect the person's dignity but increase his total and relative well-being immensely.)

Finally, it should be apparent by now that dignity cannot stand as the sole basis on which to isolate immoral punishments. For what about offenders who do not have the capacity for autonomy, or who lack a sense of justice? If dignity is the only basis for imposing or withholding punishment, it seems to follow that all types of punishment in response to individuals lacking the capacity for autonomy or sense of justice are acceptable. But, of course, this is not the case. It is also wholly contrary to the Kantian approach to dignity, which claims that every human has a dignity that should be respected.

7.4 Conclusion

From the investigations presented in this chapter it follows that we should be very sceptical about the idea that we can identify and isolate immoral punishments by appealing to the concept of dignity. The chapter does not show, or imply, that reference to dignity should not be used at all in discussions of the moral limits of punishment. It is just that advocates of dignity need to explain in more detail how this moral factor can be used as a guiding principle when it comes to identifying immoral kinds and severities of punishment. True, the concept of dignity can be used as a way of conveying, in very few words, that one is against certain kinds of punishment; but so can the expression 'yuk!'. For the present, we should use alternative and more plausible accounts of morally acceptable punishment. Such alternative accounts could refer, for example, to the rights, or the suffering, of the punished individual, or to the special or general prevention (deterrent effect) of crimes secured by punishment.

Let me reiterate that this chapter does not argue, or conclude, that there are no immoral punishments. It argues merely that the ways of identifying such punishments (by means of the 'rationale from dignity') are, to say the least, underdeveloped and offer little guidance. As I have already said, it is necessary either to develop the dignity-based approaches somewhat, or to move to other, seemingly more plausible justifications, when seeking to argue that some punishments are immoral.[42]

Notes

1. For example, compare R. A. Duff (2005), 'Punishment, Dignity and Degradation', *Oxford Journal of Legal Studies*, 25:1, 141–55; M. Nussbaum (2004), *Hiding from Humanity* (Princeton, New Jersey: Princeton University Press); R. G. Singer (1979), *Just Deserts* (USA: Ballinger Publishing Company); J. G. Murphy (1979), *Retribution, Justice and Therapy* (Dordrecht, the Netherlands: Reidel); A. Von Hirsch (1993), *Censure and Sanctions* (Oxford, UK: Clarendon Press); and J. Q. Whiteman (2003), *Harsh Justice: Criminal Punishment and the Widening Divide between America and Europe* (Oxford, UK: Oxford University Press).
2. Agreeing that imprisonment is a morally acceptable method of punishment, one could at the same time hold the *conditions* of certain uses of imprisonment (for example, not being able to receive conjugal visits, no access to

entertainment, news and education or being required to do hard labour etc.) are morally unacceptable; or one might find certain *systems* of punishment (for example, Sharia Law), in which imprisonment is in use, morally unacceptable.

3. Von Hirsch (1993), ch. 10.
4. D. E. Scheid (1997), 'Constructing a Theory of Punishment, Desert, and the Distribution of Punishments', *The Canadian Journal of Law and Jurisprudence*, 10:2, 441–506, see p. 499.
5. Although a certain kind or amount of punishment is considered to be morally unacceptable, it does not follow that such punishments therefore should be legally banned. However, in the context of this chapter it is the case that when criminal justice ethicists claim that a punishment is morally unacceptable it is the assumption that the punishment in question should be legally prohibited.
6. See, for example, Scheid (1993), 497–8; Nussbaum (2004), 227–49; and J. Kleinig (1998), 'The Hardness of Hard Treatment', in A. Ashworth and M. Wasik (eds), *Fundamentals of Sentencing Theory* (Oxford, UK: Clarendon Press).
7. An exception is J. Ryberg (2004), *The Ethics of Proportionate Punishment: A Critical Investigation* (Dortrecht, The Netherlands: Kluwer Academic Publishers), 131–40.
8. *Times* (2008), vol. 171, 26/27, 3.
9. M. J. Meyer (1995), 'Dignity, Death and Modern Virtue', *American Philosophical Quarterly*, 32, 45–57.
10. I. Kant (1998), *Groundwork of the Metaphysic of Morals* (Cambridge, UK: Cambridge University Press).
11. In defining 'deontology' I follow Shelly Kagan, who categorizes deontology as a moral theory which puts restrictions on certain kind of acts (for example, harming individuals) even though such acts would maximize the good. See S. Kagan (1998), *Normative Ethics* (Boulder, USA: Westview Press), 73.
12. L. Kass (2002), *Life, Liberty, and Defence of Dignity: A Challenge for Bioethics* (San Francisco, US: Encounter Books).
13. R. Beyleveld and R. Brownsword (2001), *Human Dignity in Bioethics and Biolaw* (Oxford, UK: Oxford University Press).
14. N. Bostrom (2005), 'In Defence of Posthuman Dignity', *Bioethics*, 19:3, 202–14.
15. As an exception to this trend, see the European Convention of Human Rights, in which the word 'dignity' is not used at all.
16. Cf. Kant (1998) and T.E. Hill (1992), *Dignity and Practical Reason in Kant's Moral Philosophy* (Chicago, US: Cornell University Press).
17. Kant (1998).
18. Murphy (1979).
19. Ibid. 233.
20. Id.
21. Ryberg (2004), 136.
22. Murphy (1979), 233. The treatment of a person as a non-human animal rather than a human being has been investigated by many philosophers discussing the moral aspect of punishment. The wording here can change a bit – some (for example, Kant) talk about acts that do not respect the 'humanity' in each person, while others talk about the 'inhumanity' of such acts.

23. Kleinig 287.
24. Ibid.
25. Kleinig 287–9.
26. Kleinig 288.
27. Ideally, Kleinig should also make it clear whether this distinction has any moral relevance. I will not pursue this matter. I merely mention that, if everything else is equal, it seems morally worse to permanently deprive a person of the *capacity* to pursue his goals (at least, if the goals are morally acceptable) than to prevent that person from being able to *act* in pursuit of such goals for a short period of time.
28. A. Von Hirsch and Andrew Ashworth (2005), *Proportionate Sentencing: Exploring the Principles* (Oxford: Oxford, UK: University Press), 83 seem to accept a combination of Gerstein's and Murphy's views (discussed in this chapter: see subsections 7.2.3 and 7.2.4) when they say that 'penal measures be objectionable ... [when] These are the interventions that destroy (or substantially interfere with) a convicted person's ability to behave as a human being capable of feeling, reflection, and choice: by inducing states of extreme terror, depression, and the like'.
29. And, following Rawls, it should come as no surprise that he is talking about the 'desire to act in accordance with the principles that would be chosen in the original position', J. Rawls (1999), *A Theory of Justice*, 2nd edn. (Oxford, UK: Oxford University Press), 275.
30. R. S. Gerstein (1974), 'Capital Punishment – "Cruel and Unusual"? A Retributivist Response', *Ethics*, 85:1, 75–9.
31. Ibid. 79, my emphasis.
32. Ibid. 78.
33. Id.
34. Id.
35. Id.
36. Compare, for example, Gerstein (1974), Spigelberg (1970) and Nussbaum (2004).
37. Gerstein (1974).
38. Spiegelberg (1970), 60.
39. Id.
40. Nussbaum (2004), 131–49.
41. I here take it for granted that whether or not punishment P affects a person's well-being is a necessary condition of the moral evaluation of P. So adherents of the dignity approach can either be pluralist in one way (claiming that dignity and other values like well-being are morally important in themselves) or pluralist in another way (claiming that dignity is of instrumental value relative to another value). Alternatively, they could be monists, claiming that dignity is all that morally matters in itself and that well-being is only of instrumental value relative to the value of dignity.
42. Thanks to Jesper Ryberg, Jakob v. H. Holtermann and Nils Holtug for valuable comments to an earlier version of this chapter. Also thanks to the participants at the ISUS conference at Berkeley University September 2008.

8
Punishment and Torture

Stephen Kershnar

In this paper, I argue that punitive torture is permissible. David Boonin puts forth a plausible account of legal punishment. He argues for the following (weaker) definition of 'legal punishment'.[1]

(1) P's act, a is a legal punishment of Q for offence o if and only if
- (a) *Official:* P is a legally authorized official acting in his or her official capacity,
- (b) *Offence:* P does a because P believes that Q has committed o,
- (c) *Intention:* P does a with the intent of harming Q, and
- (d) *Disapproval:* P's doing a expresses official disapproval of Q for having committed o.

Exactly what torture consists of varies.[2] On my account, one person tortures a second if and only if the first intentionally imposes very intense suffering on the second. This allows for torture designed to make someone's life worse (for example, punitive and sadistic torture), torture designed to benefit third parties (for example, interrogational torture), and torture designed to benefit someone (for example, therapeutic torture). Examples include severe sleep deprivation, electric shock, water boarding, pins shoved under fingernails, beatings, dog rape, and mutilation.

A critic of my definition might claim that it is too broad in that it includes sadistic sexual acts, boxing, and the performance of works of art intended to be extremely upsetting to their audiences. The same is true for the pain that religious ascetics might inflict on one another. The critic might continue, we also do not think that torture includes the kind of water boarding, sleep deprivation, and extreme hunger that is imposed on some members of the Special Forces. With the exception of Special-Force training, I doubt that the other activities usually involve enough suffering to count as torture. With regard to the Special Forces, my intuition is that these treatments are torture. My argument, however, does not depend on whether such treatments are torture. If the treatment consisted of rape by dogs, anal penetration by electrically heated instruments, intentional jaw breaking or connective tissue tearing, and so on, I suspect that most people would intuit that this is torture and this chapter is intended to focus on such treatments.

There are other challenges to the above definition of 'torture'. While I do not think this argument depends on it, I will touch on it because there might be concerns related to this issue. Michael Davis defines torture as 'the intentional testing of a sentient, helpless being's ability to bear suffering against that being's will and indifferent to his welfare'.[3] There are several problems with this definition. First, if testing is a necessary part of torture, than punitive torture in which the victim's suffering has already been taken into account is impossible, and it's not. Second, if the torturer has to be indifferent to the tortured victim's welfare, then therapeutic torture is impossible, and it's not. An interesting portrayal of such torture occurs in Anthony Burgess, *Clockwork Orange* (W. W. Norton and Company, Inc., 1962). However, it is not clear that ordinary language supports my position rather than Davis's. Perhaps this condition should be added to the above definition. Third, a person can validly consent to something that temporarily blocks his will (for example, consider Odysseus) and in that case Davis's definition makes it unclear whether persons can consent to torture.

In 'What's Wrong with Torture?' *Philosophy & Public Affairs* 33 (2005), 1–33, David Sussman argues that torture essentially involves a disruption of the victim's moral autonomy.[4] One problem with this account is that it doesn't account for the torture of non-autonomous beings like animals and the mentally disabled. A second problem with this account is that torture need not disrupt the victim's moral autonomy. For example, persons might retain their moral autonomy even while being caned, beaten, and so on. This in part explains why in rare cases we expect certain persons not to divulge secrets even when subjected to intense pain.[5]

Other accounts define 'torture' as something that 'is inflicted by or at the instigation of or with the consent or acquiescence of a public official or other person acting in an official capacity'. This definition comes from 'The Convention against Torture and Other Cruel, Inhuman, or Degrading Treatment or Punishment', adopted by the United Nations General Assembly.[6] This fails to recognize that torture can occur via persons other than officials, for example, Mafia dons, prison sadists, and revolutionaries.

In the next part of this paper, I set out the argument for punitive torture. In the last part, I consider objections.

8.1 Argument for punitive torture

8.1.1 Argument

My argument focuses on the following case: *Rape-Murder*.

Al batters and then rapes Betty. Afterward he is worried that she will tell the police, so he kills her. Al is fully responsible for his actions. Following statutory law, the state tortures him as a means of punishing him. It subjects him to severe sleep deprivation, water boarding, and a few beatings over a few weeks and then lets him go. Al prefers the torture to the other likely punishment (lengthy incarceration or death), although he gets no say in the matter. In addition, the torture is publicized and this deters other would-be aggressors. In so doing it brings about better results than alternative actions such incarceration, execution, or merely letting him go.

I shall assume that in this case the state has legitimate authority over its citizens. This ensures that the state has a right to punish.[7] This right rests on whatever gives the state legitimate authority over its citizens. This might be consent, fairness, rationality, and so on.

Here is my argument.

(P1) If there is no side-constraint against punitive torture and no overriding consequentialist reasons against it, then punitive torture is permissible.

(P2) In *Rape-Murder*, there are no side-constraints against punitive torture.

(P3) In *Rape-Murder*, there is no overriding consequentialist reason against punitive torture.

(C1) Hence, in *Rape-Murder*, punitive torture is permissible. [(P1)-(P3)]

(P4) If in *Rape-Murder* punitive torture is permissible, then punitive torture is sometimes permissible.

(C2) Hence, punitive torture is sometimes permissible. [(C1), (P4)].

It might be helpful here to go over a few of the central concepts in this argument. An act is grounded by a consequentialist reason when it is permissible, or would be permissible other things being equal, in virtue of the fact that it brings about a better outcome than any other act available to the agent. Except in cases of incommensurate goods, the better outcome is one that maximizes the good. An act is grounded by a non-consequentialist reason when it is grounded by a reason that is not a consequentialist one. A side-constraint is a non-consequential-ist reason to refrain from doing an action. My argument consists of a defence of the premises.

8.1.2   Premises

8.1.2.1   Defence of Premise (P1)

Premise (P1) states that if there is no side-constraint against punitive torture and no overriding consequentialist reason against punitive tor-ture, then it is permissible. The idea here is that in general an act is wrong only if it fails one of these conditions. This premise, then, rests on a more general theory of permissible actions.

It might also be thought that an act that is otherwise permissible might be wrong if it prevents an individual from satisfying an imperfect duty. An imperfect duty is a duty that is owed, but not to any particular person and, perhaps, not to do any particular type of act.[8] An example is charity. A person might have a duty to be charitable even though she has discretion as to whom to help and how to help them.

In this context, these duties are not relevant because we can posit that in *Rape-Murder*, the state or people imposing punishment have already satisfied their imperfect duties. Also, it is worth noting that like conse-quentialist duties, imperfect duties are mysterious because they posit duties that are not owed to anyone. On some accounts, this is a good reason to think that they don't exist.

8.1.2.2   Defence of Premise (P2)

Premise (P2) states that at least in *Rape-Murder*, there are no side-constraints against punitive torture. This in turn rests on two assump-tions. First, if something fails to satisfy a side-constraint, then it infringes on someone's moral right. Second, in *Rape-Murder*, no one's moral right is infringed. Both assumptions require defence.

a. Assumption #1: If something fails to satisfy a side-constraint, then it infringes on someone's moral right

The first assumption (if something fails to satisfy a side-constraint, then it infringes on someone's moral right) itself rests on two notions. The first notion is that if an act is wrong because it violates a side-con-straint, then it wrongs someone. The second notion is that if someone is wronged, then her right is infringed.

The first notion fails if there are free-floating wrongs. A free-floating wrong is one that does not wrong anyone.[9] Candidate free-floating wrongs involve degradation, attitudinal wrongs, and exploitation. The arguments for free-floating wrongs usually rely on either Kantian premises or the claim that they best explain our intuitions. In the next section, I discuss such objections and argue that there are no free-floating wrongs, but even if there were they would not be present in *Rape-Murder*.

The second notion fails if there are ways to wrong someone without infringing on her rights. If we view a right as a claim and a claim is a duty owed to one by another, then it is difficult to understand how this can occur. After all, if one person satisfies all of his duties towards a second, then it is intuitively hard to see how the first wrongs the second.

One might argue that one person can wrong a second if the first has a moral reason not to do certain things to a second, even if the reason does not ground a duty.[10] This might be the case on a utilitarian account, where one person, Charles, has a reason not to steal David's car not because Charles owes David a duty but because there is a utility-based reason not to do so and this reason focuses on David's well-being. I have my doubts whether such an act wrongs David because the wrongness of the action is explained in terms of the utility of the state of affairs and David's well-being is only part of this state of affairs. In any case, the utilitarian reason is not present in *Rape-Murder*.

b. Assumption #2: In Rape-Murder, no moral right is infringed

The second assumption is that in *Rape-Murder*, no one's moral right is infringed. This rests on a forfeiture theory. Because this theory forms the centrepiece of my argument for punitive torture, let us go through the argument for it. The first step in the argument is to note that our intuitions support a pre-institutional right to punish. To see this, consider the following case: *Striking Back*.

> In the state of nature, Frank batters, rapes, and sodomizes Gina. Because of what Frank has done to Gina, she strikes him, thereby intentionally causing him to suffer temporarily. Her strike causes temporary pain, but no lasting suffering, disability, or harm. Frank does not intend or know that Gina will strike him or otherwise cause him to suffer, nor does he consciously disregard the fact that she might do so.

Intuitively, Gina's act is just. Just acts are ones that do not infringe on anyone's moral rights. It intuitively seems that Gina does not infringe on Frank's right because Gina does not owe Frank compensation or other residue duty. If Gina does not infringe on Frank's right, or does so in accord with justice, then one of four things happens.

First, Gina's act might not infringe on Frank's right because his right to his body is complex, having something like the following content: *Gina-and-others-have-a-duty-not-to-touch-Frank's-body-unless-it-is-necessary-for-just-punishment-or-just-defense-etc.* This content will result in a right that is indistinguishable from forfeiture theory because it has the same implications for just punishment. However, this theory is unhelpful because the just-punishment condition makes reference to a person's right to his body and that is what is at issue.

Second, Gina's act might permissibly trump Frank's right. A reason (or an act done from a reason) trumps a right if it infringes on a right and the agent is justified in doing so. However, if Frank's right is infringed, whether trumped or not, then Frank is owed compensation or at least some other residue duty, for example, an apology. Intuitively, Frank is not owed either.[11]

Third, Frank might voluntarily lose or suspend his right. This might occur via consent or promise. A person does something voluntarily only if he does it intentionally (that is, with purpose, knowledge, or recklessness) and this is not true here. Hence, Frank does not voluntarily suspend or lose his right.

Fourth, given the failure of the above three theories, Frank's right must be forfeited. This is the *Forfeiture Theory*. On this account, this forfeiture is a primitive feature of how rights work. That is, forfeiture does not depend on a more fundamental theory of rights or morality.

On this account, forfeiture occurs only with regard to the victim. Again, this is a primitive feature of rights. The victim's agents may act on her behalf, but she alone has the right to punish. An exception occurs when she transfers it to someone else. In the state of nature, it is difficult to understand how when one person attacks a second, this changes the rights of third parties. Just as the property rights of third parties are not affected by transactions involving others, the same intuitively seems to be true with regard to their right to punishment. In addition, if in the state of nature, the right to punishment were not held by the victim alone, then if a third party acts on his own and imposes punishment on a wrongdoer then either the victim would not be able to justly punish the wrongdoer or there would be no proportionality-limit on just punishment. Both intuitively seem incorrect.

In addition, the right forfeited is either the right in question or an equivalent right. This is in part because otherwise punishment would be impossible in some cases. For example, a blind man who blinds another could not be punished. Nor could anyone punish a man who does not own a car and steals one from another. Note whether the right that is lost has a limited scope in time or whether the right is only temporarily lost is a distinction without a difference, because both descriptions are equivalent and there is no reason to prefer one over the other. On this account, the forfeited right acts as the ceiling on the amount of just punishment.

The right to punish is a claim to non-interference against the wrong-doer. The right to punishment is accompanied by a liberty against the victimizer to impose punishment. This liberty is an absence of a duty owed to him not to impose punishment. This right is usually, if not always, accompanied by a power over the claim. A claim is a duty owed by one individual to another. A power is the moral standing to eliminate, modify, or leave in place this duty.

The state has a legal right to punish individuals because it has or may exercise individuals' moral right to punish. The state may do so because individuals transfer their right to punish to the state or give permission for the state to act on their behalf. This is similar to other principal-agent contracts. They do this by whatever legitimates the state, probably actual consent. If this transfer creates a state monopoly in the right to punish, then state gains a monopoly over just punishment.

There are a host of standard objections to actual consent theory of state authority. Among them that consent is not given and if it is given then it is involuntary. It is also objected that even if consent is given and is both voluntary and fair, it is superfluous because other duties (for example, the duty of fair play) legitimate the state.[12] If these objections succeed, and I doubt they do, then whatever grounds state authority explains how the transfer of the right to punish occurs or alternatively how permission is given to exercise another's right to punish.

Note that the forfeiture theory explains why punishment is just, not why it is permissible. This is illustrated if it is possible to have a moral right to wrong actions.[13] *Forfeiture Theory*, then, does not provide a complete explanation of why punishment is permissible. However, when linked to a theory of right actions, it does so. For example, if one holds that an act is wrong only if it wrongs someone and that an act wrongs someone only if it infringes on her right, then the theory provides a complete explanation.[14]

Underlying this theory is the notion that if a state has a right, then it must get it from an individual or individuals. Hence, individuals separately or collectively cannot transfer more rights than they have to the state, although they can transfer less. If an individual may (in some sense) exercise a right and she transfers the right to the state, then the state may also exercise it. Whether the state may do so depends on issues such as whether there can be a right to wrong and whether the right was transferred in a way that makes its exercise depend on certain conditions that are not currently met. The conditions under a law-governed society are significantly different than those in the state of nature, but this does not eliminate the right to punish. It might, however, affect the conditions under which it may be exercised.

In *Rape-Murder*, Al forfeits his right against being raped and his right against being killed or a set of rights that is equivalent to the rights against being raped and killed. If torture is less severe than being raped and killed or an equivalent set of permitted activities, then forfeiture allows for it. Hence, in *Rape-Murder*, Al's right is not infringed. No one else's right is infringed. Punitive torture does not wrong his family because they do not own Al or his body and do not have a right that the state allow him to be present in their lives, support them, and so on. Punitive torture also does not infringe the rights of those state employees who impose the torture. So long as they give voluntary and fully informed consent to do so, their rights are not infringed even if the punishment psychologically harms them. Outside of Al, his family, and those state employees who impose punitive torture, there is no other person who might plausibly be thought to have her right infringed.

8.2.1.3   *Defence of Premise (P3)*

Premise (P3) states that in *Rape-Murder*, there is no overriding consequentialist reason against punitive torture. The case assumes this fact.

8.1.2.4   *Defence of (P4)*

Premise (P4) states that if in this case punitive torture is permissible, then punitive torture is sometimes permissible. This is true by definition.

8.1.2.5   *Other cases*

There is some reason to believe that punitive torture instituted regularly via the law would in general bring about desirable consequences. In theory, an increase in expected punishment brings with it an increase in deterrence and reduction in recidivism.[15] There is evidence for this theory. For example, increasing the probability that criminals will be punished has this effect.[16] Torture might be a cheaper way of providing the same expected punishment as long-term incarceration. In addition, there is some evidence that norms affect behaviour more when they are more salient and punitive torture would likely make certain norms more salient.[17]

Merely showing that punitive torture has a deterrence function is not enough to show that it brings about the best consequences, because the deterrence-related gains might be outweighed by its costs or because other approaches (for example, rehabilitation) might have as good effects at less cost. Even if punitive torture does not bring about the best consequences, opponents of punitive torture still need to show that the consequentialist losses are strong enough to override the state's (or perhaps the victim's) right to punish the offender. Given the largely silent literature on when rights are overridden and given the incredible benefits of deterrence, for example fewer homicides, this is difficult to show.[18]

8.2. Objections to the argument for punitive torture

Here I focus on objections to Premise (P2), the claim that in *Rape-Murder*, there are no side-constraints against torture. I do so because Premise (P1) is straightforward and dependent on a plausible account of permissible action. One might reject it, for example, if permissible actions are actions that reflect particular virtues, but a discussion of such theories is beyond the scope of this paper.[19] Premise (P3) is true by hypothesis. Premise (P4) is analytic.

8.2.1 Objection #1: Reject (P2) because the right against torture is inalienable

An objector might claim that because autonomy grounds rights, or at least some rights, these rights are inalienable. The idea here is that since autonomy grounds rights, that same ground can't permit the loss of autonomy.[20] So, for example, a person could not waive or forfeit a right against being lobotomized or a treatment so harsh that it reduces him to the level of an animal. Because a tortured person is not autonomous, at least during the period in which he is tortured, the right against torture is inalienable. This objection is independent of whether autonomy is viewed as a set of capacities or the exercise of these capacities.

This objection misconstrues the nature of rights that are grounded by autonomy. Autonomy includes a person's reflexive choice over whether to continue to be autonomous and, if so, the degree of autonomy to have. As a result, autonomy grounds the moral standing by which a person may control the shape and continuation of his autonomous life. In other words, self-determination permits a being to decide whether to continue to be self-determining and, if so, the degree of self-determination he shall have in the future. Since autonomy-grounded rights protect the choice whether to retain these rights, the rights protecting autonomy may be alienated.

The objector might respond that the existence of a reflexive right to give up one's autonomy is inconsistent with the respect for the value of autonomy.[21] The problem with this is that it misconstrues the value of autonomy. The value of autonomy does not rest on the notion that one should have a *maximal amount of control* over one's life, where the amount of control is the product of the significance of the choices and number of choices that a person can or does make. On this account, autonomy would permit a great deal of paternalistic coercion (for example, banning cigarettes) as a means of increasing the duration, and therefore amount, of control over their lives. Rather, the value of autonomy has to do with *narrative control*, the ability to shape one's life according to self-chosen principles. This can allow for a shortening of the number of choices, for example, via physician-assisted suicide, or a lesser quality of choices, for example, via the taking of recreational drugs that dull one's thought processes, so long as it is done in accord with a person's own principles.

Narrative control even allows for the choice to live with lessened or no rationality, because continued rationality might not be part of a person's life plan. This is analogous to the way in which an author is autonomous with regard to her work when she writes short stories rather than lengthy novels, even though the former involves a smaller number of choices about her characters and perhaps also less significant choices about them. *Narrative control* requires that a person be able to exercise reflexive control even when this disables or eliminates some first-order control. This might occur, for example, when a person gives informed consent to be addicted to some drug.

If the value of autonomy focuses on the *maximal amount of control*, this still need not rule out torture. Let us distinguish the short-term and long-term effects of torture. The two need not coincide and in the long term torture might, in some cases, increase the opportunity for or likelihood of autonomous thought, perhaps by giving the attacker, during recovery, more time and a less distracting atmosphere, by which to reshape his beliefs, values, intentions, and so on. A critic might claim that this is foolish. She might note that by all reports, a routine torture such as extreme sleep deprivation is an agonizing experience (that ultimately leads to death), which, like sensory deprivation, undoes the most basic capacities of self-directed thought. This description likely describes the short-term effects of many, if not all, tortures. However, it is possible that in the long term, torture causes the individual to reshape his life according to self-chosen principles. Perhaps it does so when an individual is recuperating and wondering how such a horror could have befallen him. Such a scenario is possible, however unlikely. If so, torture is not *per se* wrong, even if it is in the vast majority of cases.

8.2.2   Objection #2: Reject (P2) because it is wrong to turn a person's agency against himself

David Sussman argues that torture is wrong because it forces a victim to turn his agency against himself.[22] This explains why it is worse than other forms of brutality and cruelty.

> Torture does not merely insult or damage its victim's agency, but rather turns such agency against itself, forcing the victim to experience herself as helpless yet complicit in her own violation. This is not just an assault on or violation of the victim's autonomy, but also a perversion of it, a kind of systematic mockery of the basic moral relations that an individual bears both to others and to herself.[23]

He also argues that torture is wrong because it involves a person experiencing his body ceasing to be his and becoming another's.

> In a sense, his body ceases to be his, to be the substance in which he expresses his own attitudes, intentions, and feelings in a way that can be meaningful for others as a form of self-expression. Since the victim cannot effectively reassert himself physically against the assault (by fighting, fleeing, or shielding himself), his body becomes the medium in which someone else realizes or expresses his agency.[24]

This objection to torture captures an interpretation of the Kantian notion that torture fails to respect the dignity of the victim as a rationally self-governing agent.[25]

The first problem with this objection is that it is not clear how it works in cases in which the torturer seeks to impose punishment rather than use the victim to gain information. In such a case, the victim's body is not expressing anyone else's agency any more than an incarcerated prisoner is doing so.

The second problem is that, even in the case of interrogation, it is hard to see how this argument works. If a person is his body, then saying that his body is being used against himself just is saying that he is made to do certain things to which he does not consent. It is hard to see how this varies from incarceration, military conscription, or other involuntary punishments. If a person is not his body, then this is no different from using other things he cares about (for example, his family's well-being, money, and reputation) to guarantee that someone doessomething he does not want to do. This might be objectionable, but it is hard to see what is distinctively wrong about torture as opposed to other forms of rights-infringing leverage. Even if we focus on the fact that it uses a person's body against himself, incarceration does a similar thing by confining his body and thereby preventing him from leaving.

Sussman might instead be arguing that torture is wrong because it removes autonomy. It does so because of the difficulty of reasoning when experiencing extreme pain. If, however, the wrongness of torture is filled out in terms of the removal of autonomy then the torture is wrong for the same reason that murder, involuntary lobotomies, and other rea-son-ending acts are wrong. This undermines Sussman's central claim that torture is a unique wrong.

8.2.3 Objection #3: Reject (P2) because torture reflects contempt for the victim

On some completely different accounts of justice, an act that is neither exploitative nor rights-infringing can express contempt for a person and thereby fail to respect her as a person.[26] In general, a behaviour expresses an attitude just in case its asserts that the attitude is true or endorses it in some other way. This is probably a function of the agent's motive, intent, or the social understanding of her act.[27] For example, where the agent is motivated by the view that the man towards whom she acts has less intrinsic value than other persons, she intends to convey that view, and that is how her act is generally understood, her act expresses contempt for him. On some accounts, this expression is independent of whether the attitude or proposition is actually conveyed to an audience on a particular occasion and, on some accounts, on all occasions. In the case of criminals, the contempt likely involves the notion that the criminal has less intrinsic value than do other people.

One response here is that no such attitude is being taken towards the person being tortured. Rather this is a case of respecting her choice in the context of a fair set of rules. On this account, we respect the per-son as an equal by respecting her decisions. This fits with some Kant-inspired justifications of punishment.[28]

A second response is that this misconstrues justice. This is because justice focuses on the person who is acted on (that is, the person to be tortured), not the agent (that is, the torturer). The focus on the former rather than the latter provides a better explanation of what is involved in wronging a person. I think it also provides a better explanation of the non-consequentialist liberty that a person has to pursue his own projects, but I will not address this issue here. Given that it is a property of the person acted on (for example, his suffering or his autonomy) that explains why he may not be treated in certain ways, the wrongfulness of certain actions is a function of what is done to him. The attitude the agent takes towards the person towards whom he acts is relevant to judging the agent's blameworthiness, viciousness, and dangerousness, but not the act itself.[29] Agent-centered theories focus on things such as the rationality of the agent's action or the intrinsic badness of his attitude. In so doing, they presuppose that the treatment in question is bad or wrong rather than explain why it is bad or wrong. That certain acts (for example, battery and murder) fail to properly respect a person at least in part explains why desiring, intending, or willing them is wrong or bad.

Third, even if torture expresses the notion that criminals have less value than others, this does not disrespect them if they do have on average less value. To see that they do, consider the following two worlds. The first consists of one million good persons. The second consists of one million murderers. In both worlds there are equal levels of average and total well-being and in the latter world the legal regime has negated the wrongdoers' future threats through behavioural conditioning (similar to that portrayed in *Clockwork Orange*). The first world intuitively seems better.[30] The best explanation of this intuition and ones like it is that intrinsic value depends at least in part on the desert-adjusted value of persons having a given level of well-being.[31] On this account, a person's desert determines whether and the degree to which his doing well makes the world a better place. Since murderers, batterers, and other violent criminals often have negative desert, their well-being often counts for less in making the world a better place and might even make it worse.

8.2.4 Objection #4: Reject (P2) because torturing offenders is a free-floating wrong

Even if a torturer doesn't wrong the person being punished, he might still act wrongfully if he commits a free-floating wrong. An act is free-floating wrong if it is something a person should not do but that doesn't wrong anyone. Three purported types of free-floating wrongs are exploitation, indecency, and the failure to satisfy a consequentialist duty. We can ignore this third ground because consequentialist duties are distinct from justice-based ones.

Exploitation occurs when a person in a stronger position uses his stronger position to gain an unfair share of the benefits from a transaction.[32] The weaker party usually agrees because he is desperate and lacks reasonable alternatives. He is thus pressured by external circumstances into an unfair agreement. Since the weaker party validly consents to the transaction and usually benefits from it, exploitative transactions do not infringe on the party's moral rights and arguably do not wrong him. Still, such transactions intuitively seem wrong. Because punitive torture does not involve a transaction, this type of free-floating wrong is irrelevant.

Indecency involves interactions that are unnatural and, if observed, would cause a reasonable observer to feel disgust, nausea, or extreme emotional unrest. Examples include self-mutilation, fetishism, bestiality, and sexual interactions involving excrement. The reasonable observer should not be confused with a statistically average observer since the statistically average observer might get upset over a number of events (for example, surgery, gay male sex, and naked obese men) that are not indecent. It is hard to explain why indecent behaviour is wrongful given that some interactions that are indecent involve interactions that are fully informed, validly consented to and mutually beneficial.

Even if indecency is wrong, it is not clear that punitive torture is indecent. In some cases, it is likely that a reasonable person with sufficient knowledge about the criminal and his options would not feel disgust, nausea, or extreme emotional unrest if the latter were subject to treatment such as intense sensory or sleep deprivation, extremely loud noises, and violent shaking. One response here is to say that no amount of knowledge would change the response of a reasonable observer to watching someone scream and gyrate as electricity is sent through electrodes attached to his genitals. The responder might claim that my claim to the contrary relies on a definition of 'torture' that is misleading because it includes lesser forms of cruel treatment.[33] Here the responder and I seem to be at an impasse due in part to different visions of the reasonable observer.

8.2.5   Objection #5: Reject (P2) because the state acts unjustly when it uses an unreliable procedure

An objector might assert that the right to punish requires that the state or other agent have used a reliable procedure by which to identify the person or persons who may be punished.[34] The objector might continue that persons who engage in punitive torture typically use unreliable procedures in identifying who ought to be punished for serious crimes like murder and rape and thus who would trade down to torture. One concern with this objection is that the empirical claim is controversial. While there have been concerns about the unreliability of the procedure leading to capital punishment, it is not clear that the risk of punishing innocents in other contexts is inordinately large.[35] In part, the problem here is one of identifying what is an inordinately large risk.

This objection claims to show our whole criminal justice system is unjust. The problem with this objection is that it does not show that punitive torture is wrong. The wrongfulness of using an unreliable procedure is that it subjects persons to an unjustifiable risk. This is analogous to playing Russian roulette on someone.[36] This is wrong regardless of whether the person at risk is killed and the wrong is independent of the killing were it to occur. An unreliable criminal justice system wrongs all community members. It is an additional injustice only if an innocent person is tortured. Also, torture is similar to imprisonment in that in some cases we can fully compensate the victim.

8.3 Conclusion

In this chapter, I argued that punitive torture is permissible. My argument rested on the claim that in some cases there was neither a side-constraint nor a consequential override that made it impermissible. I then considered a range of objections. In particular, I considered objections that tried to establish that there was a side-constraint that ruled out punitive torture. These objections are that (i) the right against torture is inalienable, (ii) it is wrong to turn someone's agency against himself, (iii) torture reflects contempt for the victim, (iv) torture is a free-floating wrong, and (v) torture will be implemented via unreliable procedures. I argued that the objections all fail.

Notes

1. D. Boonin (2008), *The Problem of Punishment* (New York: Cambridge University Press), 24–5.
2. On some accounts, the term 'torture' lacks clear semantic borders, although progress can be made if we focus on types and models of torture. See J. J. Wisnewski (2008), 'It's About Time: Defusing the Ticking Bomb Argument', *International Journal of Applied Philosophy*, 22, 103–16, esp. 110.
3. M. Davis (2005), 'The Moral Justifiability of Torture and Other Cruel, Inhuman, and Degrading Treatment', *International Journal of Applied Philosophy*, 19, 167.
4. D. Sussman (2005), 'What's Wrong with Torture?', *Philosophy & Public Affairs*, 33, 1–33.
5. I owe the former point to Michael Davis, 'Torture and the Inhumane', unpublished manuscript.
6. The Convention against Torture and Other Cruel, Inhuman, or Degrading Treatment or Punishment', adopted by the United Nations General Assembly

resolution 39/46, December 10, 1984, http://www.ohchr.org/english/law/cat.htm.

7. The idea here is that a state just is an entity that claims a monopoly of the use of force in a region. It is legitimate if this claim is justified. For this account of a state, see R. Nozick (1974), *Anarchy, State, and Utopia* (New York: Basic Books), 23.

8. See I. Kant (1991), *The Metaphysics of Morals*, Mary Gregor, ed. (New York: Cambridge University Press), 65, 194, 240–2.

9. See J. Feinberg (1988), *Harmless Wrongdoing* (New York: Oxford University Press), 19.

10. For the notion that utilitarians have reasons to act rather than duties, see A. Norcross (2006), 'Reasons without Demands: Rethinking Rightness', in J. Dreier (ed.), *Blackwell Contemporary Debates in Moral Theory* (New York: Blackwell), 38–53.

11. Even if the right is trumped, it is not clear Boonin provides a convincing argument against this warranting punishment. I owe this point to Andy Cullison.

12. For the duty of fair play, see H. L. A. Hart (1955), 'Are There Any Natural Rights?', *Philosophical Review*, 64, 185; J. Rawls (1964), 'Legal Obligation and the Duty of Fair Play', in S. Hood (ed.), *Law and Philosophy* (New York: New York University Press), 9–10.

13. For a defence of the notion that there can be a right to do wrong, see J. Waldron (1981), 'A Right to Do Wrong', *Ethics*, 92, 21–39.

14. Examples of acts that might be considered wrong but do not wrong anyone include free-floating wrongs, acts done from an improper motive, and acts that prevent an agent from satisfying his imperfect duties. Examples of these can be seen in J. Feinberg (1988), *Harmless Wrongdoing* (New York: Oxford), 18–25, G. E. M. Anscombe (1981), 'Modern Moral Philosophy,' in *The Collected Moral Papers of G. E. M. Anscombe: Ethics, Religion, and Politics* (Oxford: Basil Blackwell), 26–42; I. Kant, *The Metaphysics of Morals*, 65, 194, 240–2.

15. The theory can be seen in R. Cooter and T. Ulen (2004), *Law and Economics* 4th edn. (Boston: Pearson), chs 11–12.

16. The empirical evidence can be seen in A. M. Polinsky and S. Shavell (2000), 'The Economic Theory of Public Enforcement of Law', *Journal of Economic Literature*, 38, 45–76; I. Ehrlich (1996), 'Crime, Punishment, and the Market for Offenses', *The Journal of Economic Perspectives*, 10, 43–67. See R. T. Wright and S. H. Decker (1994), *Burglars on the Job* (Boston, Northeastern University Press), especially 91ff; S. Cameron (1988), 'The Economics of Crime Deterrence: A Survey of Theory and Evidence', *Kyklos*, 41, 301–23; P. E. Tracy, M. E. Wolfgang, and R. M. Figlio (1990), *Delinquency Careers in Two Birth Cohorts* (New York, Plenum Press); V. K. Mathur (1978), 'Economics of Crime: An Investigation of the Deterrent Hypothesis for Urban Areas', *Rev Econ and Stat*, 60, 459–66. There is concern as to whether amount of punishment and probability of punishment act in an analogous manner. See John Henderson and John Palmer (2002), 'Does More Deterrence Require More Punishment? [or Should the Punishment Fit the Crime?]', *European Journal of Law and Economics*, 13, 143–56.

17. For the claim that norms affect behaviour more when they are more salient, see Cialdini et al. (1990), 'A Focus Theory of Normative Conduct: A Theoretical

Refinement and Reevaluation of the Role of Norms in Human Behavior', in *Advances in Experimental Social Psychology* (New York: Academic Press), 201–34; L. Berkowitz (1972), 'Social Norms, Feelings, and Other Factors Affecting Helping and Altruism', in L. Berkowitz (ed.), *Advances in Experimental Psychology* (New York: Academic Press), 6. For the notion that Norm expression is an important part of punishment, see J.-R. Tyran and L. Feld (2006), 'Achieving Compliance when Legal Sanctions are Non-Deterrent', *Scandinavian Journal of Economics*, 108, 135–56; R. Cooter (1998), 'Expressive Law and Economics', *Journal of Legal Studies*, 27, 585–608; D. Kahan (1998), 'Social Meaning and the Economic Analysis of Crime', *Journal of Legal Studies*, 27, 661–72; C. Sunstein (1996), 'On the Expressive Function of Law', *University of Pennsylvania Law Review*, 144, 2021–31. For the notion that norms affect behaviour more when people focus on them, see C. Bicchieri (2006), *The Grammar of Society: The Nature and Dynamics of Social Norms* (Cambridge: Cambridge University Press).

18. The discussion of overrides can be seen in J. J. Thomson (1990), *The Realm of Rights* (Cambridge: Harvard University Press), ch. 6; S. Brennan (1995), 'Thresholds for Rights', *The Southern Journal of Philosophy*, 33, 143–68; S. Brennan (1995), 'How is the Strength of a Right Determined? Assessing the Harm View', *American Philosophical Quarterly*, 32, 383–93. They concern the clearer notion that people's interests are relevant to when a right may be infringed and that the total amount of interests at stake and minimum for the affected parties are also relevant.

    In 2005, the latest available numbers, there were 16,692 people who were the victims of homicide. See Statistical Abstract of the United States 2009, Table 301, http://www.census.gov/compendia/statab/. The estimates of the value of a life vary. On one study the value of an average life in the United States is $5 million; on another, it is $7 million. Both use 1990 dollars. For the first, see D. Costa and M. Kahn (2004) 'Changes in the Value of Life, 1940–1980', *Journal of Risk and Uncertainty*, 29, 159–80. For the second see C. K. Viscusi (2008) 'How to Value a Life', *Journal of Economics and Finance*, 32, 311–323. Using the low-end estimate, the value of the lives lost is $83 billion. Given that in 1993, there were 24,526 homicides, different policies are able to affect the rate of homicide.

19. See, for example, G. E. M. Anscombe, 'Modern Moral Philosophy', 26–42.

20. The idea for this objection comes from J. Murphy (1979), 'Cruel and Unusual Punishments', in *Retribution, Justice, and Therapy* (Boston: Dordrecht), 223–49. Some opponents of torture focus on torture being an assault on the defenceless. H. Shue (1978), 'Torture', *Philosophy and Public Affairs*, 7, 124–43. It is hard to see how being defenceless, as opposed to be being bad at defence, is morally relevant unless it entails the presence of protective rights.

21. An analogous claim can be seen in John Stuart Mill who argues that the principle of freedom does not allow persons to be free not to be free. J. S. Mill (1978), *On Liberty*, E. Rapaport (ed.) (Indianapolis: Hackett), ch. V, sec. 11, 101–2.

22. See Sussman, 28–33. A similar argument can be seen in Kleinig, 'Ticking Bombs and Torture Warrants', 619–20.

23. Ibid., 30.
24. Ibid., 31–2.
25. See Sussman, 19.
26. In context of punishment, this idea can be seen in T. Metz (2000), 'Censure Theory and Intuitions about Punishment', *Law and Philosophy*, 19, 491–512; J. Hampton (1992), 'An Expressive Theory of Retribution', in W. Cragg (ed.), *Retributivism and Its Critics* (Stuttgart: F. Steiner Verlag), 1–25; I. Primoratz (1989), 'Punishment as Language', *Philosophy*, 64, 187–205. In bringing up this theory, I do not mean to endorse it. My view is that as a non-consequentialist justification of punishment it is superfluous because it presupposes and trivially follows from the truth of non-expressive retributivism. For an argument in support of this see M. Davis (1991), 'Punishment as Language: Misleading Analogy for Desert Theorists', *Law and Philosophy*, 10, 311–22.
27. More broadly, this might be a function of the speaker meaning, that is, what the speaker (or punishing body) in uttering a sentence (or imposing a punishment) intends to convey to the hearer. The speaker meaning consists of a nested set of intentions. Alternatively, this might be a function of meaning of the sentence (or punishment) itself. This distinction comes from H. P. Grice (1957), 'Meaning', *Philosophical Review*, 66, 377–88; H. P. Grice (1969), 'Utterer's Meaning and Intentions', *Philosophical Review*, 78, 147–77. A different but still Gricean analysis can be seen in Robert Nozick's discussion of the idea that punishment should express to the wrongdoer that his act was wrong and to show him its wrongfulness. R. Nozick (1981), *Philosophical Explanations* (The Belknap Press of Harvard University Press), 366–74, esp. 371.
28. See, for example, Herbert Morris (1968), 'Persons and Punishment', *The Monist* 52, 475–501; Jeffrie G. Murphy (1973), 'Marxism and Retribution', *Philosophy & Public Affairs* 2, 217–43.
29. The notion that nonconsequentialism is closely tied to virtue is found in P. Foot (1985), 'Utilitarianism and the Virtues', *Mind*, 94, 273–83.
30. The idea for this argument and example comes from W. D. Ross (1988), *The Right and the Good* (Indianapolis: Hackett Publishing Company), 138.
31. See Feldman, 'Adjusting Utility for Justice: A Consequentialist Reply to the Objection from Justice', 154–74; T. Hurka (2001), *Virtue, Vice, and Value* (New York: Oxford University Press), chs 1–2; Thomas Hurka (2001), 'The Common Structure of Virtue and Desert', *Ethics*, 112, 6–31; S. Kagan (1999), 'Equality and Desert,' in L. Pojman and O. McLeod (eds), *What Do We Deserve?* (New York: Oxford University Press), 298–314; N. Feit and S. Kershnar (2004), 'Explaining the Geometry of Desert', *Public Affairs Quarterly*, 18, 273–98.
32. Such an account can be found in Wertheimer, *Exploitation*.
33. I owe this response to Michael Davis.
34. This idea for this notion comes from Robert Nozick's notion that there is a natural right against an unreliable procedure being used to determine who may be punished. Nozick, *Anarchy, State, and Utopia*, 104–6.
35. The Innocent Project claims that since 1992, there have been 15 people on death row who have been exonerated. The Innocence Project, 'After 21 Years in Prison – Including 16 on Death Row – Curtis McCarty is Exonerated Based on DNA Evidence', http://www.innocenceproject.org/Content/575.php.

See, also, M. Radelet et al. (1992), *In Spite of Innocence* (Boston: Northeastern Press); M. Radelet and H. A. Bedau (1987), 'Miscarriages of Justice in Potentially Capital Cases', *Stanford Law Rev.*, 40, 21–90. This last article has come under fire. See S. Markman and P. Cassell (1995), 'Protecting the Innocent: A Response to the Bedau-Radelet Study', *Stanford Law Review*, 41, 121–61.

36. This analogy comes from Nozick, Ibid., 105.

9
Punishment and Public Opinion

Jesper Ryberg

What role, if any, should public opinion play when it comes to the question of how society should react to people who have violated the law; that is, what is the moral significance of the view or mood of the public when it comes to sentencing matters? In the following, this question will constitute the focal point; there are, I believe, several reasons for directing attention to this particular issue.

First of all, it is a fact that, over the past two decades or so, increasing attention has been paid to public opinion as part of the development of sentencing policy. Public opinion has become a standard reference point for politicians in their advocacy of penal reforms (often in the direction of more severe sentencing). For instance, a typical way of making the point was used by Tony Blair when he said 'there are more prison places, sentences are longer and sentences are tougher but if you look where the public is on this issue, the gap between what they expect and what they get is bigger in this service than anywhere else and we have got to bridge it'.[1] Similar expressions of the view, that penal policy and practice should be adjusted in accordance with public views on the matter, have been made by influential politicians of many other Western countries. The reverse idea – that legislation as well as individual sentencing decisions by the courts is supposed to educate or lead public opinion – seems to have very little current resonance. On the contrary, what is held to constitute public opinion is apparently attributed a crucial justificatory role when it comes to sentencing policy and practice. But if that is so, it certainly becomes natural to ask whether this position can stand further scrutiny, that is, whether the alleged justificatory role of public opinion in relation to sentencing is itself justified.

That there are reasons to be sceptical with regard to the justificatory force attributed to public opinion has been underlined by several law scholars, criminologists and other academic researchers. In fact, sentencing initiatives introduced by politicians with references to the fact that they mirror public opinion are often discussed under the heading 'penal populism' or 'populist punitiveness'.[2] The meaning of these terms is, obviously, not to indicate that a sentencing policy is popular in the sense that it carries widespread public approval. On the contrary, 'populism' is used in its pejorative sense. What this means is not simply that a certain policy is advanced to please the voters. Though few would probably consider this a noble motive, it is nevertheless hard to regard it as genuinely problematic if, in the end, this policy turns out to be justified. The right policy for the wrong reasons is much less problematic than a case where popularity is pursued at the cost of a well-founded sentencing policy. And it is precisely in such a case that the accusation of populism appears apposite.[3] However, this obviously prompts the question as to whether the fact that a sentencing political initiative reflects public opinion is something which in one way or another carries any justificatory weight. That is, whether popularity and justification, so to speak, come in the same package. If this is the case, then the populism accusation may less often be justified. Thus, not only the more general political movement towards greater public consultation, but also the reaction in terms of populism accusations, makes it reasonable to subject the justificatory role of public opinion in relation to penal policy to a closer examination.

Though there exists a very comprehensive empirical literature concerning public views on sentencing, the discussion on the *moral significance* of public opinion is far more limited. No theorists, to my knowledge, defend the view that sentencing legislation and practice should be determined exclusively on the ground of public opinion. A number of theorists, on the other hand, seem to favour the view that public opinion should have some limited role to play in relation to sentencing. However, when judgements along these lines are presented, they are in many cases not very thoroughly sustained. Perhaps this is not surprising. The relevance of public attitudes to sentencing clearly depends on what is regarded as the overall purpose of sentencing.[4] Thus, an answer itself presupposes a sustained answer to the more basic question concerning the justification of sentencing; which means that one is moving directly into a more complicated theoretical field that does not allow for simple answers. For this reason – that is, more precisely, in the absence of an attempt to deliver a solution to the question of the justification of punishment – what I shall do in the following is not to defend one final answer concerning the justificatory role of public opinion on sentencing. More modestly, the idea is to consider the significance of public attitudes seen from the perspectives of the traditional penal theoretical positions. The purpose of this chapter thereby is to specify under which conditions public attitudes may be relevant in relation to sentencing and to clarify in what sense public opinion may be relevant. The relevance of the latter question relates directly to the fact often emphasized in the empirical studies of public opinion, namely, that it is far from clear what is meant by 'public opinion' when references to its justificatory power are presented.

Though empirical research has been conducted with regard to various aspects of public views on sentencing, what I shall do in this chapter is to delimit the investigation to the question of the relevance of public opinion in relation to how severely different crimes should be punished. The ethical significance of public attitudes to this question will then firstly be considered from a utilitarian outlook and subsequently from a retributivist point of view. Before embarking on this scrutiny, however, one final comment is needed. It might be felt that the assumption that one has to consider the basic purpose of sentencing – and thus engage in traditional penal theory – in order to clarify the justificatory significance of public opinion is somewhat premature. After all, within a democratic framework it is hard to reject the claim that what basically justifies political decisions is that they represent the *vox populi*. Thus, in the case that one favours democracy – the argument goes – nothing further is required in order to justify a certain policy on penal levels than to establish that this policy reflects public opinion on the matter. In fact, this argument is now and then contended in political debates. However, it faces several problems.

First, it is certainly not unproblematic to suggest that the fact that there is democratic support for a certain decision is sufficient to make the decision morally right. A purely procedural criterion of rightness – such as the one that would follow by holding an act or decision right because it represents the vote of the majority – implies that any act or decision in principal can become right no matter how horrendous it may seem. A much more promising suggestion is to contend that there are strong arguments in favour of democracy and that these arguments establish that we are well-advised to follow the decisions made within the demo-cratic framework. However plausible this sounds, it is clear that the above argument faces another simple problem, namely, that it does not follow from the fact that one subscribes to democracy that individual political decisions should represent the voice of the people. All modern democracies are representative systems with various individual deci-sions made which do not necessarily represent the view of the public. This is also the case with regard to the criminal justice system. Criminal law is not formed by the people but by representatives and sometimes sentencing commissions, while individual sentencing decisions are made by a judiciary system where the distance from the public, through various steps of delegation, is even larger.[5] But this does not change the fact that we are still talking about sentencing within a democratic system. Thus, in order for it to hold water, the argument not only presupposes subscription to democracy but also to a particular version of a democracy of direct nature (or with representatives strongly bound by what constitutes the prevailing opinion of the public). Whether such versions of democracy are preferable to other less direct versions is a complicated question, which obviously cannot be settled within the scope of this chapter. For the present it is sufficient to note that the inference from the subscription to democracy to the conclusion that a sentencing policy should reflect prevailing public attitudes is not as straightforward as it may appear. And that the argument apparently presupposes a democratic system very different from the system we are familiar with in most Western countries today. Thus, in sum, there still seems to be room for the sort of considerations to which we shall now turn concerning the role that should be attributed to public opinion within a penal theoretic framework.

9.1   Consequentialism and public opinion

What role does public opinion on sentencing play if one adopts a consequentialist point of view, such as, say, a standard utilitarian view on sentencing? The simple answer is that the fact that there exists a divergence between, on the one hand, what constitutes the correct utilitarian answer as to how severely different crimes should be punished and, on the other, public attitudes to whatever a utilitarian approach would prescribe, does not constitute a reason for revising the prescribed penal levels. However, obviously this answer is beside the point. The question we are addressing is not whether the correct utilitarian answer to sentencing should be adjusted in accordance with public attitudes but rather whether the public attitude may itself be part of what constitutes the correct utilitarian answer. Furthermore, the relevant question is not whether the public knows enough or is qualified to be able to identify what constitutes the right punishment scheme seen from a utilitarian point of view. In their advocacy of disregarding public views on sentencing, Bagaric and Edney contend that: 'Seeking public views on sentencing is analogous to doctors basing treatment decisions on what the community thinks is appropriate or engineers building cars, not in accordance with the rules of physics, but on the basis of what lay members of the community "reckon" seems about right'.[6] However, clearly this analogy only concerns the identification of the right sentencing policy, that is, it does not suffice to establish that public views on sentencing may not in some way be of relevance in relation to utilitarian sentencing. Thus, in order to clarify the relation between utilitarian sentencing and public opinion what one will have to consider is, firstly, whether there are any ways in which public views on how severely criminals should be punished may become relevant in the utilitarian calculus and, secondly, if this is the case, how this would affect the utilitarian sentencing prescriptions. Let us consider each question in turn.

Even though a discrepancy between the public attitude to sentencing and actual sentencing practice is often highlighted as something which has undesirable consequences, it is less often made clear what precisely these consequences are supposed to consist of. However, an obvious answer is that a mismatch may have consequences in terms of impaired confidence in the criminal justice system. An argument along these lines is presented by Julian Roberts when he contends that 'if sentencing practices diverged widely and consistently from public opinion the legitimacy of the judicial system would be compromised' and, further, that if an imagined sentencing system ignored proportionality considerations then, once these 'penal anomalies' came into public attention, 'confidence in criminal justice would surely decline'.[7] Now, it seems obvious to interpret this confidence-based reasoning as a consequentialist argument. However, it is also clear that, in order to assess this argument, more needs to be said on what the outlined consequences amount to. The question is why does an impaired public confidence constitute a problem within a utilitarian framework?

From the outset it is not clear that a lack of confidence *per se* is of significance from a utilitarian point of view. It is a fact that the public in many Western countries expresses a limited confidence in the criminal justice system and that, when people are asked to indicate the confidence they have in different branches of the criminal justice system, the courts score less than most other branches (for example, the police).[8] In fact, it is not uncommon to talk of 'the crises of confidence in the courts'.[9] However, the fact that someone believes that the courts are dealing unsatisfactorily with crime need not in itself have any significance with regard to what is valuable from a utilitarian outlook. Whether this is so depends upon what type of quality of life theory one is adhering to as a utilitarian. For instance, on the ground of a hedonistic theory of well-being it does not seem to be the case that the mere belief that someone, say the court, is not doing a good job, need have any concomitant implications in terms of pleasure or pain. Thus, how can a lack of confidence in the courts or dissatisfaction with existing sentencing patterns become significant for the utilitarian? Several answers come to mind.

A first possibility is to point to the strong feelings that often seem related to people's assessments of how the criminal justice system, or the court in particular, is operating. It is a fact that, even though expressions of a lack of trust – or of a divergence between what one regards as appropriate sentencing levels and what constitutes the sentencing practice at the courts – may well be nothing more than mere factual statements, they are often accompanied by some sort of emotional reaction. This reaction may vary in strength from minor feelings of indignation to more powerful feelings of frustration or anger. If this is the case, that is, if the public dissatisfaction with sentencing practice gives rise to these kinds of feelings, then clearly we are closer to something which even a hedonist utilitarian would have to take into account in the outline of relevant consequences. In fact, this is what Bentham had in mind when he said that a 'portion of superfluous pain is ... produced when the punishment is unpopular: but in this case it is produced on the part of persons altogether innocent, the people at large'.[10]

A second possibility concerns the ways in which people act in relation to the courts or perhaps other parts of the criminal justice system. It is a well-known fact that police-work often depends, to some degree, on public confidence. If people do not trust the police and consequently are less willing to cooperate when this is required, this may seriously affect an essential part of the police-work (for example, the apprehension of criminals). Likewise, it might be held that a lack of confidence in the courts may make people less cooperative when they take part in the court process – for example, as witnesses or jury members – and that this may in the end have serious consequences such as, for instance, mistaken convictions or sentences. In so far as distrust has these kinds of implications it is obviously something which is of relevance from a utilitarian point of view. Again, Bentham is well aware of this possibility when he notes that 'When people are satisfied with the law, they voluntarily lend their assistance in the execution: when they are dissatisfied, they will naturally withhold that assistance; it is well if they do not take a positive part in raising impediments'.[11]

A third way in which public dissatisfaction may turn out to have relevant consequences is if a lack of confidence prompts people to take the law into their own hands. The feeling that the existing sentencing order or a sentence in a particular case is totally out of step with what justice requires may lead people to attempt to pursue justice themselves. That punitive reactions outside the control of the criminal justice system may have terrible consequences, no matter whether they affect innocent persons or someone who is guilty of a crime, is a well-known fact and is obviously something a utilitarian would have to take into account.

A final possibility is that distrust can be imagined as leading into crime in a broader way than is the case when people take the law into their own hands. As Robertson and Darley have noted the 'compliance power of the criminal law is directly proportional to its moral credibility'[12]. In other words, it may be the case that a failure of the criminal justice system to capture the public perception of justice may undermine the perceived legitimacy of the system and, in the end, compliance with the law. Once again, this is something which would be highly significant from a utilitarian point of view.

What the foregoing shows is that there are several ways in which a failure of the criminal justice system when it comes to reflecting public attitudes to sentencing may have consequences of a sort that would figure in a utilitarian calculus. The next question of course is whether the existence of these possible outcomes can be empirically sustained. That this is a complicated question becomes obvious when it is kept in mind that the issue we are addressing is not merely whether there exists a lack of public confidence in the courts, but rather whether public attitudes have any justificatory weight in relation to the question of how severely the criminal justice system should deal with crime. Consider, for instance, a situation in which some people decide to take the law into their own hands. This type of decision may spring from a powerful feeling of anger – as when someone seeks to avenge a crime committed against a family member – or a feeling of disgust – as when people persecute someone guilty (or assumed guilty) of paedophilia. However, people acting out of such vindictive feelings may have no idea of the severity of the actual punishment which the offender has received or perhaps will receive for having committed the crime. What happens within the framework of the criminal justice system may sometimes be regarded as irrelevant in relation to the wish for revenge; which means that the punishment imposed by an avenging party is not necessarily a result of dissatisfaction with court sentencing. The same is the case if we consider the possible link between dissatisfaction with the criminal law and compliance. Merely to establish that there is a correlational relation between dissatisfaction and reduced compliance will not do as empirical evidence. What we need to know is something about cause and effect. Or, put into more general terms: in order to establish that public attitude to sentencing is something which the utilitarian ought to take into account, it needs to be shown – or at least made probable – that the outlined types of consequences actually follow from a discrepancy between public perceptions of sentencing and the criminal law or existing penal practice.

Now, as initially mentioned, the point here is not to present an argument to the effect that public opinion should (or should not) have any justificatory weight, but more modestly to consider under which conditions this would be the case. Thus, to what extent it is possible to provide the suggested empirical evidence is something which will not be pursued any further in the following. Rather, let us *ex hypothesis* assume that some of the suggested consequences can in fact be empirically substantiated. What would this imply? Would this be sufficient to commit the utilitarian to adjust – at least to some extent – sentencing law or practice in accordance with public opinion? That the answer must be in the negative is clear. In fact, there are several reasons as to why this conclusion would be premature.

The first reason follows from the simple fact that utilitarian action-guidance rests on a weighing of pros and cons. It may well be the case that a mismatch between public attitudes to sentencing and the sentencing practice at the courts has undesirable consequences and that these consequences could be avoided by adjusting sentencing to whatever the public perceives as appropriate. But obviously this kind of adjustment may itself have a number of undesirable implications which would have to be weighed against what is gained. Put in less general terms: even if it is correct that by increasing sentencing one could avoid public frustration and implications of a lack of confidence, such as the taking of the law into one's own hands or a reduced compliance with the law, there may be costs to be placed in the opposite scale. The most obvious costs include the extra amount of hardship that would be inflicted on the offenders who are being punished more severely, as well as the side-effects this would have on the relatives and other people associated with an offender. Moreover, there are extra costs in terms of the simple fact that punishing offenders is expensive. The money that this would require could have been channelled into other well-being-enhancing societal institutions (for example, within healthcare, education and so on). What this means is that, in order to determine what would follow from a utilitarian point of view, further considerations are needed concerning the strength and extent of the suggested costs. Since it is obvious that harder sentencing will affect for the worse all offenders who are punished, the challenge one is faced with from the outset is that of establishing that these costs are counterbalanced by what is gained by making up for a discrepancy between actual sentencing and public attitudes to sentencing. That this is the case is not something that can be taken for granted.

The second reason as to why the costs associated with a discrepancy between actual sentencing and public views on sentencing does not justify the conclusion that the utilitarian ought to adjust the former to the latter, relates to the simple fact that utilitarianism does not imply that an act is right just because performing it would have better consequences than not performing it. Rather, what utilitarianism implies is that one should pick the very action, from the whole set of alternative options, that produces the best outcome. That this is important in the present context becomes clear if one takes a closer look at what characterizes public views on sentencing. One of the insights repeatedly emphasized by social scientists is that it makes a major difference whether people express their views on sentencing in general or in relation to individual and more well-described cases. Though several explanations can be given as to why people react more punitively when responding to the general questions – such as whether they regard sentencing levels as too lenient, too severe, or about right – the dominant view clearly is that there is a relation between the levels of punitiveness and the levels of information. As Karen Gelb has recently put it, there is 'substantial evidence that the public's lack of knowledge about crime and justice is related to the high levels of punitiveness reported as a response to a general, abstract question about sentencing'.[13] Furthermore, when people are provided with more detailed information about crime and punishment issues their level of punitiveness decreases to a point where their judgements are in line with – sometimes even below – the sentences given by judges in actual cases.[14] Now, on the one hand, it is obvious that when it comes to assessing the consequences of an act it is not in itself important whether the party carrying out the act is correctly informed. Dissatisfaction with the criminal justice system resulting in a public feeling of frustration or a diminished degree of public compliance with the law is not a less serious problem, in the sense that these consequences are less significant in the utilitarian calculus, just because they are fostered on the ground of ignorance. On the other hand, if this is the case, that is if the consequences follow from a lack of knowledge, this means that there may be alternative ways in which these consequences could be avoided. If there is a gap between what the public believes constitutes that actual sentencing pattern and what it regards as appropriate sentencing, and if this gap has undesirable consequences, then it seems that there are two tracks to follow in the attempt to remedy the problem: either adjusting sentencing to public opinion or bringing public opinion in accordance with what constitutes the appropriate level of sentencing.[15] Given the alternatives between sentencing more severely and engaging in what Bentham at one point called 'the art of public education' it is obvious – for reasons outlined above – what would be preferable from a utilitarian point of view. Bentham, himself, emphasized the importance of the latter when he, in more general terms, held that 'Every nation is liable to have its prejudices and its caprices, which it is the business of the legislator to look out for, to study, and to cure'.[16] Now, this obviously prompts the question as to what extent it will actually be possible to increase the public level of knowledge on crime and punishment issues. That more could be done in this respect than has been the case in many countries can hardly be denied. Moreover, a number of proposals have been developed with the goal of mitigating the crisis of confidence in the courts.[17] However, in the present context I shall not engage any further in such considerations. The point here is merely to emphasize the possibility of alternative ways of dealing with undesirable consequences that might follow from a mismatch between (perceived) sentencing and public attitudes.

What can be concluded on the ground of the above considerations is the following. Considering the significance of public attitudes to sentencing it certainly cannot be excluded that such attitudes may have a role to play within a utilitarian framework. However, it is also clear that the inference from, on the one hand, the fact that there exists some sort of mismatch between public views on sentencing and sentencing law or practice to, on the other, the conclusion that a more severe sentencing scheme ought to be adopted, is far from straightforward. What this inference requires in order to hold is, firstly, that one is able to establish, or at least make probable, that this mismatch has undesirable consequences, that is, that these consequences would not have followed had there not been a mismatch. Secondly, even if such consequences – as, for example, a lack of confidence or diminished compliance with the law – can be shown to follow from the existing sentencing practice, it also has to be shown that they outweigh the costs of increasing sentencing practice. The fact that these costs, both for the offenders who are sentenced more severely and for society at large, may be comprehensive, makes it dubious whether this premise can be sustained. Finally, even if this is the case, it also has to be shown that other less costly alternatives to increased sentencing – such as increased public information – are not viable options. Thus, all in all, it is clear that there is no simple route for justifying harsher punishments by reference to public opinion within a utilitarian sentencing scheme.

9.2   Retributivism and public opinion

Retributivism constitutes the traditional rival theory to the utilitarian view on sentencing. As is often emphasized, the retributivist approach has dominated the penal theoretical field over the last three or four decades. Leaving aside the fact that retributivism has been given very different forms in the modern literature, let us roughly say that retributivism is a deontological theory that justifies punishment by reference to the desert of the offender. The question then is: does the retributive approach leave any room for public opinion? That is, should the public view on sentencing have a role to play when it comes to the determination of the just deserts of offenders? Even though references to public opinion in modern retributivist literature are rare, there nevertheless seems to be some doors open to the possibility of letting considerations of public views into a desert-based approach to sentencing. Let us consider these possibilities in turn.

An explicit attempt to invoke public view on sentencing within a retributivist penal scheme has been presented by Malcolm Davies, who regards public opinion as crucial with regard to the cardinal retributivist idea of proportionality in sentencing. In order to provide an answer as to how severely different crimes should be punished, the retributivist has to answer the question of how the scales of crime gravity and punishment severity should be linked. What Davies contends is that '[w]ith sentencing policy there is no ocean floor on which to anchor the system of proportionality. Ocean floors are variable in depth as well as out of sight to the spectator, but at sea level that which floats is visible. And this is where the tariff of sentencing should start – with what is visible and floats on a sea of public acceptability'.[18] Unfortunately, this metaphorical way of presenting his thoughts leaves it somewhat unclear precisely what Davies has in mind. Several interpretations are possible.

The first is to interpret the proposal as a type of anchor point theory. One of the ideas which have been defended by modern retributivists is that the crime scale and the punishment scale should be linked at the bottom and top of the scales. However, the questions as to what constitutes the most lenient punishment, and why this particular punishment should constitute the appropriate response to the least serious crime, have not been made very clear by theorists favouring this type of answer to the anchor problem.[19] The same is the case with regard to the upper anchor point, that is, with regard to what constitutes the most severe punishment and why this punishment is the one that should be imposed for the most serious type of crime. However, perhaps these challenges could be overcome simply by holding that 'the tariff of sentencing should start' by the punishment which the public regards as appropriate for the least serious crime. Correspondingly, the upper anchor point could be determined on the ground of what the public regards as the fitting punishment for the most serious crime. By identifying the upper and lower anchor points in this way – with all the punishments for the other crimes falling in between these points – one could hold that the anchor problem has been solved.

However, on closer scrutiny this proposal faces several problems. Whether the question of punishment distribution can plausibly be resolved by a theory of anchor points depends on how crimes and punishments are scaled. Suppose first that we are considering a mere ordinal matching of crimes and punishments. In that case the matching is faced with an obvious 'bunching' problem. That is, this sort of matching opens up the possibility of letting the punishments for different crimes float freely, as long as the ordinal order of the punishment of crimes is observed. For instance, one could punish the theft of $100 with a particular fine, the theft of 200$ with a slightly larger fine, and finally the theft of 300$ with several years of imprisonment. As long as one is operating within the lower and upper anchor points and the order of the crimes is maintained in the respective punishments, the proposal allows for what seem highly arbitrary jumps in the way the punishment of crimes is distributed. In fact, this is precisely the reason why most retributivists who have considered the issue hold that the matching of the two scales must somehow account for the *spacing* between the crimes on the gravity scale. Let us therefore assume that this is the case, that is, that we have some sort of interval matching of the scales which manages to reflect the comparative differences in seriousness between different crimes. Even though this from the outset seems more plausible, the suggested solution to the anchor problem still faces problems. As we have seen, the central part to the proposal is that the anchor points should be determined by reference to what the public regards as the proper punitive responses to respectively the least and the most serious crimes. Now, given an interval matching the two anchor points are sufficient to make the punishments for all other crimes fall into place. But what if the punishments for these crimes do not reflect the views of the public? Even though the upper and lower anchor points are determined by the view of the public, it need not be the case that the public view accords with all the punishment levels that follow from an interval matching of the two scales.[20] But if this is so, then it seems that the suggested solution to the anchor problem becomes somewhat arbitrary. It is simply not clear why it is the top and bottom of the scales that should be determined by public opinion and not some of the other punishments which reflect the view of the public (and on the ground of which an interval matching might just as well be constructed!). There are further problems facing the theory and to these we shall shortly return. However, before doing so it is worth considering one possible way of meeting this objection of arbitrariness.

It might be suggested, that Davies' proposal could be interpreted somewhat differently. Rather than a theory concerning anchor points, the idea of holding that the tariff of sentencing should float 'on a sea of public acceptability' might imply that *all* the punishments of the different crimes should be determined on the ground of public opinion. More precisely, the retributivist might hold that, as long as the basic ordinal proportionality constraint is observed – that is, a more serious crime is always punished more severely than a less serious crime, while equally serious crimes are punished equally severely – one simply determines the precise punishments for each crime on the scale by consulting the public view on the matter. If one abandons the idea of an interval matching and returns instead to the more simple model of a purely ordinal matching, then this would leave room for the possibility of determining the punishment for each crime on the ground of public opinion. This proposal would avoid the above accusation of arbitrariness directed against the anchor point model. Moreover, it would provide an answer to the problem of under-determination that usually follows from a purely ordinal matching (namely, that this type of matching does not provide a final answer as to how different crimes should in the end be punished). Thus, have we here reached a plausible solution to the anchor problem by letting recognition of public opinion operate within the framework of the retributivist idea of a proportionalist distribution of punishment?

The answer depends upon a further simple question, namely, why should we accept this solution? It is a fact that a number of retributivists have engaged in moral considerations of cardinal proportionality and have sought to develop what they regard as plausible solutions to the anchor problem.[21] Thus, it is clearly not sufficient merely to present the outlined proposal; what is needed is a justification. That is, we need to know why this proposal should be accepted rather than any other theory of anchoring. But what would such an argument look like? The reason provided by Davies rests on his denunciatory retributive view on punishment. Roughly, what he suggests is that the idea of *the public* is founded on the idea of shared beliefs which are institutionalized in social relations. Moreover, 'denunciation reassures citizens that the values that underpin their way of life and the rights, rules and responsibilities that go with these values are worthy of condemnation if breached'.[22] In an almost Durkheimian style he holds that '[w]e collectively define what sort of people we are by denouncing the type of people we are not'.[23] This is why, from a denunciatory-retributive perspective, 'the system of proportionality should be floating on the waves of public consent, not hidden in the invisible mud of the ocean floor'.[24] An argument, with a clear affinity to Davies', might be suggested as a part of a more general expressionist-retributive view on punishment. For instance, Roberts sustains the view that a desert-based model of sentencing cannot ignore public perceptions by holding that it 'would make little sense for the sentencing process to express censure on behalf of the community, yet pay no attention to public opinion regarding the kinds of offences and offenders which in the eyes of the community are seen as being most worthy of condemnation'.[25] Even though this, strictly speaking, sounds like an argument concerning ordinal proportionality it might be suggested that the censure-on-behalf-of-the-community argument applies with the same force in regard to how severely crimes should be punished.[26] In sum, it might be held that a retributive view on punishment distribution implies, on the one hand, that ordinal proportionality is observed and, on the other, that punishment levels should be determined by public perceptions and, finally, that this is due to the fact that the purpose of the punishment system is to convey appropriate condemnatory messages on behalf of the community. Thus, apparently it is possible to provide some sort of justification of the outlined model of retributive penal distribution.

In order to assess this type of justification, one would have to engage in more thorough considerations of the sort of expressionist theory on the ground of which the justification is based. However, this would go far beyond the purpose of the discussion in this chapter. As mentioned, the more modest goal here is to examine under which conditions public opinion might have a role to play with regard to punishment distribution. Thus, let us for the sake of argument assume that the suggested argument can stand up to further scrutiny. What would this imply with regard to the way in which public perception is drawn into the question of setting penal levels? As far as I can see, there are two important restrictions relating to a retributivist invocation of public opinion on punishment severity.

The first restriction concerns a topic that has been comprehensively discussed in modern criminological literature, namely, the general lack of knowledge of the public on crime and punishment issues. To illustrate the point, consider a simple analogy. Suppose that the head of a firm has decided to give an extra bonus to the staff and that she wishes this bonus to reflect the degree to which each employee has contributed to the benefit of the firm. That is, the bonuses should be distributed in accordance with the individual desert of each employee. In order to make the bonus system operational, it is decided to set up some levels of bonuses. The employees who score the highest on a number of performance parameters (such as the amount of overtime work, the number of products produced, or whatever) receive the largest bonus, while employees who score less on these parameters receive a minor bonus, and so on. Now, suppose that after the bonuses have been distributed it turns out that the information on the ground of which they were given was mistaken. The parameters have not been correctly selected, that is, they do not reflect the degree to which someone has benefited the firm. Should we say that the employees have got the bonuses they deserved? Obviously, the answer is in the negative. If what matters is the benefit of the firm, then the fact that the distribution was based on misinformation constitutes an obvious reason to revise the parameters and to admit that those employees with the best performances – that is, who have benefited the firm the most – have not been rewarded accordingly. The employees have not got what they deserve; and the reason is that desert presupposes correct information with regard to what constitutes the desert-base (that is, the features on the ground of which desert is determined). Now, this simple insight has obvious consequences if we return to our discussion of punishment distribution.

Firstly, if public views should be consulted in order to determine how seriously different crimes should be punished, then it must be presupposed that the public is correctly informed with regard to what constitutes the desert-base for the distribution of punishment. That is, the proposal presupposes that people are correctly informed with regard to the aspects of a crime on the ground of which desert should be determined. For instance, if people happen to under- or overestimate the harm which a particular type of crime causes to its victims, then the subsequent judgement of what constitutes the proper desert of the offender is likely to be mistaken. Obviously, the same is the case if people are misinformed with regard to whatever other aspects of a crime – beyond harm – the retributivist believes should be considered part of the desert-base.

Secondly, the significance of being correctly informed is not only of relevance with regard to crimes. Of equal importance is the degree of information concerning the object of desert, that is, with regard to the nature of different types of punishment. If, for instance, one tends to underestimate the severity of a particular type of punishment or if one mistakenly believes one punishment to be more severe than another, then, once again, one's judgement as to what constitutes a deserved punitive reaction for a certain crime might well be mistaken.

That a proper ascription of just deserts to criminals presupposes correct information with regard to different aspects of the nature of crime and punishment is not a fact of which the importance is merely academic. On the contrary: on the grounds of research studies carried out in various countries, criminologists have repeatedly underlined the fact that people in general are often misinformed in various ways with regard to questions of crime and punishment. As Roberts et al. put it: 'As with crime rates, public misperceptions of the sentencing process and sentencing trends abound'.[27] Thus, in this light it obviously becomes not only theoretically but also practically highly pertinent to recognize that, if one holds that sentencing levels should – within the framework of a retributive theory of justice – be determined by consultation of the public view on sentencing, then one has to presuppose that public judgements are informed; that is, that they are formed on the ground of correct information with regard to all the aspects which the retributivist regards as significant for the determination of the seriousness of crime and the severity of punishment. In the same way that one should reject the idea that the above-mentioned head of the firm succeeded in giving her employees the bonuses they deserved, so should one reject misinformed public perceptions of just deserts as an instrument for setting penal levels.[28]

The second restriction that has to be placed on the invocation of public views on sentencing within a retributivist theory of punishment does not concern the informational background for public judgements but the reasons behind such judgements. To illustrate the point, consider again a simple analogy. Suppose this time that the head of a firm knows that there is hard competition and that there is a risk that some employees might decide to switch to a rival firm. In order to prevent this, she decides to give a bonus to the employees. More precisely, a number of bonus levels are set so that those employees who are estimated as most likely to switch to a rival receive the largest bonuses, while those estimated as being less likely to change jobs, receive the smallest bonuses. Should we say that, when the bonuses are distributed in this way, the employees get what they deserve? Once again the answer is obviously in the negative: the distribution was not based on desert but on some sort of preventive scheme. Now, the lesson to be learnt from this example if we return to the question of punishment distribution is quite simple. The fact that a list of penal levels can be extracted by surveys of public views on sentencing does not imply that this list is one that can plausibly be adopted within a retributive theory of penal distribution. The fact that people believe that a certain number of years in prison constitutes the proper punitive reaction to a particular crime will not do as part of a retributive scheme unless it is the case that this judgement is in fact based on considerations of desert. If the judgement is founded on another distribution pattern – for instance, on the belief that if this crime is responded to by a particular number of years in prison, then this will have desirable consequences in terms of crime prevention – then the resulting penal level cannot plausibly be incorporated into the retributivist scheme. As in the case of the distribution of bonuses to employees, it is obviously premature to jump from the fact that something is distributed in a certain way – say, that the public ascribes punishment of varying severity to crimes of varying gravity – to the conclusion that this distribution pattern is one of desert. Thus, the second obvious condition that has to be placed on the invocation of public views on sentencing is that these views are in fact based on desert.

In sum, what the foregoing considerations indicate is that, even if it can be established that the public view on sentencing should have a role to play within a retributivist theory of punishment, this is not tantamount to the claim that all one has to do is make a survey of what the public regards as the proper punishments for different sorts of crimes. On the contrary, it has to be presupposed that public perceptions are fully informed in the relevant respects and that these perceptions reflect considerations of just deserts. Obviously there is nothing that prevents social scientists from trying to carry out studies in which these conditions are satisfied. However, since there is no reason to believe that such conditions are satisfied in typical cases where people indicate how they believe different crimes should be punished – in fact, as indicated, there are reasons to believe that the conditions are not usually satisfied – there seems to be little room within a retributivist scheme for drawing on actual public attitudes to sentencing.

9.3   Conclusion

The movement towards greater consultation of the public on matters of sentencing naturally prompts the question as to whether – and under which conditions – this sort of consultation is ethically justified. There are good reasons to hold that the mere fact that penal law or practice reflects public opinion does not *per se* establish that the law or practice is ethically right. Furthermore, it does not follow from the fact that one subscribes to democracy that the question as to how severely different crime should be punished – which has constituted the main issue of this paper – should reflect the existing public view on sentencing. Thus, the assumption behind the previous considerations has been that whether public opinion should have a role to play must depend on whether there is room for public views on sentencing within a theory which seeks to justify and thus identify the goal of punishment. Since it would be a task much too comprehensive for the paper to consider what constitutes the most plausible theory of punishment, what has been done here is more modestly to consider whether public views should have a role to play seen from the perspectives of the traditional rival views on punishment. What we have seen is the following.

Firstly, whether to sentence criminals in a way that does not reflect the public view on sentencing has undesirable consequences – for instance, in terms of a decreasing confidence in the courts, or an increased tendency of people to take the law into their own hands – is obviously an empirical question. However, even if it is taken for granted that failure with regard to mirroring public views would have undesirable consequences, it does not follow from a utilitarian view that the sentencing law or practice should be adjusted to the public view. As argued, it may be the case that this kind of adjustment has even more undesirable consequences and, even if this is not so, it may be possible to prevent the consequences in other and more desirable ways than by adjusting the distribution of punishment in accordance with public perceptions.

Secondly, from the outset it has been seen that there is no obvious room for including public opinion in a retributive view on punishment distribution. However, one possibility is to use public opinion as delivering anchor points. But, as argued, this proposal seems highly arbitrary. Another and more radical suggestion is that the punishment for all crimes should be determined by public opinion. But this would mean that the retributivist would basically have to give up standard considerations of ordinal proportionality. A final proposal is that public views on sentencing should determine the precise punishment levels as long as ordinal proportionality is observed. But obviously this proposal has to be sustained by some sort of rationale. As indicated, it may be possible to present an argument to this effect. Whether this argument is stronger than the arguments which some retributivists have presented in favour of other solutions to the question of how the punishment and crime scales should be linked is still an open question. However, even if this is assumed to be the case, the proposal would still have to presuppose that the two outlined conditions – that public views are fully informed and reflect considerations of desert – are satisfied.

Thus, though the foregoing considerations do not exclude the possibility that it may sometimes be justified either on utilitarian or retributivist grounds to let public opinion have a role to play when it comes to the distribution of punishment, they nevertheless establish that a justified invocation of public opinion presupposes that a number of conditions are satisfied. However, as indicated, it does not seem obvious or even likely that these conditions are in fact satisfied in the way in which public opinion is invoked by policy-makers. Even though there is no space here to engage in analyses of some of the various tough-on-crime initiatives that have been taken in Western countries over the latest decades, the nature of the outlined conditions nevertheless gives reason to fear that it is correct when it held that these initiatives – even if popular – are rightly characterized as populist in the initially mentioned sense of the term.

Notes

1. *The Guardian*, 9 June 2006.
2. See, for instance, A. E. Bottoms (1995), 'The Philosophy and Politics of Punishment and Sentencing', in C. Clark and R. Morgan (eds), *The Politics of Sentencing Reform* (Oxford: Clarendon Press). For a more recent comprehensive discussion, see A. Freiberg & K. Gelb (eds) (2008), *Penal Populism, Sentencing Councils and Sentencing Policy* (UK: Willan Publishing).
3. See J. V. Roberts et al. (2003), *Penal Populism and Public Opinion: Lessons from Five Countries* (Oxford: Oxford University Press), 'Introduction'.
4. See also, D. Golash and J. P. Lynch (1994–5), 'Public Opinion, Crime Seriousness, and Sentencing Policy', *American Journal of Criminal Law*, vol. 703, pp. 703–32.
5. See, for instance, F. Zimring, G. Hawkins and S. Kamin (2001), *Punishment and Democracy* (USA: Oxford University Press), chapter 10.
6. M. Bagaric and R. Edney (2004), 'The Sentencing Advisory Commissions and the Hope of Smarter Sentencing', *Current Issues in Criminal Justice*, vol, 16, 129.
7. J. V. Roberts (2008), *Punishing Persistent Offenders* (Oxford: Oxford University Press), 211.
8. See, for instance, M. Hough and J. V. Roberts (2004), 'Confidence in Justice: An International Review', London: Home Office, Research, Development and Statistics.

9. See D. Indermaur, 'Dealing the Public In: Challenges for a Transparent and Accountable Sentencing Policy', in Freiberg and Gelb (eds), *Penal Populism, Sentencing Councils and Sentencing Policy*.

10. J. Bentham (1988), *The Principles of Morals and Legislation* (New York: Prometheus Books), 198.

11. Ibid. 199.

12. P. Robinson and J. Darley (1995), *Justice, Liability, and Blame: Community Views and the Criminal Law* (Boulder: Westview Press), 6.

13. K. Gelb, 'Myths and Misconceptions: Public Opinion versus Public Judgment about Sentencing', in Freiberg and Gelb (eds), *Penal Populism, Sentencing Councils and Sentencing Policy*, 74.

14. See, for instance, J. V. Roberts et al., *Penal Populism and Public Opinion*.

15. Obviously, these two approaches could also be combined.

16. J. Bentham, *The Principles of Morals and Legislation*, 199.

17. See, for instance, D. Indermaur, 'Dealing the Public In: Challenges for a Transparent and Accountable Sentencing Policy'.

18. M. Davies (1993), *Punishing Criminals* (Westport: Greenwood Press), 17.

19. See the discussion in J. Ryberg (2004), *The Ethics of Proportionate Punishment. A Critical Investigation* (Dordrecht: Kluwer Academic Publishers), chapter 4.

20. It should be mentioned, though, that people usually seem to subscribe to a proportionate distribution of punishments. See, for instance, J. Roberts, *Punishing Persistent Offenders*, 210–12.

21. See, for instance, A. von Hirsch (1993), *Censure and Sanctions* (Oxford: Clarendon Press). Or, for a very different solution, D. E. Scheid (1997), 'Constructing a Theory of Punishment, Desert, and Distribution of Punishment', The *Canadian Journal of Law and Jurisprudence*, vol. 10 (2), pp. 441–506.

22. M. Davies, *Punishing Criminals*, 14.

23. Ibid. 15.

24. Ibid. 17.

25. J. Roberts, *Punishing Persistent Offenders*, 85.

26. After all, the idea of the expressionist view is that the severity of a sanction expresses the stringency of the censure or blame.

27. J. Robert et al., *Penal Populism and Public Opinion*, 24.

28. However, it should be underlined that the discussion is somewhat more complicated when it comes to the question of setting general penal levels. When we are considering individual cases of sentencing, what is required is that one is informed with regard to all things that count in relation to the determination of desert. However, it is less obvious what this means when, alternatively, we are considering general sentencing levels.

10
Punishment and Discrimination

Kasper Lippert-Rasmussen

All kinds of punishment can be discriminatory, but for capital punishment the charge of discrimination has played a central role in arguments for its abolishment. David Baldus concluded in a study that 'the odds of a death sentence for those who kill whites in Georgia are 4.3 times higher than the odds of a death sentence for those who kill blacks'.[1] In 1987 this work was used to challenge the execution of death row prisoner, Warren McClesky, in the Supreme Court on the grounds of an 'unfair racial bias in the administration of the death penalty in Georgia'.[2] The Supreme Court dismissed the argument, but the debate about how discrimination bears on the justifiability of punishment has continued. In 1997 the American Bar Association called for a moratorium on the death penalty partly because of 'the continuing problem of racial bias in the administration' of it.[3]

Discrimination against someone takes place only if some entity (a person, a company, a court, a law and so on) treats individuals differently on the basis of group membership such that the interests of members of different groups, broadly construed, are differentially affected or are intended to be so. Discrimination may take place even if the relevant differential treatment does not result in people's interests being differentially affected: it is enough if such an effect is intended.

Differential disadvantageous treatment is a necessary, but not a sufficient condition of discrimination. There are many ways in which a group can be treated less favourably than another without this group being discriminated against.[4] First, some people think that discrimination is necessarily unjust. Thus, if it is just that paedophiles who molest children are punished, they are not discriminated against even though the legal system treats them disadvantageously compared to those with non-paedophile sexual desires.

Second, not all groups can suffer discrimination even if they can suffer disadvantageous differential treatment. Some distinguish between socially salient groups – that is, groups perceived membership of which structures social interactions in a lot of different contexts, for example, men, homosexuals, blacks, disabled – and socially, non-salient groups, for example, people with one 'F' in their name, arguing that only the former can be discriminated against.

Third, not just any causal background of differential treatment suffices for discrimination. Women were on average older than men in the USSR twenty years after WWII because millions of male Red Army soldiers had died. Suppose also that Soviet laws were in place prior to WWII that systematically favoured older people over younger. Even though these laws would on average treat women more favourably than men in 1965, they did not indirectly discriminate against men given the coincidental and sex bias-unrelated nature of the causal background of this differential treatment. The case is different from firing and promoting on the basis of seniority in a company that has only recently started to hire African-Americans due to past racist attitudes, which does constitute indirect discrimination.[5]

Most forms of discrimination are unjust and discrimination in punishment seems particularly objectionable. First, a fundamental legal value is that of equality before the law. Because discrimination, by its very nature, involves unequal treatment, discriminatory punishment unavoidably clashes with the equal legal status of all.

Second, punishment has a different status than discrimination by private individuals. It is carried out in the name of the state and is thus authorized by all of us. Hence, discriminatory punishments have a communicative and symbolic dimension that many forms of private discrimination do not. This seems particularly obvious in the case of severe punishments such as capital punishment. Noting that the punishment that one receives in the US for 'murdering an African-American is often significantly less than the [punishment one receives for] murdering anyone else', Michael Cholbi infers that '(i)mplicitly, then, the lives of African-Americans are treated as less valuable than the lives of others'.[6] On one account, wrongful discrimination is discrimination that demeans the victim, and to demean someone is to treat this person 'as not fully human or not of equal moral worth'.[7] If Cholbi is right, discriminatory capital punishment appears to be one of the most demeaning and, thus on the account mentioned, most wrongful forms of discrimination.

To set the stage for an exploration of the moral qualities of punitive discrimination, section 10.2 of this chapter distinguishes between different loci of legal discrimination. Focusing on the third locus, section 10.3 discusses what constitutes an adequate criterion for the existence of discrimination in sentencing. This question is complicated, partly because of how considerations about legal protection of potential victims of crime interact with considerations about equal treatment of perpetrators of crime. Section 10.4 discusses the question of what, if anything, is wrong with discriminatory punishment when we set aside all those morally problematic features with which discriminatory punishment might be contingently correlated. Section 10.5 confronts an influential response to the claim that discriminatory punishments cannot be unjust, because provided those who are as a matter of fact punished deserve their punishment, they are in no position to complain. But not being in a position to complain about a certain treatment may result from factors other than those that bear on the permissibility of this treatment. Thus, it does not follow from the putative fact that, say, a murderer, who deserves capital punishment, is in no position to complain about being sentenced to death, when he might have received a lighter sentence had he had a different race or sex, that the punishment is just.

10.1   Loci of legal discrimination

Discrimination in punishment has several loci. First, laws may discriminate. It is common to distinguish between direct and indirect discrimination and claim that, although most laws no longer discriminate directly, many do so indirectly. An official EU homepage on discrimination defines the two species of discrimination as follows:

> Direct discrimination occurs when a person is treated less favourably than another in a comparable situation because of their racial or ethnic origin, religion or belief, disability, age or sexual orientation. An example of direct discrimination is a job advert, which says 'no disabled people need apply.' ... Indirect discrimination occurs when an apparently neutral provision, criterion or practice would disadvantage people on the grounds of racial or ethnic origin, religion or belief, disability, age, gender or sexual orientation unless the practice can be objectively justified by a legitimate aim. An example of indirect discrimination is requiring all people who apply for a certain job to sit a test in a particular language, even though that language is not necessary for the job.[8]

Based on this definition, presumably, a law that stipulates that the level of punishment for crimes involving crack cocaine is significantly higher than punishments for crimes involving powdered cocaine, might – see below – indirectly discriminate against blacks provided that blacks primarily use crack cocaine and whites primarily use powdered cocaine.[9] This is so even if the law is apparently neutral – it does not distinguish for the purpose of meting out punishment between blacks and whites – and provided that there is no 'legitimate aim' that can 'objectively justify' the differential treatment.

Second, the law can be enforced in a discriminatory way. For instance, if the police are more inclined to stop black motorists and search them for drugs than to stop and search white motorists, they might arrest and prosecute more black people for possession of illegal drugs even if the underlying real crime rate in relation to possession of such drugs does not differ between the two groups.[10] The distinction between direct and indirect discrimination applies to enforcement of laws as well. It is one thing that police tactics are openly motivated by racial animosity – in that case the practice is not even 'apparently neutral'; it is another if it is formulated in entirely neutral form, for example, police makes it a top priority to combat certain kinds of crimes where a particular group is overrepresented, even though there is no justification for this priority.

Third, the way lawbreakers are punished can discriminate. This occurs whenever members of two groups do not receive equally severe punishments for crimes that, legally speaking, are not relevantly different. This kind of discrimination may not be intentional. Judges and jurors may reach the verdicts they do in ways that reflect their intention to punish some groups of criminals harder than others, or because they believe that certain crimes are graver when committed by members of some groups against members of others. But more likely discrimination in punishment takes a non-intentional form. That is, judges and jurors intend to treat members of different groups equally; they think this is what they are doing, and yet there exists a pattern of differential punishment, which is best explained by the role the legally irrelevant group membership plays.

Fourth, the way punishments are implemented can be discriminatory. Many convicts do not serve the full sentence but are released on parole, and biases may determine who gets it and when.

Below I focus exclusively on the third kind of discrimination. It is worth stressing that even if no discrimination takes place in terms of sentencing this does not imply that discrimination takes place in none of the other loci.[11] In fact, discrimination in one locus may cause greater discrimination in one of the others. For instance, John P. Pittman believes that discrimination against African-Americans in policing strategies causes more African-Americans to be apprehended and convicted. The result is statistics showing higher crime rates for African-Americans, which again causes jurors to have a 'suspicion of guilt' and thus to be more inclined to convict African-American defendants.[12]

An interesting possibility that I shall disregard is that members of a certain group are discriminated against in terms of one particular crime and discriminated in favour of in terms of others, for example, that women get harsher sentences for child molestation than men do, but lighter sentences for murdering a member of the opposite sex than men do. Here judges discriminate *between* men and women, but they may not discriminate *against* either group on the whole.

10.2   Criteria vs indicators of discrimination

Initially, it may seem easy to determine whether discrimination in punishments exists. According to the simple view, if a group receives a greater share of the total sum of punishment meted out by courts than its share of the total population, its members suffer sentencing discrimination. On this view, the fact that African-Americans are strongly overrepresented among those who receive capital punishment strongly suggests that they are subjected to capital punishment discrimination. Since overrepresentation is even more massive in the case of men in the US, the simple view implies that men are massively discriminated against.[13] Few accept the latter inference and, thus, few should accept the former. Independently of whether African-Americans suffer sentencing discrimination, we should reject the simple view.[14]

The obvious flaw with the simple view is that to the extent that crime rates differ across groups, in the absence of sentencing discrimination some groups *should* receive a larger proportion of the total punishment than their proportion of the total population warrants. This is the principal reason we do not infer from the fact that men receive a greater proportion of the total punishment than women do that men are being subjected to sentencing discrimination. No doubt, different crime rates may reflect extra-legal discrimination. If a group faces discrimination on the job market, more of its members may on average be unemployed and thus be more criminal, but this is irrelevant here given our focus on punishment. So what I shall call the complex view says that a group suffers sentencing discrimination if, and only if, its share of the total sum of crime differs from its share of the total sum of punishment.[15] This view allows that a group might receive a disproportionately large part of total punishment and yet not suffer sentencing discrimination. Indeed, consistently with this state of affairs, it may even *benefit* from sentencing discrimination in its favour.

While the complex view is less flawed than the simple view, it is still not quite right. First, suppose a certain group suffers sentencing discrimination. Presumably, this means that, on average, its members will receive harsher punishments for crimes for which members of other groups will be punished more leniently. But this could be the case, even if some individual members of this group are sentenced in a way where no discriminatory biases influence the verdict they receive. Moreover, some individual members of the group experiencing sentencing discrimination in their favour might be discriminated against and, as a result, receive harsher sentences than they would have received had biases not influenced their trials. Given what is the case on average, such cases cannot be particularly common, but the fact remains that a group might suffer sentencing discrimination even if some of its members are actually discriminated in favour of and some members of other groups are discriminated against. Hence, if two groups' shares of the total crime correspond exactly to their shares of the total punishment, we cannot infer that none of their members suffered or enjoyed sentencing discrimination. Such discrimination might be going on in individual cases even though its effects cancel each other out such that no differences show up at an aggregate level.

The second problem is that the complex view ignores which groups the victims of crime belong to. Suppose that killers of whites tend to get harsher sentences than killers of blacks; that black killers of whites are punished more harshly than white killers of whites and white killers of blacks; and that most, but not all, murders are intraracial. In that case, the complex view might imply that no sentencing discrimination exists even though discrimination might well explain differential sentencing depending on the race of the victim.[16]

The third problem with the complex view concerns how we identify the victim of sentencing discrimination. Suppose a certain group receives a greater share of the total punishment than its share of the total crime warrants. It is not clear that this implies that members of this group are victims of sentencing discrimination overall. Consider the following thought experiment: blacks receive only ten years in prison for murder, whereas whites receive twenty and murder is the only crime committed. All murders are intraracial. Suppose that the more years in prison a race-identical murderer serves, the greater the deterrent effect of the punishment is and the fewer members of the relevant community will be murdered; suppose also that the murder rates within the black and the white communities vary with the level of deterrence only.[17] Suppose, finally, that the level of punishment does not alter the fact that blacks kill blacks only and whites kill whites only, so potential black murder victims only have reason to care about the punishment meted out to black murderers at least as far as deterrence goes and the analogous point is true about potential white murder victims. Obviously, these assumptions are unrealistic, but this is beside the present conceptual point.[18] Initially, we might think that this scenario involves sentencing discrimination against whites, because the punishment whites receive is twice as severe as the punishment blacks receive for exactly the same crime, that is, murder.[19] But this is only part of the picture. For in addition to the severity of the punishment that criminals from different groups receive, we should also consider the degree to which the legal system offers protection to different groups. In the hypothetical scenario the legal system offers much less protection to blacks against the risk of being murdered than it does to whites. So rather than saying that sentencing discriminates against whites, perhaps we should say that it discriminates *against* blacks as such or blacks who are potential murder victims (because it offers them less protection than it does to white, potential murder victims) and that it discriminates *in favour of* black murderers (because it punishes them less than white murderers). Possibly one would not want to say the latter, for example, because black murderers are not a socially salient group and, thus, for conceptual reasons not a group that can be the object of discrimination (see section 10.1), or because the causes of black murderers receiving less severe punishments have nothing to do with racial prejudice against whites and so on. However, these observations are beside the point: that, unlike what the complex view implies, the consequences of a certain sentencing practice for potential victims of the crimes also bear on the question of whether group differences in terms of the severity of punishment reflect discrimination.[20]

The conclusion in the previous sentence stands even if we relax the assumption that all crimes are 'intra-group' crimes, but I will not pursue this issue further for it is irrelevant to establishing this section's main claim: it is complicated to show that discrimination in punishments exists and, of course, to show that it does not exist. In what follows I set aside these complications and assume that discrimination in punishment has been shown to exist.

10.3 The pure discrimination case

I now turn to the injustice of sentencing discrimination. I am interested in a rather narrow question: what, if anything, makes sentencing discrimination unjust or morally wrong in itself? Obviously, sentencing discrimination may be morally wrong for a lot of other reasons than because of what it is in itself. For instance, if significant sentencing discrimination exists in all likelihood people believe it exists, and their believing so may lead to a loss of trust in general and trust in the legal system in particular. Moreover, it may cause a breakdown of relations between different communities and, in extreme cases such as the acquittal of the four police officers who beat up Rodney King, to rioting. Also, it is hurtful for people to know that they, or people like them, are singled out for discriminatory treatment.[21] These are all flaws that, empirically speaking, accompany sentencing discrimination, but they are not flaws that are necessarily true of sentencing discrimination and, thus, not flaws that could explain why sentencing discrimination is morally wrong *in itself*. It is possible, even if unlikely, for sentencing discrimination to exist without these flaws. Yet, discriminatory punishment may seem unjust even if none of its victims, say, believe they are being subjected to discriminatory treatment and, thus, none of them are hurt by what they see as their being singled out for discriminatory treatment.

To focus on this rather narrow question, suppose that for any crime there is some level of punishment such that the perpetrator deserves exactly this level of punishment and suppose that justice in punishment simply is that all criminals receive exactly the level of punishment they deserve. On this view justice in punishment is retributivist and entirely noncomparative, to use a terminology coined by Joel Feinberg.[22] It is unjust if, say, men receive 10 units of punishment less than they deserve and women receive 10 units more. Given the stated assumption, this discriminatory situation is no less unjust than one in which they all receive 10 units less (or more) and in which, consequently, no sentencing discrimination exists. On the assumptions made, the question of whether sentencing discrimination is unjust *per se* translates into the question of whether sentencing discrimination entails that some people do not get the punishment they deserve, noncomparatively speaking.

There is no doubt that sentencing discrimination often involves noncomparative injustice. Take the direct legal discrimination of the 1816 Georgia statute explicitly requiring 'the death penalty for rape or attempted rape if the crime was committed by a black against a white' (and in such cases only).[23] On the impeccable assumption that there is no difference in punishment deserved for raping black and white people, there is no way that this sentencing discrimination could exist consistently with all rapists receiving the level of punishment they deserve. But sentencing discrimination is consistent with all those who are punished receiving exactly the punishment they deserve. This is very unlikely, but it is logically possible. Even if judges and jurors are systematically biased in the assessment of evidence and systematically intend to impose harsher sentences on members of some communities than members of others, they might fail to carry out their intentions and their biased assessment of evidence may be neutralized by counteracting factors, for example, that members of one community generally commit crimes in a way that makes it harder to prove that they committed them. Insofar as we find sentencing discrimination unjust even in this scenario, justice in punishment must consist of something more than all criminals receiving exactly the punishment that they deserve, noncomparatively speaking, since ex hypothesi this is what all criminals do and yet the situation is unjust.

Some defenders of noncomparative justice might bite the bullet and say that the scenario I imagine is perfectly just. Surely, judges and jurors can be criticized for the way they reach their verdicts. But unjust reasoning is different from reaching an unjust decision.[24] After all, in my scenario everyone receives a punishment that perfectly matches the one they deserve.

This response strikes me as having considerable force, even though I do not find it decisive. First, a legal system that operates in a biased way even though through sheer luck it manages always to reach the right verdicts fails to fully reflect the value of equality before the law and, thus, conflicts with an ideal of a society in which we relate to one another as equals.[25] It sends an objectionable message despite the fitting punishments it imposes and may for that reason be one that justice requires to be reformed. Second, criminals are arguably wronged even though they receive exactly the punishment they deserve and cannot complain that they are being punished more harshly than others who have committed comparable crimes.

Setting aside the way sentences are reached, I now turn to comparative justice. To test the relevance thereof, consider a slightly different scenario. Suppose we have a group of murderers all of whom deserve the death penalty. Some, but not all of them, receive it. Those who do not receive the death penalty receive some lesser punishment, say, life imprisonment.[26] Ex hypothesis, all of those who are put to death deserve to be put to death and, thus, suffer no noncomparative injustice.[27] But it is also the case that some who deserve to be put to death are not put to death. Perhaps those being put to death can complain of comparative injustice: how come they are being put to death when others who have committed comparable crimes are not? I want to ask three questions with regard to this scenario: (1) Does it involve injustice in punishment? (2) If so, is the relevant injustice greater for reflecting discrimination as opposed to pure arbitrariness? (3) If the relevant injustice is greater for reflecting discrimination, what should be done about it to reduce injustice?

Starting with the first question, it is obvious that the situation involves injustice. Or, at least, insofar as there is such a thing as comparative justice, this is one of the clearest candidates for comparative injustice. In an exchange between Ernest van den Haag and Stephen Nathanson, the former denies that, in the scenario imagined, any execution is unjust, whereas the latter thinks they all are. Van den Haag, who favours the death penalty, says: '[I]f the death penalty is morally just, however discriminatorily applied to only some of the guilty, it does remain just in each case in which it is applied'.[28] Nathanson and van den Haag both suppose that if this claim is true, the discrimination objection to capital punishment and, thus, an important abolitionist argument fails.[29] Accordingly, Nathanson, who opposes capital punishment, rejects the claim. In support of its rejection, he offers two (relevantly similar) counterexamples to van den Haag's claim, one of which is the following: 'I tell my class that anyone who plagiarizes will fail the course. Three students plagiarize papers, but only one receives a failing grade. The other two, in describing their motivation, win my sympathy, and I give them passing grades'.[30] In this case, Nathanson submits, 'the justice of giving [the plagiarizing students] what they deserve appears to be affected by the treatment of others', despite what Nathanson admits to be van den Haag's forceful rhetorical question: 'How can it possibly be unjust to punish someone if he deserves the punishment?'[31] More generally, Nathanson claims that 'the treatment of classes of people is relevant to determining the justice of' treatment of, including punishments for, individuals.[32]

Both van den Haag and Nathanson fail to consider a third view, which can concede the force of van den Haag's rhetorical question and yet is consistent with denying the justice of a discriminatory but fitting punishment. On this view, we should be more careful than van den Haag and Nathanson in our individuation of the state of affairs that we deem to be just. Specifically, the state of affairs, 'X is executed and Y receives a lighter punishment', is different from another state of affairs, 'X is executed', and, given that X and Y are equally deserving, the fact that the latter state of affairs is just does not make the former state of affairs just too. It is entirely open to an opponent of capital punishment to concede of each individual state of affairs of a deserving criminal receiving the punishment he deserves that it is just (and it is open to Nathanson to deny that it is unjust that the plagiarizing student fails), while denying the justice of the more complex states of affairs that some deserving criminals receive capital punishment and others do not. (The state of affairs of my offering to carry an elderly, fragile person's bag involves a manifestation of politeness. But the state of affairs of my offering to carry one elderly person's bag and not offering to carry another elderly, fragile person's bag does not, when they stand next to each other, I could easily carry both bags, and there is no reason why I should carry one person's bag but not the other's.) If the latter injustice is sufficiently weighty, one might answer van den Haag's rhetorical question the way he thinks the question should be answered and still oppose capital punishment. So, in sum, Nathanson might fail in showing that discriminatory sentencing undermines the justice of individual punishment, but van den Haag and Nathanson err in thinking that to oppose capital punishment, discriminatorily administered, one must deny the justice of individual cases of capital punishment.[33]

So let us turn to the second question by comparing two situations: one in which it is entirely arbitrary who receives capital punishment and who does not – say, judges simply flip a coin whenever someone is found guilty of a crime that carries the death penalty – and one in which some kind of discriminatory bias determines who gets it.[34] Arguably, the lottery situation in which any guilty person runs an equal risk of receiving capital punishment is more just than one in which, due to bias, some people do not. Both situations are unjust to the extent that some people receive lighter sentences than they deserve, but the latter involves an additional unfairness to offenders from those groups that are discriminated against: namely, that they have a smaller chance of enjoying the benefit of a lighter punishment than they deserve. Of course, it ought not to be the case that anyone receives a lighter sentence than she deserves, but given that some, but not all, do, it is fairer that everyone has an equal chance of receiving a lighter sentence.[35] This explains why the situation in which some, but not all, receive lighter sentences as a result of idiosyncratic biases is fairer than one in which some, but not all, receive lighter sentences as a result of discrimination, since, given the idiosyncratic nature of the bias, there is a sense in which all defendants bear an equal risk of facing judges and jurors who are idio-syncratically biased against them.

Turning now to the third question: what should we do about the injustice involved in the scenario that I have imagined? We accept that discriminatory punishment in the scenario that I have described is unjust and that it is more unjust, because more unfair, than the punishment lottery where some get lighter sentences than they deserve but all have an equal chance of getting a lighter sentence. So the question is how we eliminate or reduce this injustice. Basically, there are three options to consider.[36] First, we might impose mandatory capital punishment on all. This seems to be the position taken by van den Haag.[37] Second, we might refrain from imposing the death penalty on anyone. This seems to be the position taken by Nathanson.[38] Finally, we might try to neutralize the systematic bias in the legal system without ensuring a perfect match between the punishment received and the punishment deserved.

Consider van den Haag's position. We might endorse it given the assumptions on which this discussion has been conducted. Yet, once we address the plausibility of these assumptions, we might be more critical. For provided that biases have a deep influence on how discretion in capital punishment is exercised, there is reason to believe that such biases will influence who among deserving as well as non-deserving defendants gets capital punishment, even if discretion is eliminated. For instance, biases may influence who is prosecuted and convicted for crimes that carry mandatory capital punishment.

Now consider Nathanson's position. Suppose we agree that discriminatory punishment is unjust. Does it follow that we should stop imposing it?[39] Note, first, that Nathanson is not suggesting that we refrain from punishment altogether. His proposal is that we continue to punish murderers with long term imprisonment rather than impose capital punishment on anyone. If we canvass the criticism of van den Haag that, in practice, biases will influence sentencing even if discretion is eliminated, it would seem difficult to argue that biases will not influence sentences lighter than capital punishment as well.[40] If so, Nathanson's proposal will not eliminate the injustice of discriminatory sentencing and – again: given the assumptions made – it will result in the additional injustice that more people will be punished more lightly than they deserve to be punished. The question is whether it will reduce the injustice of discriminatory justice in such a way that it more than outweighs the additional noncomparative injustice of some people not receiving the capital punishment they deserve.

With regard to the last question, it should be noted that in practice the death penalty is imposed on very few people relative to how many people are convicted of crimes that might in principle be punished by death. This suggests that the additional noncomparative injustice will be relatively small.

With regard to the former question, it might be argued that the injustice of discrimination depends on the importance of the benefits and harms involved in the discriminatory practice.[41] So discriminatory ticketing for parking offences is less unjust than discriminatory capital punishment, even if the two discriminatory practices are identical in all other respects than the severity of the harm involved in the punishment, that is a small fine versus death. So if capital punishment involves a much greater harm than, say, a lifetime in jail, the injustice involved in discriminatory capital punishment is much greater than the injustice involved in discriminatory lifetime imprisonment.[42] Still, if we argue that the noncomparative justice involved in eliminating capital punishment is small because few people receive capital punishment, it seems we are also committed to saying that the reduction of the injustice of going from discriminatory capital punishment to discriminatory lifetime imprisonment is small because of the relatively few people involved. A further issue is whether there are alternatives to eliminating capital punishment that eliminate discriminatory sentencing, but do not reduce the number of people deserving capital punishment who receive it. This is where the third alternative comes into the picture.

Suppose, for instance, that rather than receiving a death penalty, defendants receive a death penalty lottery ticket where the risk of losing varies between the two groups that are being discriminated between such that this differential risk eliminates the overrepresentation of one of these groups within the relevant penal category. So to take the case of the death penalty in the US: if you're a black defendant you do not receive a straightforward capital punishment verdict, but rather a lottery ticket that gives you, say, a 25 per cent chance of capital punishment. Or if you are a white defendant charged with a crime for which death penalty could be imposed you do not get a life-term imprisonment sentence. Rather, you get a lottery ticket that gives you a certain risk of receiving the death penalty. I am not putting this forward as a serious proposal. But note that given the assumptions on which the discussion is based, it is hard to see why it is not better than Nathanson's proposal. True, it involves an arbitrary unfairness in terms of who among the pool of comparable defendants receives the death penalty, but as I argued above, this unfairness seems smaller than the unfairness involved in differential capital punishment rates reflecting discrimination against certain groups. Also, unlike Nathanson's proposal the capital punishment lottery does not let people who deserve capital punishment off the hook.

I conclude that given the assumptions made and insofar as discriminatory capital punishment constitutes an injustice it is not clear that the best alternative to the present practice is to abolish capital punishment altogether. It is worth stressing that this conclusion is different from a defence of capital punishment. First, a number of considerations other than justice bear on whether capital punishment should be abolished.[43] Second, the discussion has been conducted on the basis of a number of assumptions that might be rejected, for example, the retributivist assumption that murderers generally deserve capital punishment, and that discriminatory biases affect only whom among those who deserve the death penalty actually receive it.

10.4   The no-complaint argument

In the final section I address an argument – the 'no-complaint argument' – that seems to show that discriminatory punishment may be just:

(1) It is true of all those who are punished either that they deserve the punishment they get or that the punishment they get is comparable to the harm they have imposed on the victim.
(2) If one deserves the punishment one gets or when it is comparable to the harm one has imposed on one's victims, one cannot complain about one's punishment.
(3) Hence, none of those punished is in a position to complain about being punished.
(4) If no one is in a position to complain about being punished, no one is punished unjustly.
(5) Hence, none of those being punished is punished unjustly.
(6) If none is being punished unjustly, the scheme of punishment is just.
(7) Hence, the scheme of punishment is just.

So, by way of illustration, suppose that all who are sentenced to death are murderers who deserve capital punishment and for whom the harm is comparable to what they imposed on one or several of their victims, then (1) is true in their case. It follows from this and (2) that these people cannot complain about being sentenced to death. Since they are not in a position to complain about their punishment, none of them is being punished unjustly (by (4)), and accordingly the scheme of capital punishment is just (by (6)). If this argument is sound, discriminatory sentencing is just provided that no one receives a punishment they do not deserve. This conclusion is favourable to van den Haag's position.

Other versions of this argument are suggested by remarks by Jeffrey Reiman (who ultimately rejects the death penalty) and Saul Smilansky (who discusses punishment in general and, thus, takes no stand on capital punishment in the work quoted). Reiman entertains a Kantian argument in favour of capital punishment which he takes to imply that 'a rational being cannot complain of being treated in the way he has treated others, and where there is no valid complaint, there is no injustice, and where there is no injustice, others have acted within their rights'.[44] Similarly, Saul Smilansky writes that: 'morally, a person cannot complain when others treat him or her in ways similar to those in which the complainer freely treats others'.[45]

I concede the first two premises of the argument. There is a clear difference between a complaint of being subjected to capital punishment put forward by a convicted serial killer on his own behalf and a complaint from a human rights activist with no criminal record on behalf of the convicted serial killer. Suppose the killer says: 'Human life is sacred and therefore you should spare mine'. It seems right to dismiss the complaint – 'Look who's talking' – on the ground that the serial killer is not in a position to complain given his own violation of the very norm to which he appeals. In a wide range of cases, there is a sense in which one is not in a position to complain about a certain treatment when that complaint is based on an appeal to the very norm that one has violated to an equal or greater degree.

My primary quarrel with the argument is with premise (4). I want to put forward two objections. First, it is important to be precise about what the punishees are not in a position to complain about. While it may be true that they are not in a position to complain about being punished, it does not follow that they are not in a position to complain about the following: that they are being punished, while others who are equally deserving of punishment are not. This complaint could be put forward even by a murderer (not guilty of similar differential treatment of his victims). So one might say: 'True, I am not in a position to complain about being sentenced to death given that I am murderer, but I am in a position to complain about being sentenced to death when other equally deserving murderers get off much more lightly'. Accordingly, (4) is false: one might be treated unjustly even if one is not in a position to complain about one's punishment as such provided one is in a position to complain about some conjunctive fact of which this is an essential part.

Second, even if we set aside the objection of the previous paragraph there seems to be a wide range of situations when someone is not in a position to complain about how he is being treated where this does not show that he is not being treated unjustly. For instance, it seems an unjustly harsh punishment to torture someone for torturing others even if a torturer is not in a position to complain about being tortured. Similarly, a person who believes that there is no such thing as freedom of speech might not be in a position to complain about the police preventing him from voicing his opinion.[46] Yet, those of us who believe in the right not to be tortured and a right to freedom of speech might agree that he cannot complain about the way he is being treated and yet also agree that it would be unjust to torture or silence him.

For these reasons, one can be treated unjustly even if one is not in a position to complain about being treated that way *per se*. Hence, even if it is true that those being sentenced under a discriminatory system of sentencing deserve the punishment they receive – which is highly unlikely in any case – and, for that or some other reason, are not in a position to complain about their punishments, this treatment might be unjust. Accordingly, the no-complaint argument fails to establish that discriminatory sentencing may not be unjust.

10.5   Conclusion

It is complicated to establish the absence of sentencing discrimination and it is hard to determine its overall magnitude due to how discrimination against groups of lawbreakers interacts with discrimination against groups of potential victims of lawbreaking. To the extent that it exists, it is unjust if there is such a thing as comparative justice. Given retributivist premises, it may in some cases of discriminatory sentencing be more just to let the unjust sentencing system continue than to abolish it. Finally, it may be true of a criminal who receives the punishment he deserves through discriminatory sentencing that he is in no position to complain about his punishment even if it is false that his being punished involves no injustice.

Notes

1. M. L. Radelet and M. J. Borg (2000), 'The Changing Nature of Death Penalty Debates', *Annual Review of Sociology*, 26, 43–61, 48. But see Cassell, P. (2004),

'In Defense of the Death Penalty', in H. Bedau and P. Cassell (eds), *Debating the Death Penalty: Should America Have Capital Punishment?* (Oxford: Oxford University Press), 183–217, 203–5.

2. Radelet and Borg, 'The Changing Nature of Death Penalty Debates', 48.
3. Ibid., p. 48.
4. I discuss the concept and wrongness of discrimination in K. Lippert-Rasmussen (2007), 'Discrimination: What is it and What Makes it Morally Wrong', in T. Petersen, J. Ryberg and C. Wolf (eds), *New Waves in Philosophy: Applied Ethics* (Basingstoke: Palgrave MacMillan), 51–72; K. Lippert-Rasmussen (2006), 'The Badness of Discrimination', *Ethical Theory and Moral Practice*, 9.2, 167–85; K. Lippert-Rasmussen (2007), 'Private Discrimination: A Prioritarian, Desert-Accommodating Account', *San Diego Law Review*, 43, 817–56.
5. G. Ezorsky (1991), *Racism and Justice* (Ithaca, NY: Cornell University Press), 24–6.
6. M. Cholbi (2006), 'Race, Capital Punishment, and the Cost of Murder', *Philosophical Studies*, 127, 255–82, 268. See also R. L. Kennedy (1988), '*McClesky V. Kemp*: Race, Capital Punishment, and the Supreme Court', *Harvard Law Review*, 101, 1388–443, 1391. According to Radelet and Borg most post-*Furman* US Supreme Court decision – a decision reducing discretion in the imposition of the death penalty intended to restrict the influence of biases, notably racial biases, in the use of capital punishment – studies 'conclude that for crimes that are comparable, the death penalty is between three or four times more likely to be imposed in cases in which the victim is white rather than black', Radelet and Borg, 'The Changing Nature of Death Penalty Debates', 47.
7. D. Hellman (2008), *When Is Discrimination Wrong?* (Cambridge, MA: Harvard University Press), 35.
8. http://ec.europa.eu/employment_social/fdad/cms/stopdiscrimination/resources/glossary/ ?langid=en#I [accessed 1.2.2010].
9. S. L. Myers Jr. (1993) 'Racial disparities in sentencing: Can sentencing reforms reduce discrimination in punishment?', *University of Colorado Law Review*, 64, 781–808, p. 790; Anonymous (2001) 'The Rhetoric of Difference and the Legitimacy of Capital Punishment', *Harvard Law Review*, 114.5, 1599–1622, p. 1619. But see R. Kennedy (1994) 'The State, Criminal Law, and Racial Discrimination: A Comment', *Harvard Law Review*, 107, 1255–78, pp. 1267–70.
10. See the discussion of '"disproportionate" investigation' in M. Risse and R. Zeckhauser (2004), 'Racial Profiling,' *Philosophy & Public Affairs*, 32.2, 131–70, 140–2.
11. Discrimination taking place outside these loci could also bear on the moral status of legal discrimination. For instance, Reiman believes that 'unjust discrimination in the recruitment of murderers undermines the justice of applying the penalty under foreseeable conditions in the United States', J. H. Reiman (1985), 'Justice, Civilization, and the Death Penalty', *Philosophy & Public Affairs*, 14.2, 115–48, 133 n22.
12. J. P. Pittman (1997), 'Punishment and Race', *Utilitas*, 9.1, 115–30, 117–18. See also B. Stevenson (2004), 'Close to Death: Reflections on Race and Capital Punishment in America', in Bedau and Cassell (eds), *Debating the Death Penalty*, 76–116, 87.

13. 'Between 1977 … and 1996, 301 men and only one woman were executed in the United States', P. E. Devine (2000), 'Capital Punishment and the Sanctity of Life', *Midwestern Studies in Philosophy*, 24, 229–43, 241 n23.
14. W. J. Bowers and G. L. Pierce (1980), 'Arbitrariness and Discrimination under Post-Furman Capital Statutes', *Crime & Delinquency*, 26, 563–632, 575.
15. The notions of total punishment and total crime are rather complicated entities, but I disregard the complications that this raises for the purpose of exploring the basic thought. One complication is recidivism. Suppose we think that the second murder is worse than the first and thus deserves harsher punishment. In that case, the second murder should count for more in relation to the measure of total crime than the first.
16. Bowers and Pierce (1980), 'Arbitrariness and Discrimination under Post-Furman Capital Statutes', 573, 577.
17. It is unclear if the deterrent effect of capital punishment is greater than long-term imprisonment, Radelet and Borg (2000), 'The Changing Nature of Death Penalty Debates', p. 47. If capital punishment does not have a greater deterrent effect than long-term imprisonment, an argument in favour of the former is undermined, but it is not in itself an argument *against* capital punishment.
18. They are not wholly unrealistic, however: 'About 80 percent of violence occurs among persons of the same race', Kennedy (1994), 'The State, Criminal Law, and Racial Discrimination', 1255 n2.
19. Van den Haag notes that since 'most black murderers kill blacks, black murderers are spared the death penalty more often than are white murderers … The motivation behind unequal distribution of death penalty may well have been to discriminate against blacks, but the result has favored them', E. van den Haag (1986), 'The Ultimate Punishment: A Defense', *Harvard Law Review*, 99.7, 1662–9, 1664; see also E. van den Haag (1985), 'Refuting Reiman and Nathanson', *Philosophy & Public Affairs*, 14.2, 165–76, 173, where he argues that '[t]he practice invidiously discriminates against black victims of murder'.
20. Randall Kennedy stresses this concern (1988), '*McClesky V. Kemp*', 1422, 1425. He thinks that 'the main problem confronting black communities in the United States is not excessive policing and invidious punishment but rather a failure of the state to provide black communities with the equal protection of the laws', Kennedy (1994), 'The State, Criminal Law, and Racial Discrimination', 1256, 1259.
21. J. Feinberg (1974), 'Noncomparative Justice', *Philosophical Review*, 83.3, 297–338, 318.
22. Feinberg believes that retributive punishment has both a comparative and a noncomparative element, 'Noncomparative Justice', p. 311.
23. Bowers and Pierce (1980), 'Arbitrariness and Discrimination under Post-Furman Capital Statutes', 757.
24. T. Scanlon (2008), *Moral Dimensions: Permissibility, Meaning, and Blame* (Cambridge, MA: Belknap Press of Harvard University Press), 27.
25. E. Anderson (1999), 'What is the Point of Equality?', *Ethics*, 109, 287–337.; S. Scheffler (2003), 'What is Egalitarianism?', *Philosophy & Public Affairs*, 31.1, 5–39; J. Wolf (1997), 'Fairness, Respect, and the Egalitarian Ethos', *Philosophy & Public Affairs*, 27, 97–122.

26. For the sake of argument, I assume that, for some crimes, it is true that the criminal deserves the death penalty and that the death penalty is always a harsher punishment than life imprisonment.
27. Feinberg discusses some comparable examples in Feinberg (1974), 'Noncomparative Justice', 313–18. He thinks that they involve unfairness and comparative injustice, but that, generally speaking, claims of noncomparative justice are superior to claims of comparative justice.
28. E. Van den Haag (1978), 'The Collapse of the Case Against Capital Punishment', *National Review*, 31, 397; Quoted from S. Nathanson (1985), 'Does It Matter if the Death Penalty is Arbitrarily Administered?', *Philosophy & Public Affairs*, 14.2, 149–64, 151. Elsewhere, van den Haag distinguishes between equal justice (all get what they deserve), unequal justice (some, but not all, get what they deserve) and equal injustice (no one gets what they deserve) arguing that the former is best and that unequal justice is better than equal injustice, van den Haag (1985), 'Refuting Reiman and Nathanson', 174. It is unclear why he does not think that 'better' here means 'better in terms of justice'.
29. 'Discrimination or Capricious Distribution thus Could not Justify Abolition of the Death Penalty', van den Haag (1986), 'The Ultimate Punishment', 1662–63.
30. Nathanson 156.
31. Ibid. 157, 156.
32. Ibid. 160.
33. For a different response to van den Haag, see J. Reiman and L. P. Pojman (1998), *The Death Penalty: For and Against* (Lanham, Maryland: Rowman & Littlefield Publishers), 118–21.
34. In cases involving significant racial bias, McDermott would consider the punishing agent illegitimate and, thus, object to the assumption that those being punished receive a legitimate punishment even if, by sheer coincidence, the punishment is identical to that which they deserve from a legitimate punishing agent, see D. McDermott (2001), 'A Retributivist Argument Against Capital Punishment', *Journal of Social Philosophy*, 32.3, 317–33, 326, 328.
35. Note that here I disregard unfairness to potential victims. Arguably, members of groups who face a higher risk of being murdered might argue that this is unfair and that if the only way to eliminate this unfairness is to impose harsher sentences on people who murder members of this group, it might be less unfair, all things considered, that some groups of defendants receive harsher punishments than others for crimes that are identical except for the extrinsic features that some group of potential victims face a higher risk of being subjected to this crime than others.
36. Indisputably, a legal system in which all criminals receive exactly the punishment they deserve is best. The interesting question concerns situations in which a legal system cleansed of all discriminatory biases is unfeasible.
37. Philip Devine agrees that this is what the discrimination concern motivates even if he thinks capital punishment is hardly ever justified, Devine (2000), 'Capital Punishment and the Sanctity of Life', 232.
38. Cholbi thinks a moratorium is warranted until the discriminatory bias has been eliminated, Cholbi (2006), 'Race, Capital Punishment, and the Cost of Murder', 270–7.

39. It does not follow from the fact that some penal practice is not perfectly just, nor from the fact that it is unjust because discriminatory, that we should eliminate it altogether. The consequences of having no penal practice as opposed to a flawed one might be disastrous.

40. Unless we suspect that the death penalty 'strikes at deep-seated racial prejudices in a way that milder penalties do not', Reiman (1985), 'Justice, Civilization, and the Death Penalty', 134 n22; Bowers and Pierce (1980), 'Arbitrariness and Discrimination under Post-Furman Capital Statutes', 574.

41. For example, J. Greenberg (1986), 'Against the American System of Capital Punishment', *Harvard Law Review*, 99.7, 1670–80, 1678 n42.

42. 'death is a much more severe punishment than imprisonment', Nathanson, 'Does It Matter if the Death Penalty is Arbitrarily Administered?', p. 161.

43. See, for instance, Reiman in Reiman and Pojman (1998), *The Death Penalty*, 107–18.

44. Reiman (1985), 'Justice, Civilization, and the Death Penalty', 124. Cp. I. Kant (2006 [1798]), *Metaphysics of Morals* in P. Kleingeld, *Toward Perpetual Peace and Other Writings Politics, Peace, and History* (New Haven: Yale University Press), 6:334.

45. S. Smilansky (2007), 'The Paradox of Moral Complaint', in his *Ten Moral Paradoxes* (Oxford: Blackwell Publishing), 90–9, 91.

46. J. Rawls (2000), *A Theory of Justice*, rev. ed. (Cambridge, MA: Harvard University Press), 190.

Index